MAKING SENSE OF ADULT LEARNING

Dorothy MacKeracher

Culture Concepts Inc.
Publishers
Toronto Canada

ISBN 0-921472-26-9
International Small Press Finalist Award 1997
Second printing January 1998

Canadian Cataloguing in Publication Data

MacKeracher, Dorothy
  Making sense of adult learning

Includes bibliographical references and index.
ISBN 0-921472-26-9

1. Adult learning. I. Title.

LC5225.L42M33 1996   374   C96-931585-6

Culture Concepts books are available at special discounts for bulk purchases as premiums, or for fund raising, sales promotions or educational use. Please contact us at:

Culture Concepts Inc.

69 Ashmount Crescent
Toronto Ontario Canada M9R 1C9
Telephone: 416-245-8119   Fax: 416-245-3383

The author's opinions and selected facts do not necessarily represent those of the publisher; nor does the publisher claim any responsibility for accuracy of sources provided by author.

Printed and bound in Canada

CONTENTS

DIAGRAMS

INTRODUCTION

This book grew out of a project begun in 1979 under the direction of Donald H. Brundage, then a faculty member of the Department of Adult Education, Ontario Institute for Studies in Education, affiliated with the University of Toronto. At the time, I was a financially needy, single parent working on my doctoral dissertation in Adult Education. Don had obtained a small research grant, from the Ontario Ministry of Education to do a literature search and write a report on adult learning principles; I was hired as his research assistant.

In the previous year, the Ministry of Education had been involved in a wide-ranging inquiry into declining enrolments in the province's elementary and secondary schools. One of the findings of that inquiry* was that the need and demand for schooling by adult learners, particularly the under-educated, would likely increase in the near future. A ministry official decided that background information on adult learners and on the learning processes typical of adult learners would help in planning and implementing programs for adults within the elementary and secondary school system. The research project resulted in a report entitled, *Adult Learning Principles and Their Application to Program Planning (ALP Report).*

The ALP Report was intended for teachers and planners who had been trained to work with children and adolescents and who might find themselves working with adult learners. In addition to sections on the characteristics of adult learners and the learning situation, the report also dealt with the retraining and professional development of such educators and with issues related to program planning. The complexities of the issues involved were reduced to relatively easy-to-understand principles applicable in a wide variety of settings. The Ministry published the 126-page report, as it publishes all its funded research, under a "blue cover" and set the purchase price at $3.00. Over a period of twenty years, the price gradually rose to $6.00. No figures are available to tell us how many K-13 educators actually purchased or used the report. However, we do know that it was purchased and used by many students in adult education programs across North America and by practising adult educators working in Canada, Asia, Australia and the West Indies. The Ministry stopped publishing the report in 1993.

In 1995, Thelma Barer-Stein, a colleague from my days as a student in OISE's Department of Adult Education, asked if I would consider revising the ALP Report. Don encouraged me to go ahead. He had retired in 1991 and was not interested in giving up his hard-

---

* Jackson, R. W. B. (Chair) (1979) **Implications of declining enrolments for the schools of Ontario.** Final report of the Commission on Declining School Enrolments in Ontario. Toronto, ON: Ontario Ministry of Education.

earned leisure. I am grateful to Don in many ways: finding work for me when I badly needed money; encouraging me to become a researcher; providing personal support as I struggled to complete my doctoral dissertation; giving full credit to the work I had done on the ALP Report; and giving me permission to write this revision without him.

When I left Toronto, in 1986, to take a faculty position at the University of New Brunswick, Don and I had plans to revise the ALP Report. We wrote letters back and forth and made plans but neither could find time to actually do the work. We had two unresolved discussions about what should be included in the revised text: I wanted to include a section on a topic I was then calling "social learning," and Don wanted to include a section on "transcendent learning." Neither of us understood completely what the other was talking about. I now understand that I was sorting out issues related to relational or connected learning, a way of learning much discussed in feminist literature; and I understand Don's concern to be about transpersonal or spiritual learning, a focus of learning discussed mainly in therapy and counselling literature.

This book is based on the ALP Report, but offers some major revisions. The references have been updated. New sections have been included on gender and cultural differences in learning, spiritual learning, learning styles, and physical learning. **Ideas about using the learning principles have been incorporated into each section.** The book has been written for students who are preparing to become adult educators. It is not intended to be an authoritative commentary on, or theoretical statement about, the learning done by adult learners. Rather I hope to provide those with a limited background in adult education with some basic ideas about how to work with adult learners in a variety of formal and informal settings. Since 1986, I have been writing course notes on learning and development for students in graduate and undergraduate adult education courses at the University of New Brunswick; and the students in these courses have helped me revise and clarify my ideas and have encouraged me to write for a wider audience.

My assertions are presented first as ideas which are drawn in part from adult education literature, and in part from personal experience. At the end of each section, these ideas are summarized as a series of *learning principles* offering generalized ideas about adult learners and the nature of their learning.

Some of the learning principles are formulated *facilitating principles* to plan and implement activities designed to assist adults in their learning. Some learning principles have no corresponding facilitating principles, however, because there is little that a facilitator can do to change the circumstances under which the learning principle operates.

This book is organized into ten chapters. The first chapter examines some background issues and assumptions which guided me in writing this book. Chapter Two examines models for matching learner characteristics to facilitating activities and considers some characteristics of adult learners which affect learning. The third through the seventh chapters describe five aspects of learning — the emotional, cognitive, social, physical and spiritual aspects. Chapter Three discusses **emotional aspects of learning,** Chapter Four explores **cognitive aspects of learning** and cognitive development. Chapter Five considers **social aspects of learning** and examines some of the ways in which social issues affect learning. Chapter Six examines **physical aspects of learning** and what is involved in learning a physical skill. Chapter Seven explores **spiritual aspects of learning** by considering learning which goes beyond body and mind.

Chapter Eight, **Cycles and Styles in Learning,** explores learning cycles and learning styles. Chapter Nine, **Strategies and Models in Facilitating,** examines basic methods and models for facilitating adult learning. Chapter Ten, **Putting the Ideas Together,** offers some advice to novice adult educators on putting the disparate ideas I have presented in the book into actual practice.

It is not necessary to read the chapters in order although it would be wise to read Chapter One first because it establishes the terminology and general perspective used throughout the book. At the end of various chapters and sections within chapters, I have provided **Learning and Facilitating Principles.** The format of these principles is not consistent throughout the book because different topics seemed to lend themselves to different types of principles. I would encourage you to actively develop your own learning and facilitating principles. Mine tend to emerge from the context in which I do most of my work — formal, university level (undergraduate and graduate), credit programs. If my work was more predominantly in nonformal and not-for-credit programs I would have phrased the principles somewhat differently.

I discovered, on the basis of the feedback I received from several early readers of the manuscript, that I continue to cling stubbornly to my assimilative learning style. I learn and work in ways which place a strong emphasis on reflection and conceptualization. The most prevalent feedback I received was "put in more examples" and "put in more of yourself." I realized that I still lack the consciousness of an accommodative learning style (emphasizing testing in reality and concrete examples). I know how to use examples and why it is sometimes helpful to write in the first-person singular, but I forget to do it because the examples do not seem relevant to me and I view my experiences as unimportant to anyone else. Now that my consciousness has been raised (again), I may do better in future writing tasks.

The chapter which worried me the most was the chapter on spiritual learning (Chapter Seven). It worried me because so many of the ideas were based on my concrete experiences and so much of the writing seemed experimental in that it did not conform with my perception of good academic writing. On reflection, I can see that the first half of the chapter was written from an accommodative learning style, a style foreign to my normal learning. I worried because I had no way to assess it for myself. Chapter Seven emerged over the Spring and Summer — indeed new ideas are still emerging — as I struggled with some concerns related to other work activities. I think of the chapter as a "work in progress;" every time I re-read it, I find something else I want to add.

ACKNOWLEDGEMENTS

I would like to gratefully acknowledge the contributions made to this book by some wonderful friends and colleagues. My special thanks to Don Brundage for his support over the past fifteen years, and to Thelma Barer-Stein for persevering with me throughout the project. Over the past ten years, I have been privileged to have some very remarkable students in my various courses at U.N.B.; many of them took the time to give me feedback on my course notes and to point out places where I needed to write more clearly. I have incorporated their ideas in this book wherever possible.

I want to extend my special thanks to my colleagues, Liz Burge, Ellen Herbeson, Pat Post and Marg Wall, who read the entire manuscript and gave me excellent feedback. Kathleen Howard and Diane Abbey-Livingstone read Chapter Seven and convinced me that I was on the right track. Lisa Kay, Margaret English and Yolanda Clowater were patient enough to assist me with typing the manuscript and letters and with other frustrating details. And Jeanette Robertson's computer skills made the various illustrations and diagrams look much more "professional" than my hand drawings.

Finally, I want to thank my family — Mary, David and Gordon — who survived my days as a graduate student and helped me to grow in ways which I never thought possible. They have encouraged me every step of the way through their love and companionship, and their wonderful sense of humour.

Dorothy MacKeracher
Fredericton, NB
October, 1995

Assumptions about Learning and Adult Learners

1

Some underlying Assumptions and Ideologies

Before beginning a detailed consideration of the characteristics of adult learners and the many aspects of the learning processes, I would like to set out some of the underlying assumptions and ideologies which have informed me. My description of these is by no means exhaustive and most will be elaborated in later chapters, in terms most commonly found in adult education literature. Also included where these appear to be important, will be disagreements about these assumptions.

I find it hard to present a comprehensive description and explanation of learning in a short definition. By the end of this chapter, you may find that you have some important questions remaining unanswered or points on which you disagree.

My view of learning is very complex because my learning style allows me to see learning from many sides. One metaphor which helps me understand the complexities of learning is a kaleidoscope. In my kaleidoscope, each aspect of learning brings a new colour to the overall picture:

* ❖ the emotional side brings pain and pleasure in hues of red;
* ❖ the physical side brings the intensity of orange;
* ❖ the cognitive side brings the sparkle of yellow;

❖ the social side brings the depth of greens and blues; and

❖ the spiritual side brings the serenity of indigo and deep purple.

Only when all the colours are brought together can we see the wonder of the rainbow connection that I understand as being the learning process.

I would like to present the full spectrum of the learning process as a whole image, on one page, in one compact, colourful, three dimensional model. But it can't be done. So bear with me. You may have to read to the end of the book before I get around to your most cherished questions or points of disagreement.

THE LEARNER CENTRED APPROACH

My understanding of learning is based on a learner centred approach to learning and teaching interactions.

The learner centred approach focuses primarily on the learner and the learning process, and secondarily on those who help the learner learn.

Only when I centred my attention on the learner and the learning process, did I begin to understand what competent adult teaching, facilitating, training, planning, advising, and counselling processes would be like.

Those approaches which are **not** learner centred might focus primarily on:

❖ the **content (knowledge or skills)** to be learned, and how that content is organized and presented;

❖ the **technologies to be used** as an aid to learning and how they limit or enhance learning or

❖ the **facilitator** and his or her facilitating[1] activities.

In these approaches, learners would be perceived in terms of their competency to learn the knowledge or skills, respond to technologies, or participate in facilitating activities.

An approach that is *not* learner centred, would view the learner as someone who responds to the facilitator, facilitating activities, resources or technologies. These responses would be judged in comparison to "correct responses" and the facilitator's advice would be viewed as a prescription to be followed.

The learner and the learning process are paramount in the learner centred approach used in this book.
The more we know about the basic processes of learning and the unique strategies used
by individual learners to carry out learning activities,
the more effectively we can design appropriate activities and resources to facilitate that learning.

In the learner centred approach, the learning process is assumed to be paramount, while facilitating is regarded as a responsive activity adapting to the learner's activities and natural learning process. The content to be learned is identified by the learners as knowledge or skills they need, for themselves, their work or the world around them, or to solve problems. The resources selected are those most likely to enhance the learners' preferred styles of learning. Any advice from the facilitator can be viewed, not as a prescription to be followed, but as a description of one direction among several alternatives.

This approach is presented here, not as the "best" way to approach learning and facilitating interactions, but as the approach that I find works best and as one viable alternative which is particularly useful with adult learners.

All approaches to learners and learning are
useful in some contexts, with some learners, and for some content.
Decisions about facilitating activities, content, resources and technologies must
be the focus of the planning which precedes any learning-facilitating interaction.

Learning as it is described in this book cannot be equated with schooling and education. Whether formal or informal, these are a means for delivering services and programs within which learning may occur. Learning is something done *by* the learner rather than something done *to* or *for* the learner. Learning proceeds independently of, and sometimes in spite of, education and schooling.

LEARNING IS A NATURAL, EVOLVING PROCESS

*Most writers agree that learning is
a natural, evolving process originating within the learner and
growing from the learner's need to interact with the environment.*

Learning has numerous definitions. Thomas (1991, p.3) describes the word "learning" as having two basic meanings of 'possession' and 'process':

1. learning in terms of its objectives and outcomes, as an "intangible *possession* that people work to acquire";
2. learning as a valuable *process* in itself; as something people do rather than as something they acquire.

Like breathing, learning is a normal function of living. And like breathing, learning can be hindered by inadequate activities and impaired resources or it can be enhanced by appropriate activities and improved resources. The activity of breathing stems from a need to reduce carbon dioxide and increase oxygen levels in the blood. Unexpected conditions may interfere with the act of breathing but not the need to breathe.

*The activity of learning stems from a need to
make sense of experience,
reduce the unknown and uncertain aspects of life to a manageable level, and
act skillfully in ensuring one's survival and security.
Unexpected conditions may interfere with the act of learning but not the need to learn.*

Humans are 'meaning making' organisms. Perry (1970) states that what an organism does is organize and what a human organism organizes is meaning. The most fundamental thing we do with our life experiences is to organize them by making sense of them and giving them meaning (Kegan, 1982). The experiences humans must organize include both those which we sense (feel) from the internal environment within our bodies, and those which we sense (see, hear, smell, taste, touch) from the external environment around us.

Learning activities are designed to help us:

❖ make sense of the chaos and confusion of raw, uninterpreted experience;

❖ reduce the unknown aspects of life to a manageable level,

❖ develop ways to predict how to respond, interact, and

❖ influence our own particular space in life.

Learning throughout life

Current theories on brain function suggest that the human brain is intensely aggressive and is designed to allow for learning throughout life (Hart, 1983). According to these theories, learning occurs as the brain extracts sets of meaningful patterns from the confusion of daily internal and external experience. These patterns are then organized into *meaning perspectives* (Mezirow, 1991) and *programmed structures* (Hart, 1983) which control and guide further learning.

According to such theories, three conditions are required for learning (Hart, 1983):

1. Enough raw data or experiences must be provided, with enough repetitions and variations on themes to allow differences in patterns to emerge.

2. Enough time and freedom from threat must be provided to allow the patterns to emerge naturally.

3. Sufficient prior meaning perspectives and programmed structures must exist in the learner's mind to handle new experiences productively.

If adult learners do not already possess perspectives and strategies for handling new material, then the learning activities must provide opportunities to learn them (Hart, 1983; Thibodeau, 1979; Feringer, 1978; Hebb, 1972).

Learning is a normal physiological-psychological activity which does not require external pressure or encouragement to begin and which proceeds out of inner drives fuelled by interpersonal energy rather than out of external pressure fuelled by rewards and punishments.

The basic problem confronting any facilitator is not how to motivate learning, since it happens both normally and naturally; but rather how to avoid setting up disincentives and obstacles which retard, block, or de-motivate learning. Once these are operating, however, the facilitator must take steps to neutralize or remove them, thereby allowing the learning process to return to its normal level of activity. If adults are not blocked in their learning activities, the facilitator can enhance learning by adding positive external conditions which encourage, influence and reinforce learning (Wlodkowski, 1985; Hart, 1983; Pine & Boy, 1977).

In this book, therefore, learning is defined as
a process of making sense of life's experiences and
giving meaning to whatever `sense' is made;
using these meanings in thinking, solving problems, making choices and decisions; and
acting in ways which are congruent with these choices and decisions as
a means for obtaining feedback to confirm or disconfirm meanings and choices.

Learning results in relatively permanent changes not only in meanings and behaviours but also in the ways one goes about making meaning, thinking, making choices, acting, and ultimately making sense.

Learning involves five components:
1. the cognitive or mental
2. the social or relational
3. the affective or emotional
4. the motor or physical
5. the spiritual or transpersonal.

These five components of learning form the core of this book and will be discussed in detail in the chapters that follow.

LEARNING IS A DIALECTICAL PROCESS

I understand learning to involve a *dialectical process.* That is, learning is characterized by interactive, constitutive, and transformative dimensions (Basseches, 1984; Kegan, 1982).

A dialectical process involves an internal or external discussion
which explores alternative viewpoints in order to develop
an integrated viewpoint synthesized from the best aspects of all alternatives.

The interactive dimension

Learning is *interactive* because we make meanings through exchanging information with our environment, most particularly with other persons.

1. We *receive meanings* from others, in person or through the resources they develop, in the form of information and ideas;
2. we *develop meanings* from our own experiences; and
3. we *integrate both sources of meaning* into a constructed whole.

As learners, how much we are willing to

❖ adopt, unchallenged, the meanings provided by others, is a measure of our *dependence*;

❖ create meanings for ourselves without reference to others, is a measure of our *independence*;

❖ develop shared meanings in interactions with others is a measure of our *interdependence*.

---

*Because learning is interactive,
our ability to communicate is an important feature of
our ability to learn.*

Meaning is conveyed through our shared vocabulary (semantics), grammar (structure or syntax) and non-verbal expressions. Meaning is also conveyed through and influenced by the context in which the interactions occur and through the ways in which power and control is distributed among the persons who are interacting.

The constitutive dimension

While we are not genetically programmed to respond to our world in a fixed way, as would a clam or a bee for example, we are programmed to constitute (invent, create) and make sense of our world by experiencing it directly through our senses, discerning patterns within experiences, and assigning meaning to these patterns. Learning is constitutive (composed, invented, socially constructed) because it involves a process of endowing the world around us with social meaning. It is "social" in the sense that we engage in this process with others. As humans, we not only endow our world with meaning, we have no choice but to do so (Hart, 1983; Kegan, 1982).

This process of sense-making helps us describe and explain what has happened in the past and to predict what might happen in the future. We use our explanations and predictions to develop behaviours that will give us some control in order to obtain outcomes which are more favourable to us. That is, we each invent our own "theories" about how the world works based on our experiences, perceived patterns and assigned meanings. A learner, in effect, is his or her own researcher and theorist about how the world works (Hunt, 1987; Kelly, 1955).

A theory explains what has happened in the past, predicts what will happen in the future, and implies ways to control or respond to what is happening in the immediate present.

The meanings we assign to reality and our personal theories about life and reality provide us with a *cognitive representation of the real world.* This is a personal mental map or model that is never an exact replication of the real world, but only an approximation of it[2] . Our personal models or maps always include many omissions and distortions. Once we have developed this personal model of reality, we experience it as if it had an objective reality of its own. We then take this "objectified reality" for granted, legitimizing it as "the truth" and as a description of "the real world."

Since our objectified reality was created from personal experience, we each place our "self" at its centre. To question what we take for granted may question our very existence; to have someone else question what we take for granted may feel like a personal rejection. When we deliberately re-examine meanings and taken-for-granted personal models of reality, we may feel uncomfortable and anxious. When these are questioned by someone else, we may feel distressed or disoriented.

To the extent that we share with others similar meanings for experiences, we also share similar models of reality and similar explanations about how to act as human beings. These shared models become our "cultural understanding". Gaining agreement about appropriate meanings is a basic problem for any social group. The meanings and model of reality most often shared by members of any given social group are those created by the dominant members of that group.

Without shared models, we would feel confused.
With shared models we tend to assume, unless we ask,
that everyone else's model and meanings are the same as ours.
Such assumptions frequently create conflict, confusion, and distress.

The transformative dimension

Learning is *transformative* because it has the potential for developing change. Personal meanings and the personal model of reality can be changed during interactive and constitutive processes. One may retreat from such changes and return to what is already known. But learning normally results in the development of new or modified meanings; these can be used to reconstitute previously existing explanations and predictions.

The personal model of reality which I use now is not an accumulation of everything I have learned over my lifetime. Rather, I continually revise previous meanings to make them more congruent with my current meanings. For example, once I thought of myself as a "bad mother". Now I understand I am a "good mother" because I created numerous opportunities which challenged my children to develop and mature.

Transformations occur through *differentiation* (separating, distinguishing) and *integration* (connecting, combining) (Basseches, 1984; Chickering & Reisser, 1993):

Differentiation occurs through identifying greater detail within selected aspects of the knowledge, skills or values being learned; or through becoming aware of differences between one's own meanings and those of others.

Integration occurs when greater detail and different meanings are combined with previous detail or meanings, thereby modifying them.

Mezirow (1995, 1991) describes three levels or types of transformations:

1. **Our meanings** (or the content of our personal model of reality) can be transformed by modifying our knowledge, skills or values.

2. **Our premises** (or how we come to know what we know and why we value what we value) can be transformed by reflecting and modifying the processes which underlie our meanings. Premise transformation also transforms our meanings.

3. **Our perspectives** (or the general framework and cultural understandings which underlie our entire model of reality) can be transformed by reflecting on and modifying its premises or underlying assumptions.

In the process of these transformations, our personal model of reality is transformed in whole or in part and associated premises and meanings are revised.

Meaning transformations occur regularly as new experience informs us of deletions or distortions in our model of reality. Premise transformations occur less regularly and require a conscious effort to think critically about what we know and how we know it. Perspective transformations occur even less regularly and either require a conscious effort to think critically about the assumptions underlying our premises or appear to occur spontaneously as revelations or Ah-ha experiences.

LEARNING IS NON-NORMATIVE

What and how I learn will always be different than what you learn even if we are participating in the same activity.

What learners learn is rarely an exact copy of what the facilitator intended them to learn. The learner always modifies what is presented through their own model of reality. Facilitating activities may seek normative results; that is, the facilitator may seek to obtain learning results which are consistent and predictable for all learners and congruent with pre-established goals. Obtaining normative outcomes may be appropriate in the training of plumbers or electricians or in the professional development of doctors or nurses. Such results are rarely attained because the individual's own internal resources will always modify what the facilitator seeks to obtain.

THE LEARNING PROCESS IS CYCLICAL

There are many ways to describe the overall learning process. I have used the combined ideas of several writers, including Jarvis (1987), Boud, Keough and Walker (1985), and Kolb (1984), to develop Diagram 1 *The Basic Learning Process* describing learning as a cyclical process in which four basic phases are repeated continuously. The knowledge and skills learned in one cycle are recycled and revised through subsequent cycles.

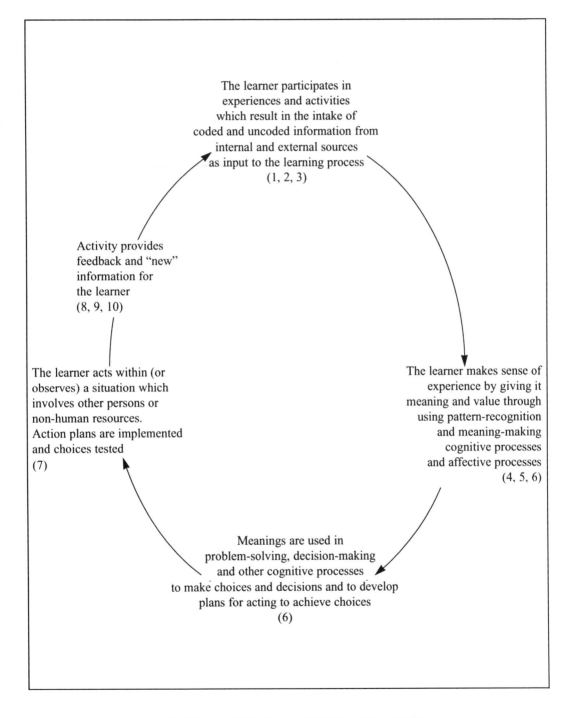

The learner participates in
experiences and activities
which result in the intake of
coded and uncoded information from
internal and external sources
as input to the learning process
(1, 2, 3)

Activity provides
feedback and "new"
information for
the learner
(8, 9, 10)

The learner makes sense of
experience by giving it
meaning and value through
using pattern-recognition
and meaning-making
cognitive processes
and affective processes
(4, 5, 6)

The learner acts within (or
observes) a situation which
involves other persons or
non-human resources.
Action plans are implemented
and choices tested
(7)

Meanings are used in
problem-solving, decision-making
and other cognitive processes
to make choices and decisions and to develop
plans for acting to achieve choices
(6)

1. THE BASIC LEARNING PROCESS

I have attempted to make the diagram self-explanatory but some additional comments may help. The numbers used for the following points refer to the numbers found in the diagram.

1. Learning always occurs within a specific context which contributes directly and indirectly, to whatever is learned. Context is difficult to represent in a diagram; think of this book as the context for this diagram, a context affected by the assumptions and ideologies which you are now reading.

2. The richness and accuracy of the information taken in through experiences and activities will be limited by the information available within the learning context, and by the acuity of the learners' sensory receptors, focus of attention, and prior expectations. These factors in turn, are affected by such variables as age-related changes, physical health, cognitive style, previous experience as well as existing knowledge and skills.

3. The intake of information is controlled by the learners. What is taken in is rarely an exact replica of the information presented.

4. The meanings and values used to make sense of incoming information or new experiences are drawn from those which currently exist within the learner's model of reality. If no meanings or values can be found in memory applicable to the incoming information, then the learner will need to create new ones or modify existing ones.

Learning, therefore, is affected greatly by memory and by the meanings and personal model of reality held there.

---

5. Cognitive processes can be conscious or subconscious. Conscious processes tend to use words as representational markers, although they also make use of feelings and images. Much of learning is subconscious (below or beyond conscious awareness) and may use feelings or images, but is unlikely to use words. Formal and shared learning experiences tend to involve deliberate conscious processes, and therefore use words as representational markers.

From an observer's perspective, both conscious and subconscious learning can be inferred from changes in observable behaviour. From a learner's perspective, conscious learning can be known through introspection, self-awareness and self-observation; while subconscious learning can be inferred from changes perceived in one's own behaviour and through altered states of consciousness such as hypnosis, psychotherapy, dreams, and meditation.

6. Learning in group settings proceeds more effectively if learners can verbalize the cognitive processes they are using, either in writing or orally. Adults learn to distrust non-verbal, non-representational, and subconscious learning because it is difficult to verbalize and is often perceived by others as illogical or irrational. The process of verbalizing cognitive processes is sometimes described as "cognitive apprenticeship" (Brandt, Farmer, & Buckmaster, 1993).

7. A decision to act may result in behaviour as fleeting as a shift in the focus of the eyes or as complex as a decision to change one's occupation. Fleeting and simple decisions occur too rapidly to rise to consciousness. Complex decisions are more likely to be made at a conscious level and may take longer to make as well as to implement.

8. Useful feedback tells learners about the results of their activities in comparison to expected outcomes. Feedback is a form of information and is subject to the same distortions as the original information. It is more effective when it is provided from an external source, such as a trusted other. Information from feedback provides the learner with a sense of success or failure.

9. Feedback becomes reinforcement for learning particularly if learners value their own performance or value the feedback they receive from others. Reinforcement in turn, can provide the learner with a feeling of reward (if the feedback is what the learner expected and is willing to accept) or of punishment (if the feedback is not what the learner expected or is willing to accept).

10. When feedback and reinforcement are immediate, their value to the learner is enhanced. Immediate feedback can be seen by the learner as part of the learning cycle. Delayed feedback is often seen as unassociated with the learning cycle.

Alternative activities and possibilities in the learning cycle

Many alternative activities and strategies are possible within each phase of the learning cycle. For example, learners may prefer information which:

❖ is visual as compared to auditory;

❖ comes from feelings which originate internally as compared to sensations which originate externally;

❖ comes from non-human resources, (books, manuals) as compared to human ones; or

❖ is based on one's own interpretation of experience as compared to the interpretations of others; and so on.

The basic phases in the learning cycle can help the learner to advance (through changes) in spiral fashion in desired directions. A learner can opt out of the process by retreating to the safety of existing knowledge, skill or values, by stalling or by foregoing the focus of one learning process and engaging in another. As learners we can begin at any of the four phases involved and work through the sequence. As facilitators, we can use the model to select our starting activities and to guide subsequent activities.

How does facilitating relate to learning?

Our present understanding of the relationship between facilitating and learning is very limited. Research on teaching and facilitating consistently shows that the facilitator's effects on learner achievement are unstable and that most facilitating behaviour is unrelated to learner outcomes (Candy, 1987; Pratt, 1979).

The best predictor we have is the B-P-E model proposed by Lewin (1951) which states that

Behaviour is a function of the interaction between Person and Environment: $B \to f (P, E)$.

This relationship has been reiterated and extended by several authors (Knowles, 1990; Bortner, 1974; Hunt & Sullivan, 1974; Kidd, 1973a). The facilitator can be thought of as a very influential component of the learning Environment through the provision of guidance, structure, information, feedback, reinforcement, and support.

What we do know is that learning as a process
should guide the facilitating processes, rather than the other way around.

LEARNING INVOLVES LEARNING TO LEARN

The concept of learning to learn is endorsed and promoted by educators at all levels of the educational system. Whether we know it or not, when we learn we are also learning how to learn. Like learning, "learning to learn" can be thought of as a goal or outcome as well as a process (Candy, 1990).

As a goal, learning to learn challenges individual learners to develop skills and knowledge which will allow them to learn more effectively in various contexts and settings.

As a process, learning to learn consists of two groups of interrelated processes and activities (Smith, 1990):

1. The *intrapersonal* which includes such skills as critical thinking, self-reflection and self-control.

2. The *interpersonal* which includes such skills as engaging in and reporting on the interactive dimension of learning in the ongoing dialectical process.

Candy (1990) describes learning to learn as involving higher-order cognitive skills that rest on increased self-awareness and self-control.
These higher-order cognitive skills include:
problem solving, critical thinking and planning for learning purposes.

Such skills must also be accompanied by appropriate attitudes. Critical thinking, for example, "does not consist merely of raising questions or of indiscriminate scepticism" but also comprises attitudes and behaviours which taken together, can be labelled "the critical spirit or critical attitude" (Candy, 1990, p.45). The critical approach to learning involves calling into question established knowledge and the assumptions which inform it (Brookfield, 1987).

Self reflection also includes skills and special attitudes which call on individuals to accurately describe not only their own physical and social activities but also their mental activities and emotional responses in learning situations. The individual therefore, must adopt a self-critical attitude as part of learning to learn. Both critical and self-critical attitudes can have potentially positive or negative outcomes. They are a necessary precursor of change; yet they sometimes create distress which can slow or even stop the learning process.

Of the three levels of transformations described by Mezirow (1995, 1991), transforming premises and transforming meaning perspectives contribute to learning to learn.

1. *Transforming premises* requires an assessment of the processes through which we create meaning in order to determine dysfunctional processes. Meaning or concepts can be changed without radically altering the model of reality within which they are integrated, but a change in our ways of learning can transform it.

2. *Transforming meaning perspectives* involves consciousness-raising, self-reflection, critical thinking and awareness of the constraints within which one's personal model of reality was developed and operates.

---

*Through such activities, the individual becomes aware
of distorted, incomplete or repressed information and interpretations which
underlie the entire model.
Perspective transformation involves both a critical reappraisal of the supporting assumptions and
the development of new assumptions and a transformed model of reality.*

'Learning to learn' is described in the literature under a variety of terms: second-order change (Watzlawick, Weakland & Fisch, 1974); reflection-on-action (Argyris & Schön, 1974; Schön, 1987); meta-formal schemata (Basseches, 1984); metacognition (Novak & Gowin, 1984); metalearning (Maudsley, 1979); deutero-learning (Bateson, 1972); and paradigm shift (Inglis, 1994; Barker, 1993; Koestler, 1964).

It is clear from the literature that not all adults have developed the learning skills necessary for learning to learn in conscious and deliberate ways (Collett, 1990; Candy, 1987). Those who have such skills appear to be more productive learners than those who do not. It is also clear that the most effective learning requires not only self-reflection and self-direction but also input from external sources and objective observers. Without input from others the individual learner can become stalled in self-perpetuating errors and false assumptions (Candy, 1987).

ALL ADULTS CAN AND DO LEARN

The work of Allen Tough (1979, 1978) clearly shows that adults engage in a wide variety of learning activities in response to their daily needs and problems. They may not define these activities as "learning" since there may be no apparent connection between the activities and formal schooling or the educational system; but the activities are clearly recognizable as learning activities.

Recent work in fields related to adult education indicate that adults of all levels of intelligence, all ages, and all stages of development up to the moment of death are capable of learning.
Adults experience a sense of well-being when they do learn and when their environment supports and encourages learning.

These implications are to be found in the works of developmental psychologists such as Chickering and Reisser (1993), Fiske and Chiriboga (1990), Levinson (1986), Basseches (1984), Kegan (1982), Gould (1978), and Vaillant (1977); in the works of educational gerontologists such as Birren and Bengtson (1988); Peterson (1983), and Neugarten (1976); in the works of thanatologists such as Imara (1975) and Kübler-Ross (1970); and in the works of educators of adults who experience mental and learning challenges such as Sutcliffe (1990), Simpson (1979) and Vanier (1970).

ADULTS ARE NOT MATURE CHILDREN NOR ARE CHILDREN IMMATURE ADULTS

The literature in the field of adult education describes a basic conflict between the nature and characteristics of adults as learners in comparison with those of children. Some writers (Cranton, 1989; Hart, 1983; Houle, 1972) maintain that learning is learning and is the same at every age. Other writers (Knowles, 1990, 1970; McKenzie, 1977) maintain that adult learning and child learning are both qualitatively and quantitatively different. Still other writers avoid the issue by discussing the wide variations found among adult learners (Squires, 1993; Flannery, 1993b).

My reading and experience persuade me that the internal cognitive and physiological processes involved in learning may indeed be similar in both adults and children, since they are based on biological and cognitive processes which are not markedly different. However, the social, emotional, developmental and situational variables which affect learning processes are different for adults and children. Baltes, Reese and Lipsitt (1980) provide a conceptual model which helps put variables affecting learning into perspective. They state that lifelong learning and development are influenced by three major factors:

1. **Biological and environmental factors** and traditional age-related experiences, such as socialization and education, are very influential in childhood and adolescence, decline during adulthood and begin to rise again during the later years beginning with such experiences as compulsory retirement.

2. **Historical factors** are associated with the events and contexts of each passing era and are specific to each generation, age cohort and social group to which an individual belongs. Examples include being 20 years old during World War II and being 18 years old when AIDS became a significant problem. Historical factors are very influential during adolescence and young adulthood but decline in influence in later years.

3. **Life events** are specific for each person. Examples include having a parent die when one is a child; developing cancer as a young adult; deciding to return to college in middle age. Life events are cumulative and rise steadily in influence from childhood to old age.

The joint impact of the three influences, mediated through the knowledge and strategies of the developing individual, accounts for differences in learning characteristics between childhood and adulthood.

They also account for differences in learning characteristics between young adults and older adults, and between men and women, issues which will be addressed in Chapters Two and Five.

Adult and childhood learning differences

The major differences I have summarized in Diagram 2, are sometimes aspects of a continuous and ongoing characteristic, as in the accumulation of experience, or they may be aspects of a discontinuous characteristic, as in the shift from concrete to abstract thought. This summary helps us to understand people's behaviour, but is not meant to reflect universal absolute differences. It is drawn from the work of Knowles (1990), Brundage and MacKeracher (1980), McKenzie (1977) and Kidd (1973a).

ADULTS	CHILDREN
• have extensive pragmatic life experiences which tend to structure and limit new learning. Learning focuses largely on transforming or extending the meanings, values, skills, and strategies acquired in previous experience • experience major pressures for change from factors related to social and work roles and expectations, and from personal needs for continuing productivity and self-definition • have learning needs related to current life situations • have the capacity for using generalized, abstract thought • are likely to express their own needs and describe their own learning processes through verbal activities which allow them to negotiate and collaborate in planning their own learning programs • have an organized and consistent self-concept and self-esteem which allows them to participate as a self separate from other selves and capable of acting independently of others • are assigned a responsible status in society, and are expected to be productive	• have fewer pragmatic life experiences. Learning focuses largely on forming and accumulating basic meanings, values, skills, and strategies • experience major pressures for change from factors related to physical growth, demands for socialization, and preparation for future social and work roles • have learning needs related to developing organized patterns for understanding future experience • are more likely to use specific, concrete thought • are likely to express their own needs and learning processes through non-verbal activities, which leads to planning by "expert" observers and interpreters • have a relatively less organized and consistent eslf-concept which allows them to perceive themselves as a self-separate from but dependent on others • are assigned a non-responsible status in society, and are expected to play and learn

2. DIFFERENCES BETWEEN ADULTS AND CHILDREN AS LEARNERS

The characteristics of adult learners will be considered in greater detail in Chapter Two. The list provided in Diagram 2 is based on chronological age and social definitions of childhood and adulthood, and does not take into consideration additional differences based on gender, race or social class. Gender in particular, may have an important effect on learning and will be discussed in greater depth in Chapter Five.

TWO BASIC TENDENCIES FOR ORGANIZING HUMAN BEHAVIOUR

Adults and children show similar characteristics and behaviours relevant to learning and these seem to be organized around two complementary tendencies: *separateness* and *relatedness*. The tendency toward separateness is indicated by mastery, autonomy and separation from others, while the tendency toward relatedness is indicated by belonging, entering into relationships and being connected to others (Miller, 1986; Kegan, 1982; Gilligan, 1982; Jones, 1968).

1. The separateness tendency

This tendency relates to a sense of autonomy, independence, and personal control over one's life. Learning related to this tendency focuses on meanings, strategies, and skills required to function independently as well as values reflecting positive personal feelings of being competent, effective and worthwhile. Such learning reduces any sense of helplessness or inferiority and assists in meeting personal needs for survival, self-esteem and achievement. This type of learning responds best to behavioural or task-related feedback (Jones, 1968).

2. The relatedness tendency

This tendency relates to a sense of affection for others, interdependent behaviour and connectedness to others. Learning related to this tendency includes personal and shared meanings and values, as well as the skills and strategies necessary to function interactively, cooperatively and collaboratively with others. Such learning reduces feelings of isolation and alienation and assists in meeting personal needs for security, belonging, and affiliation. This type of learning responds best to feeling-oriented feedback (Jones, 1968).

Adult education and the two behavioural tendencies

Western adult education literature seems to assume that the tendency toward mastery (separateness) is more important than the tendency toward belonging (relatedness), particularly in relation to learning. This assumption is currently challenged by women, aboriginal learners and persons of colour. The literature is replete with the assumption that an adult is no longer dependent (see Feuer & Geber, 1988; Knowles, 1970), implying that dependent behaviours and possibly even interdependent behaviours, are immature and childlike.

Such a view presupposes that the adult is willing and able to use independent behaviours appropriate to any given situation, ignoring that adults may require dependent and interdependent behaviours in certain situations.

Adults need to be able to use different behaviours in different situations. For example, *dependent behaviours* are entirely appropriate during severe shock following personal accident or trauma, disorientation resulting from entry into an unfamiliar environment, or helplessness in the wake of catastrophes such as floods or earthquakes. In such situations, adults may need to gracefully accept assistance from others and would be foolhardy not to.

Interdependent behaviours are the hallmark of most work, family and community settings and are a crucial part of the daily functioning of most adults. The assumption that an adult is no longer dependent also ignores those adults who have never learned the basic behavioural patterns for independence or interdependence. Some adults, on first entering a learning context, may respond initially with dependent behaviours because their past (schooling) experience tells them such responses are safe.

---

*It is appropriate to view a fully functioning adult
as someone able to use dependent, independent and interdependent behaviours
in varying combinations and under varying conditions, and
that maintaining dynamic equilibrium among these is one of the developmental tasks of adulthood.*
(Josselson, 1992; Bergman, 1991; Coleman, 1976; Cross, 1976; Jones, 1968) .

Gender and the two behavioural tendencies

Some research indicates that behavioural tendencies toward autonomy and belongingness are gender-related but not gender-specific. Such writers as Baxter Magolda (1992), Tannen (1990), Lyons (1988), Belenky, Clinchy, Goldberger and Tarule (1986) and Gilligan (1982) report that women are more likely than men to use behaviours related to the belongingness tendency while men are more likely than women to use behaviours related to the separateness tendency. While the majority of men and women use a combination of these behaviours, many men place an emphasis on autonomous behaviours and many women an emphasis on belongingness behaviours.

Transcendence: The third tendency

A third tendency for organizing behaviour is less documented in the literature, but involves the tendency toward achieving what is described as "transcendence", "self-actualization", "the illuminated mind," "the third eye," or "transpersonal learning" (Wilber, 1986; Roberts, 1975; Maslow, 1970). Wilber (1986, p.72) describes this as a developmental trend in which the

> ... individual's cognitive and perceptual capacities apparently become so pluralistic and universal that they begin to `reach beyond' any narrowly personal or individualistic perspectives and concerns... [T]he individual begins to learn to very subtly inspect the mind's cognitive and perceptual capacities, and thus...to transcend them.

As this tendency develops, the

> …ego-sense is entirely subordinated, lost in largeness of being and finally abolished; a wide cosmic perception and feeling of boundless universal self replaces it …an unlimited consciousness of unity which pervades everywhere…a being who is in essence one with the Supreme Self (Aurobindo, as quoted in Wilber, 1986, pp. 73-74).

This tendency toward transpersonal or spiritual learning will be discussed in greater detail in Chapter Six.

EDUCATION IS POLITICAL

The 1975 International Symposium for Literacy, after completing lengthy discussions about the function of literacy education, declared:

> Literacy work, like education in general, is a political act. It is not neutral, for the act of revealing social reality in order to transform it, or of concealing it in order to preserve it, is political. (Final Report, 1975)

All education is part of a political enterprise, and its basic principles reflect an underlying political philosophy. Elias and Merriam (1995, p.5) describe a philosophical orientation as raising "questions about what we do and why we do it". They state that:

> …philosophy of adult education does not equip a person with knowledge about what to teach, how to teach, or how to organize a program. It is more concerned with the why of education and with the logical analysis of the various elements of the educational process (Elias & Merriam, 1995, p.8).

Writers in the field of adult education have identified a number of philosophical orientations (see Draper, 1993; Zinn, 1990; Hiemstra, 1988; Apps, 1973). The complexity and extent of these many different orientations is such that I could not do them justice in a summary. Here I focus on political philosophical orientations; those which describe assumptions about:

- ❖ how and what learners should learn,
- ❖ how learning resources should be distributed, and
- ❖ how the content and process of educational activities should be publicly supported.

Baum (1978) has proposed three political orientations which have the virtue of being practical, informative, and relatively easy to understand. They are the *liberal, conservative* and *socialistic* orientations. Each makes assumptions about learners and their individual needs; describes the learning process and associated facilitating processes; proposes how the educational system can institutionalize and operationalize a response; and predicts the consequences of the educative processes involved (Baum, 1978).

The liberal orientation
What it is
The most widely-held orientation is based on a liberal philosophy and a pluralistic and systemic approach to facilitating and to learning. A liberal orientation is described by such writers as Knowles (1990), Smith (1982), Kidd (1973a) and Rogers (1969).

This orientation is based on the presupposition that all individuals, in response to their personal life experiences, develop their own personal model of reality representing the meanings and values they have attached to these experiences and the strategies and skills they have developed during them.

Each person's model of reality is both similar to and different from the models developed by others. Since all learners bring a unique model of reality to the learning situation, they also bring unique needs and goals. In the liberal orientation, therefore, the educational system must be prepared to accept, respect, and accommodate these individual needs and goals.

The liberal orientation also recognizes the need for people to form social groups for mutual survival and security. Social interactions require individuals to communicate their models of reality to others; to comprehend and acknowledge those of others; and to develop shared aspects of a group-defined model which may be integrated with their own. The needs and goals of social groups and those of individuals are viewed as having equal importance.

The educational system needs to be able to facilitate this communicating, comprehending, acknowledging, and sharing between individuals and groups through group activities and social interactions.

The task of adult education
In the liberal orientation, the task of adult education is to provide a diverse and flexible set of programs and processes to accommodate individual and group needs. Providing democratic structures and facilitating

learning activities are more important than imposing standards for content and performance.

The facilitating activities are process-oriented and include:

- ❖ helping individuals to create, maintain, extend, and communicate their model of reality;
- ❖ testing and evaluating the utility of their model;
- ❖ comprehending the models of others; and
- ❖ developing shared aspects of a group model through group activities and dialogue with others.

The learning activities include:

- ❖ participating in new experiences;
- ❖ discovering, extending, and transforming personal models of reality;
- ❖ obtaining feedback about the utility of such models; and
- ❖ solving problems related to individual and group needs.

This orientation leads to individualized models of reality and behaviour functioning within group-defined limits. It has a tendency to value the means or processes used in learning rather than the ends or goals. It assumes that individual adults are capable of adapting to the social pressures of the group without adverse effects.

The conservative orientation
What it is
Based on a conservative philosophy and a universal and traditional approach to facilitating and learning, this orientation is the least widely-held in adult education but tends to be implicit in programs which help adults learn professional and occupational skills.

It is based on the presupposition of the existence of a known and understood objective reality and ultimate truth which should be integrated into the knowledge, values, skills, and strategies of each individual within that society or culture. Individuals acquire this objective reality through assimilating standardized public knowledge; acquiring related skills and strategies; and accepting, unquestioningly, the approved values. Individuals can be evaluated by other members of their society/culture on the basis of their ability to conform to a set of behavioural norms which are standardized by role and status.

An "objective reality" is one which exists independently of reality created by an individual. Objective reality is based on knowledge proven to be true through empirical or scientific research or divine revelation.

In the ideal society, all individuals are involved in setting standards and evaluating the performance of others. In real societies, these activities tend to be performed by the most powerful and influential members of the group. Sanctions are provided through law or custom to maintain individual commitment to this objective reality.

The task of adult education

In the conservative orientation, the task of adult education is to provide learning programs which assist all societal members to learn the basic components of the approved model of reality. The concept of universal literacy stems from this orientation (for example, every adult *should* be able to read). Other tasks focus on the provision of relatively autocratic structures and learning content, and the development of universal criteria for judging performance.

The facilitating activities are content-oriented and include:
- ❖ defining the content to be learned and setting objectives;
- ❖ planning learning activities and presenting content;
- ❖ providing feedback related to standardized criteria;
- ❖ disseminating information; and
- ❖ modelling appropriate behaviour.

The learning activities include:
- ❖ comprehending and assimilating the content;
- ❖ testing out skills and strategies; and
- ❖ accepting and responding to feedback.

This orientation leads to an objective and universal model of reality and behaviour which is prescribed by the group. It has a tendency to value goals to be reached rather than processes to be used in learning. Tending to ignore the individual needs and problems of learners, the conservative orientation leads to consistent and competent behaviour among individuals which can be publicly certified or licensed.

The socialistic orientation
What it is
The third orientation is based on a socialistic philosophy and a radical (Jarvis, 1985) or therapeutic approach to facilitating and learning. A socialistic orientation is grounded in the work of such writers as Mezirow (1991), Weiler (1988) and Freire (1985, 1973). It shares many characteristics with the liberal orientation, presupposing the same multiple individual models of reality.

The socialistic orientation differs in that it promotes the correction of those aspects of individual models which are distorted because they are based on lost, repressed, misrepresented, over-simplified or over-generalized aspects of experience.

Society itself encourages distortions by valuing some models of reality over others and by rejecting or discounting some. Valued models are those of the dominant group. For example, in Euro-American societies, the dominant group is comprised of white, middle to upper class males. The shared model of the dominant group becomes the hegemonic model of reality dominating the views of the entire society. Those individuals or groups whose models of reality are undervalued, rejected, or discounted, tend to occupy marginal positions within society. Non-dominant groups in Euro-American societies include women, racial minorities, aboriginal populations, persons with disabilities, the working class, and the poor (Weiler, 1988).

The task of adult education
In the socialistic orientation, adult education provides learning programs to assist in the recovery of lost or repressed models and traditions, to raise misrepresented aspects to a conscious level and transform them, and to persuade the larger society to change the dominant model.

The facilitating activities are issue-, problem-, or person-centred and include:

❖ assisting individuals through therapeutic or counselling-type processes; and

❖ assisting groups through consciousness-raising processes or through change processes which include destabilizing, changing and restabilizing.

The learning activities include:
- ❖ self-reflecting;
- ❖ transforming;
- ❖ re-integrating; and
- ❖ communicating alternative models of reality to others.

Socialistic orientation tends to value separate issues and problems rather than relationships between issues and problems. In the process of recovering and restructuring certain aspects of a model of reality, this orientation tends to discount whatever validity and utility the dominant model had. When used judiciously it enhances and extends the individual in positive ways and alters society in ways which enhance both individuals and society.

Summary of orientations

Although these orientations are discussed here as if they were polarities operating exclusively of one another, they are commonly found in varying combinations within one system, one institution, or even one facilitator/teacher. Educators often espouse one orientation for content and another for process. Commonly, a facilitator who believes that all learners should end up with the same content (a conservative orientation) may also encourage individual learners to use different processes (a liberal orientation).

LEARNING AND FACILITATING PRINCIPLES FOR OPTIMIZING ADULT LEARNING

Based on the research on learning and adult learners described in this chapter, we can make some preliminary assumptions about conditions affecting adult learning. Adults will learn best:

❖ **what has relevance** for them as determined by their current meanings and personal model of reality in terms derived from their needs, life tasks, roles, and personal interests. Without relevance there is little likelihood that the engagement which constitutes learning will occur.

❖ when they are **treated in ways which are consistent** with their existing description of who they are and what they are capable of doing. Most adults see themselves as responsible persons who are capable of planning actions and making decisions for themselves. They need to feel they are being treated as responsible adults who are capable of learning and of making effective use of what they have learned in the past on the basis of their own experience.

❖ when others **respect and acknowledge them** and their past experiences and personal knowledge, skills, values, and motives (that is, their personal model of reality).

❖ when their learning bears some **relationship to past experience** and can be connected to their existing meanings and personal model of reality.

❖ when they have some **sense of where they are going** in the learning process, how they will get there, and how they will know when they have succeeded. Learning is guided as much by what we predict the future will be like (as derived from our personal model of reality), as by current relevance.

CHARACTERISTICS OF ADULT LEARNERS

2

I begin this chapter by considering some characteristics of adult learners in relation to characteristics of learning situations which include facilitator behaviours, quality of the physical or social environment, the nature of resources and technologies, and so on. Five characteristics of adult learners are considered in this chapter:

1. physiological factors
2. past experience
3. time perspectives
4. the self
5. self-direction.

Other characteristics such as energy, emotions, stress and anxiety as well as motives for learning will be discussed in Chapter Three.

A word of caution.
Although these characteristics appear as separate entities,
they are inter-related and interwoven to make a complex fabric of learning.
Each affects and is affected by, every other characteristic.

As you read, think about how each characteristic relates to the others, even if the text does not provide such a discussion.

PHYSIOLOGICAL FACTORS

Physiological characteristics relate to physical well-being, sensory acuity, and the effectiveness of physiological and physical responses in learning activities. Adults reach full physical maturity by their early 20s. Until their late 40s they will experience no major physical changes other than those induced by accident, illness, stress, childbirth, and lifestyle. From the late 40s on, they may gradually become aware of two general physical changes: sensory acuity and speed of physical responses.

Sensory Acuity

With increasing age, the acuity of the sensory receptors for hearing and vision will slowly decline. Usually these declines can be corrected and may be so imperceptible that the individual remains unaware of change.

Such declines affect the quality and quantity of the information input to the learning process by reducing the accuracy and the amount of sensory information taken in. Some older adults develop coping behaviours to deal with such changes. For example, by deliberately placing themselves in relation to others so their hearing losses are minimized, or by gathering information in other ways such as lip-reading. Others cope by using information from past experience to replace unseen or unheard material (Novak, 1993; Birren & Schaie, 1977; Kidd, 1973a).

The implications of sensory changes for learning are few, particularly when the learning environment provides a wide range of repetitive information in both auditory and visual modes. In environments where a range of information is not available, the learners may begin to replace absent information in unproductive ways.

Occasionally, conditions within the learning environment may inadvertently augment sensory losses. The major age-related auditory change is loss of high frequency sounds, a condition which renders normal speech garbled and muffled. Technological devices such as lights and projectors often produce a humming sound which diminishes audible sound even further. And hard reflective surfaces may create an echo which has the same effect.

The major age-related vision changes are an increase in the eye's focal length, a mild decline in ability to discriminate between some colour combinations, and an increase in the time required to adjust vision to changes in light intensity. Older adults need printed materials which are clear and easy to read; large print is not necessary but small print should be avoided. A serif type face (type with a small line at the extremities of the main strokes of a letter) is easier to read than a sanserif type face (type that looks like this). When typed material is reproduced from reproductions of reproductions, the letters gradually lose their serifs, making the material increasingly difficult to read. Reproduce typed material from an original copy whenever possible.

Visual material for projection or flip charts using colours which provide high discrimination between letters and background such as bright red, green, blue, purple and black on an off-white or dull yellow background, are best. Other colours can be used for highlights. When using projectors (overhead, slide projector, VCR), room lights should be adjusted to improve the quality of the projection and allow learners enough time to adjust to changes in light intensity.

Speed of physical responses

The second physical change is a general reduction in the speed of response of the central nervous system. This change should have no effect on learning, except in extreme cases, provided learners are allowed to pace their own learning.

All adults are adversely affected by time constraints, older adults more so than younger adults (Arenberg, 1994).

When a change in speed of response is combined with an overall reduction in physical strength, the older learner may experience some difficulty responding effectively in novel or emergency situations. This change is the result of both a mild decline in the rate at which nervous impulses are transmitted and a general energy decline caused by combinations of poor health, poor nutrition, and poor physical fitness.

Individually, a lessening in the speed of response or a reduction in overall strength should not be a problem. When the learning or responding must be done under pressure of time, the decline in speed of response is further aggravated as it may be with temporary poor health, chronic disease, fatigue, and emotional or physical distress. All of these factors aggravate the overall effects of physical change. While sensory acuity and speed of response decline, there is no corresponding decline in the adult's ability to make meaning, or in effectiveness of learning responses (Arenberg, 1994; Birren & Schaie, 1977).

Older adults generally require more time to learn material, although experience, good health and fitness, and good learning skills will compensate for all but the most marked declines.

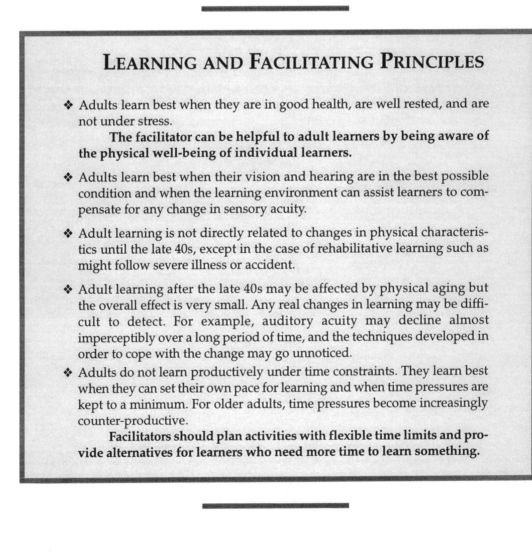

LEARNING AND FACILITATING PRINCIPLES

❖ Adults learn best when they are in good health, are well rested, and are not under stress.
    The facilitator can be helpful to adult learners by being aware of the physical well-being of individual learners.

❖ Adults learn best when their vision and hearing are in the best possible condition and when the learning environment can assist learners to compensate for any change in sensory acuity.

❖ Adult learning is not directly related to changes in physical characteristics until the late 40s, except in the case of rehabilitative learning such as might follow severe illness or accident.

❖ Adult learning after the late 40s may be affected by physical aging but the overall effect is very small. Any real changes in learning may be difficult to detect. For example, auditory acuity may decline almost imperceptibly over a long period of time, and the techniques developed in order to cope with the change may go unnoticed.

❖ Adults do not learn productively under time constraints. They learn best when they can set their own pace for learning and when time pressures are kept to a minimum. For older adults, time pressures become increasingly counter-productive.
    Facilitators should plan activities with flexible time limits and provide alternatives for learners who need more time to learn something.

PAST EXPERIENCE

The second of my five inter-related learner characteristics is prior life experiences. These are used by each learner to develop a personal model of reality which includes both meanings and values (constructs or concepts) to make sense of past experience, impute sense to current experience, and predict future experience. Life experiences are also used to develop skills and strategies (processes or procedures) for reflecting, reconstructing and organizing the past; acting, reacting and interacting in the present, and anticipating the future. Structures and processes are complementary aspects of experience. Each person's model of reality is dynamic rather than static, and is open to constant revision, expansion and transformation as the result of further experience and learning.

Differentiating Process and Structure in Learning

I think of learning as involving a duality in which both process and structure are essential and interdependent. Distinguishing between process and structure is difficult. Consider the following analogy:

> In the physical sciences we can understand matter in three different ways. We can perceive matter as being created by the organization of particles, however minute. In this perception, matter can be understood as an observable, "real" structure which has form, substance and durability.

> Or we can perceive matter as being created by the constant motion of energy. In this perception, matter can be understood as a fleeting wave, a process which passes through the present moment and is known only by the traces it leaves behind.

> Or we can perceive matter as being created by the duality of energy and particles. In this perception, matter can be described as being created by the interaction of energy and particles, process and structure.

We can consider both learning and learner characteristics as either processes or structured concepts, although we generally understand learner characteristics in structural terms and learning in process terms.

Process is constantly in motion, fleeting and transient and occurs in the present moment only.
Structure is something already existing, relatively unchangeable but observable.
We can perceive learning as being created by the **interaction of process and structure.**

To understand and describe a process we must discuss it as if it were thing-like and already in the past. Take, for example, the characteristic of self-directedness.

In **process terms**, we can think of self-directedness as something on its way to being there — a process evolving as the learner becomes more confident and the environment encourages more self-reliance. When we perceive self-direction as a process, we should be able to see the learner's behaviour change from the beginning of the process through to the end, and we should be able to describe how self-directedness emerges over time in response to an enabling environment.

In **structural terms**, we can think of self-directedness as something already there — part of the personality structure of the learner, and hence, as relatively unchangeable. Or we can think of it as some relatively unchangeable aspect of the environment, such as a programmed learning module, which demands or pulls self-directed behaviour from the learner.

We can also perceive **self-directedness as the result of the interaction of self-direction** (or lack of it) as a personality trait (structure), **and self-directedness** as a process which emerges in response to the environment. This also exemplifies the B-P-E model which we will discuss later.

Figure-ground relationships

Our personal model of reality never incorporates all our experiences but rather rests on selected experiences or generalizations about experiences.

The details of most experiences remain obscured in the background while we select aspects to form a "figure." In Gestalt psychology (Zimbardo & Ruch, 1978), a "figure" is the central pattern of our recalled and generalized experiences. In comparison to the background or "ground," the figure is that part of the experience that

- ❖ is more vivid or has more affect,
- ❖ is more complete in detail,
- ❖ has shape and is more thing-like, and
- ❖ is nearer to us in time, space or relevance.

The part of experience not selected for the figure fades into the ground accompanying the figure.

The manner in which details are selected for inclusion in a figure contributes to the distortions or deletions which are also incorporated in the figure-ground relationships within our personal model of reality.

Figure-ground relationships are an example of the interaction of process and structure. These relationships are not fixed or immutable.

In reflecting on the same experience,

❖ some individuals may perceive persons or events as figures;

❖ some may perceive processes (learning, thinking, remembering) as figures; and

❖ some may perceive both processes and structures as figures.

However we make sense of experience, we need to expend energy if we wish to overcome the human tendency to conserve existing relationships, rather than developing new possibilities.

The place of experience in learning

Some aspects of past experience have an important effect on learning. Our personal model of reality is generally understood as consisting of several tightly interwoven components. Some of these components are:

❖ **our self-system** or how we understand ourselves as persons through the meanings we give to ourselves as actors, or our self-concept, and the values we assign to ourselves, or our self-esteem.

❖ **our professional or occupational knowledge** (meanings, values, skills and strategies);

❖ **our practical knowledge** about daily living;

❖ **our cultural knowledge** about how things work in our society; and

❖ **our personal narrative or story** which tells us who we are and records our biography.

We each invest a vast amount of emotional energy in the development of our personal model of reality and place ourselves at the core of the model since we perceive reality from the centre of our own existence. When we enter into learning activities, we tend to use at least part of our energy to protect and defend our model and our self from potentially disconfirming experiences. If we lack self-confidence and feel as if some part of our model has been rejected or discounted by others, we may feel rejected or discounted as a person and become distressed.

Adults have more experience than children in the pragmatic realities of life, and have developed many patterned ways of perceiving and understanding that experience. The adult's personal model of reality simultaneously defines, creates, and restricts perceptions and understanding of new experiences. In response to today's information explosion and accelerating change, an individual's model requires constant updating and revision, at an ever-increasing rate.

Toffler (1970) discusses the "half-life" of an adult's professional knowledge and skills. For some professionals, such as computer programmers, librarians and technicians, the half-life is uncomfortably short, perhaps two years or less. For other professionals, such as educators, the half-life is much longer. In the first group, the major learning need is keeping up with change; in the second group, the major learning need is preventing stagnation.

The place of past experience in learning

Past experience is an essential component in learning,
both as a base for new learning and as an unavoidable potential obstacle.

Past experience structures the ways an adult will
- ❖ approach new experiences,
- ❖ determine what information will be selected for further attention and how it will be interpreted, and
- ❖ determine what knowledge (meanings and values) and skills (strategies, tactics and styles) will be employed first in the learning process.

If these are found unsuitable, the learner will first search back through previous experience for suitable knowledge and skills to apply indirectly. If nothing can be found, then the learner is faced with a dual challenge: first to acknowledge the inadequacy of knowledge or skills already held, (thereby questioning their self-concept as a competent person); and second to trust themselves to enter learning which will result in as-yet-unknown transformation of that self-concept. The first part of this challenge represents in some sense a failure of the existing self-concept, and the second represents risk of new failure.

The paradox for the adult, is that while self-concept must undergo partial change in the process, that same self-concept must be relied on to manage that change. The learner may respond to such situations by becoming confused or angry, withdrawing to a more comfortable environment, or avoiding learning experiences altogether. More productively, the learner can adopt a questioning and reflective stance leading to a more profound understanding of self. Past experience always enters into adult learning unless the learning experience or content is wholly new to the learner.

Adult learning focuses primarily on modifying, transforming, and reintegrating knowledge and skills, rather than on forming and accumulating them as in childhood.

We tend to assume that learning processes involved in transformations are different from those involved in formations. Mezirow (1991), Hart (1983), and Freire (1973) indicate that transformations require:

❖ greater input of energy, (the body invests considerable energy in maintaining established patterns, a conservative tendency which must be overcome first if these patterns are to be transformed);

❖ more time than formations;

❖ examination and critical reflection of established knowledge and skills at a conscious level before being altered;

❖ testing new behaviours in "safe" situations before using them in daily life, as a means for reducing potential threat to the self; and

❖ awareness of both figure and ground and the ability to perceive the relationship between the two.

Transformations are based on raising figure-ground relationships to consciousness and then reorganizing them on a new basis by bringing some of the material in the ground into the figure or moving some of the material in the figure to the ground.
This process also contributes to increasing awareness of distorted and repressed realities and to correcting them *(Weiler, 1988; Denis & Richter, 1987).*

Using past experience in learning

When we base learning principles on the notion that adults' past experiences form the basis of all learning, we may also be presupposing that the adult learner has already acquired all the knowledge and skills necessary for current learning. Such assumptions are not tested often enough and may prove erroneous.

For example, work by Piaget indicates that, as a result of cognitive development, adults have attained generalized and abstract strategies for thinking *(formal operational thinking)*. However, tests show that instead of using formal operational thinking, the average adult is more likely to use concrete and specific strategies for thinking *(concrete operational thinking)* (Thibodeau, 1979). These results do not indicate whether the concrete stage of thinking represents non-attainment of the abstract and generalized stage, or is a regression from the formal stage of thinking in response to the conditions of daily life (Arlin, 1986; Thibodeau, 1979).

If we proceed with learning activities assuming that all adult participants have all the necessary knowledge and skills and we later discover some are missing essential components, we are likely to perceive such learners as incompetent, ignorant, stupid, stubborn, unmotivated, or even deviant (Brim & Wheeler, 1966). Such perceptions would be rapidly communicated to learners through our non-verbal behaviour, creating further distress for them.

While past experience is an essential component in adult learning, using it in relation to current learning presents a problem. Many adults cannot perceive connections between past experiences and current problems. Only some parts of past experience may be relevant to the present context.

The facilitator may need to assist the learner to identify potentially relevant past experiences and to actively seek connections with the current situation.

Feringer (1978) and Ornstein (1972) suggest that past experience can be used most productively when it becomes the basis for analogy or metaphor. What appears to be a non-logical, non-rational approach to learning can be used as a method for making logical, rational sense of current experience. Their view implies that learning requiring transformation of previous experience, proceeds most effectively through such facilitating activities as brainstorming, analogies, games, simulations, metaphors, case studies, and the like.

All of these can be described as non-sequential cognitive processes seeking as wide a variety of information and ideas as possible. The learner then looks for connections among the ideas generated, identifies and narrows these through convergent and sequential cognitive processes. In this way, adult learning based on past experience becomes most productive (Denis & Richter, 1987; Feringer, 1978).

TIME PERSPECTIVES

An adult tends to perceive time as including an ever-increasing past, a fleeting and pressured present, and a finite future.

The time perspective of some adult learners is different than that of children. A child tends to perceive time as including a present and an infinite future. Children and young adults tend to measure time as "time since birth"; adults past 40 tend to measure time as "time until death" (Neugarten & Datan, 1973). This shift from an increasing span of time (time since birth) to a decreasing one (time until death) has consequences for learning.

The ever-increasing past provides an ever-increasing model of reality which can both help and hinder learning. The larger and more enriched it becomes, the greater its potential for helping or hindering. When existing knowledge conflicts sharply with what is to be learned, learners will need additional time to re-evaluate what they already know and to modify it slowly before reintegrating it back into their existing knowledge. Since life experiences accumulate over time, older learners may experience more potential conflict than younger learners.

━━━━━━━━━━━━━━━━━━━

Conflicts that cannot be resolved will be integrated into existing knowledge only very slowly, if at all. Knowledge for which the learner has no experiential base may be acquired without conflict but may not be easily understood or immediately applied.

━━━━━━━━━━━━━━━━━━━

The fleeting present involves many conflicting concerns, needs, drives, and problems. These conflicts become essential content to the learning process. Solutions to current problems, while often readily apparent to an observer, must:

1. come from within,
2. be consistent with the individual's model of reality, and
3. be implemented from the individual's own resources.

Solutions which do not "fit" are generally rejected. The pressures on an adult to resolve conflicts and solve problems quickly, make the discovery of personally meaningful solutions that much more difficult to accomplish. The perceived finite future for middle-aged and older adults tends to create the illusion of a need to hurry, to change and learn quickly, and to get on with life. This illusion also grows out of our traditional (and erroneous) beliefs that learning and education are once-in-a-lifetime activities which will provide for all future contingencies, and that learning is an activity distinct and separate from living and working (Kidd, 1973a; McClusky, 1970).

LEARNING AND FACILITATING PRINCIPLES

❖ Past experience of adult learners must be acknowledged as an active component in learning and accepted as a valid representation of their experience. Past experience can be both an enhancement to new learning and an unavoidable obstacle.

Learning is facilitated when past experience is used by both learners and facilitators as a resource for learning in some activities.

❖ Past experience becomes increasingly important and its potential for helping or hindering the learning process increases with age.

❖ Adults learn more productively when the material or processes used bear some perceived relationship to past experience, or when past experience can be applied directly to new situations.

Learning is facilitated when time and opportunities are provided to reflect on past experience, to find connections between past experience and new knowledge and skills, and to integrate these.

❖ Adults tend to experience a need to learn quickly and get on with living. They are often reluctant to engage in learning activities or content which does not appear to have immediate and pragmatic application within their life.

Learning is facilitated when learners can assess their own learning needs and select their own learning goals and directions for change. If this is not possible, then learners should have a complete understanding of the objectives which have been established by others, should be able to accept these, and should be willing to commit themselves to the selected direction for change.

❖ Past experience presents the adult learners with a paradox. In the learning experience, the knowledge (meanings and values) and skills (strategies, tactics and styles) based on past experience and forming part of the present self-concept are being changed. These changes may in turn, disconfirm or threaten the self-concept. At the same time, the self-concept must be a trusted agent in managing the learning process.

❖ Adult learning focuses largely on transforming knowledge and skills derived from past experience. This process requires more energy and more time than learning based on formation of new knowledge. It also requires that past experience be raised to consciousness, and that new behaviours be tested in safe and trusted environments.

Learning is facilitated in learning environments which are free from threat and which provide support for personal change. Learning activities need to include opportunities for testing new behaviours in relative safety, developing mutually trusting relationships, encouraging descriptive feedback, and reducing fear of failure.

❖ All adults do not necessarily possess all the knowledge and skills required for new learning activities. Acquisition of the missing components must be regarded as an essential part of all learning activities.

Learning is facilitated when the learners' existing knowledge and skills are assessed to identify their strengths and weaknesses, and to determine which components essential to the learning context may be missing.

❖ Adult learners may need considerable assistance in verbalizing and clarifying ther current problems, identifying how learning activities could help in solving these problems, and specifying these activities in terms of learning objectives and directions.

Learning is facilitated where the learning activities provide opportunities to talk about and share experiences.

Adult learning is also facilitated if

❖ past experiences are considered in relation to current experience through reflective learning activities which involve the use of imagery, mataphors, analogies and other divergent, non-sequential, cognitive processes;

❖ activities planned for the first two or three sessions of a program include a built-in factor for success and preclude the possibility of failure;

❖ learners are reassured that their learning performance will not be judged on the basis of tentative answers and experimental behaviours, and that such answers and behaviours can be modified as the learning activity progresses.

THE SELF

The fourth of my five inter-related learner characteristics is the self and its development. The ability of human beings to form abstract ideas allows them to think about themselves and how they appear to others. The process of synthesis and adaptation occurring between the inner life and outer reality produces a sense of personal continuity and sameness in the experience of feeling and being "a self."

Our sense of self evolves out of our experience with objects, other persons and the kinds of interactions we have with them.
In other words, we construct our "self" out of our experience with the object world.

This "self" which we take to be "me" and which feels so present and real to us is actually an internalized image, a composite representation, constructed by a selective and imaginative "remembering" of past encounters with significant objects [and other persons] in our world. In fact, the self...is actually being constructed anew from moment to moment. Even as a representation, it is not a fixed entity but a temporal succession of discrete images, each representing a new construction, a new synthesis, in the present moment of experience (Engler 1986, p.22).

Ordinarily, we do not experience our self in this way; rather we experience our self as having continuity and sameness across time and contexts, as being consistent in our interactions with others, and as being recognized by others on the basis of this continuity and consistency.

Even when we develop and change in terms of our knowledge and behaviour or in our understanding of ourselves, we still experience our self as having an inner core which maintains some continuity with the self we knew in childhood and adolescence.

The self is a basic and essential component of the individual's personal model of reality. It comprises meanings from various aspects of experience:

❖ physical elements contribute to the body-image,
❖ cognitive elements to the self-concept,
❖ emotional or affective elements to self-esteem,
❖ social elements to the social-self; and
❖ spiritual elements to the higher or ideal self.

In terms of learning,

...all new experiences for the learner are symbolized and organized into some relationship to the self, or are ignored because there is not a perceived relationship, or are denied organization or given a distorted meaning because the experience seems inconsistent with the structure of the self [and threatens it] (Kidd, 1973a, p.130).

A child's self-concept is in the process of being formed and each new learning experience may vary the structure but not threaten it with fragmentation or disconfirmation. The adult's self-concept is already well formed, and new learning experiences have the potential for fragmenting it or partially disconfirming it.

Adults must defend the "self" against the threats inherent in learning activities, until they are able to perceive that the worst will not happen and that change in self-concept can lead to positive results. A search of the literature on adult learning and the self-concept provides the following ideas about the function of the self-concept and self-esteem in the learning activities of adults:

❖ The fate of the self is *the* central issue in healthy personality development (Engler, 1986; Kegan, 1982; Erikson, 1968), and in learning.

❖ Adults who value their own experience as a rich resource for further learning or whose experience is valued by others are better learners (Thibodeau, 1979; Pine & Boy, 1977; Combs, 1974).

❖ Adults are more concerned with changing in the direction of their own idealized self-concept than with meeting objectives established by others (Lam, 1976; Huberman, 1974). Some adult learners hold an idealized concept of themselves which requires acting as independent learners and setting their own goals for learning. If a facilitator insists that such individuals learn in relation to pre-established goals, they may see this requirement as threatening to their self-concept.

❖ Adults learn best when they are involved in developing learning objectives for themselves congruent with their current self-concept and ideal self (Tough, 1979). Many adult learners are quite willing to accept some learning goals pre-established by the facilitator, but it helps to offer them the opportunity to set some goals for themselves.

❖ Adults with higher self-esteem and a more positive self-concept are more ready to accept change (Klopf, Bowman & Joy, 1969).

❖ There is a positive correlation between flexibility as a personal characteristic and self-esteem (Klopf and others, 1969). That is, those who have a high self-esteem are more flexible.

❖ The self is affected by each new role taken on by the learner. Role learning provides the basis for most adult learning needs (Brim & Ryff, 1980; Kidd, 1973a; Brim, 1968).

❖ The most essential component of the self in relation to learning is self-seen-as-learner (McClusky, 1970). If adults think that learning and the adventure of change are as much a part of their lives as their work and family roles, they will be more likely to enter into learning with positive and flexible attitudes. If adults think that learning is only for children or associated with a non-responsible status in society, they will not participate willingly in learning activities. The self-seen-as-learner role also appears to be an essential component in learning how to learn.

❖ Role learning is carried out not through formal, logical, or sequential processes but through interpersonal interactions, modelling, and experimenting (Goslin, 1969). The role of learner can be learned most productively when adults observe and interact with others using such role behaviour in normal daily activities, and especially when they have a safe environment to test it out.

❖ When the self-concept fails to maintain a fit between the experience of ongoing events and the satisfaction of emerging needs, individual meaning begins to diminish. Any loss of meaning leads to distress and personal crises (Hanna, 1987).

Development of the self

An unresolved issue related to "the self" lies in our conception of how the self develops. We have already seen that the self emerges as a function of our interactions with others. Traditional developmental theories tend to see all personal development as a process of differentiating one's "self" from a matrix of "others". Levinson (1978), for example, talks about "becoming one's own man".

> Development of the self presumably is attained via a series of painful crises by which the individual accomplishes a sequence of…essential separations from others and thereby achieves an inner sense of separated individuation (Miller 1984, p. 1).

Miller (1986) and Josselson (1992) question whether this accurately reflects the lives of men, and state emphatically that the ideal of a self separate from others does not fit the life experiences of most women. In our traditional models of human development as typified by Loevinger (1976), Erikson (1968), Erikson and others (1986) and Jung (1964), such ideas about separation and individuation dominate our collective view of the preconditions of mental health. These ideas are powerful because they have become prescriptions for what should happen and for what 'normal' development should be like.

Those whose life experience does not fit this traditional model, may feel that their self-concept is inadequate and their personal development has not been normal, and by extension that they are inadequate "selves" and "not-normal" as persons.

Feminist writers encourage such persons to challenge traditional knowledge whenever it is inconsistent with their personal life experiences.

> Psychology has only recently begun to consider seriously the developmental course of human connection in its subtlety and variety. Until now, psychological theory of development has occupied itself with [the explication] of the self. Self-esteem, self-control, self-awareness, and individual achievement have dominated psychological theory. Other people have been recognized only as "objects" for the gratification of instinctual needs and of the needs of the growing and differentiating self. Relationship as a goal, inter-connection as an aim — these had no place in our theories. Where the phenomena of interpersonal connection in human life are acknowledged at all, they serve merely as a backdrop for the more apparent dramas of self (Josselson 1992, p.1).

Miller (1984) and Josselson (1992) propose an alternative conception of human development, which includes the life experiences of both men and women. In their model of human development, the infant begins to develop an internal representation as a being-in-relationship, as a self which reflects what is happening between the infant and significant others.

*That is, the self is still conceived as developing in and through interactions with others, but the emphasis is placed not on the qualities of one's **separation** from others, but on the qualities of one's **connections** to others.*

Such development is promoted in interactions in which the caregiver is actively attending to the infant's needs, particularly to the infant's emotions. Miller (1984) goes on to say that the infant responds to the other in the same way — that is, to the other's emotions.

> The beginning of mental representations of the self, then, is of a self whose core — which is emotional — is attended to by other(s), and who begins to attend to the emotions of the other(s). Part of this internal image of one's self includes feeling the other's emotions and acting on the emotions coming from the other as they interplay with one's own emotions. This means that the beginnings of the concept of self are not those of a static and lone self being ministered to by another..., but much more of a self inseparable from a dynamic interaction (Miller 1984, p.3).

This early image of self as a being-in-relationship is present in infants of both sexes, but gender-biased, culturally-induced processes of socialization take over at a very early age.

Most girls are socialized and encouraged to augment their abilities to "feel as the other feels" and to practice "learning about" others. Most boys are systematically diverted into viewing themselves as a self separate from other selves. Most girls therefore, tend to develop a self-concept based on attending and responding to what is going on in relationships. Most boys tend to develop a self-concept based on standing alone, thinking and learning independently, and acting autonomously.

Kegan (1982) adopts a similar view of human development but sees the lifelong process of development moving through successive phases which alternate between an emphasis on the self-as-exclusive and autonomous, and the self-as-inclusive and relational. Lyons (1988) assessed the self-concepts of both men and women. She reported that while many men and women use a combination of both relational and autonomous concepts to describe themselves, more men rely on a self-perception as separate and independent of others, and more women rely on a self-perception as connected and interdependent.

These differences in conceptualizing self-development, raise questions about adults' participation in learning activities. Do those defining themselves in mainly autonomous or separate terms participate in learning activities in ways which differ from those defining themselves in mainly relational or connected terms? Baxter Magolda (1992) reports that, although college men and women do not differ much in what they learn, they do differ in their preferences for carrying out learning activities. Men more often than women learn more effectively in activities involving:

❖ autonomy,
❖ mastery of the material,
❖ individual achievement,
❖ working with others to challenge one's own thinking, and
❖ focusing primarily on self-directed learning even when engaged in collaborative contexts.

Women more often than men learn more effectively in settings involving:

- ❖ relationships,
- ❖ connecting learning to one's own life experiences,
- ❖ understanding the experiences of others, and
- ❖ focusing on a collective or collaborative perspective even in individualized learning contexts.

We will consider these differences again in a later chapter.

Descriptions of the self tend to be idiosyncratic. Adult learners share relatively few labels for their self-concepts. The literature tends to rely on descriptive labels which come from personality theory. For example, very few adult learners would describe themselves as a "self-directed learner," and yet many use the behaviours related to this label. They would be more likely to describe themselves as "I am someone who figures things out for myself"— hardly a label which can be used for research purposes!

LEARNING AND FACILITATING PRINCIPLES

❖ Adults enter learning activities with an organized and integrated set of descriptions and feelings about themselves which influence the learning process. The description is the self-concept; the feelings are the self-esteem.

Learning is facilitated when learning activities support opportunities to organize, understand and integrate new knowledge into existing knowledge.

❖ Adults with positive self-concept and high self-esteem are more responsive to learning and less threatened by learning environments. Adults with negative self-concept and low self-esteem are less likely to enter learning activities willingly and are often threatened by such environments.

❖ Adults are more concerned about changing in the direction of their own ideal self than about meeting standards and objectives set for them by others.

Learning is facilitated when the self-concept (description) and self-esteem (feelings) of each learner are valued as they are presented by the learner. Facilitators working with adults need to know how they conceptualize adult learners, as well as how adult learners conceptualize themselves. Where the two conceptualizations are incongruent, the facilitator should pay more attention to the learners' descriptor of themselves.

❖ Adults react to learning experiences or information as they perceive it, not as the facilitator presents it.

❖ Adults learn best when there are activities which allow them to organize and integrate new learning into their self-concept.

❖ Adults learn best in environments which provide support and safety for testing new behaviours.

❖ Adults learn best in environments which provide opportunities both for the development of interpersonal relationships with the facilitator and other learners, and for demonstrating their mastery and understanding of the content to be learned.

Other ways to facilitate adult learning...

❖ **Facilitators should be able to model behaviour which is relevant to the learners' role. This includes:**

— **valuing the role of learners as an integral part of living and as essential to living as work, social, and family roles;**

— using learning-how-to-learn strategies;
— valuing and using personal past experience as a resource for current learning; and
— valuing the role of learners as a responsible status within society.

❖ Facilitators need to be able to assist learners wishing to master the content and learn independently, as well as those preferring to discuss issues with others as a means of understanding their own experience and those of others. Both types of activities should be an integral part of all learning experiences.

SELF-DIRECTION

The fifth inter-related learner characteristic is self-direction. The idea of self-direction as a characteristic of adult learners and as an approach to learning, is probably the most discussed and debated issue in adult education (Caffarella & O'Donnell, 1988). Because I cannot possibly cover the numerous variations on the theme of self-direction, I present only the highlights. For a more detailed and comprehensive discussion, I recommend Candy's 1991 book, *Self-direction for lifelong learning*.

The term "self-direction" is problematic because few writers, researchers and educators take the time to provide a clearly functional definition. Candy (1991) points out that the term "self-directed", when applied to learning, can be either a goal of, or a process used within, learning activities; and when applied to the learner, can be either a general personal characteristic (not related to learning) or a characteristic with specific meaning for the learning process.

Self-direction as a personal characteristic

Since we are concerned here with the characteristics of learners, we will begin by considering how the term "self-directed" is used to describe people in general and learners in particular. Based on a detailed review of the literature, Candy (1991, p.125) states that a self-directed or autonomous person is able to invoke a coherent set of beliefs, values and attitudes which include viewing the self as autonomous. This serves as a basis for:

❖ conceiving goals and plans,
❖ exercising freedom of choice,
❖ using rational reflection,
❖ using will power to follow through,

❖ assessing plans and choices, and

❖ exercising self-restraint and self-discipline.

Self-direction usually includes the idea that the autonomous person has the will and capacity to complete any plans of action arrived at through planning, choosing or reflecting, without having to depend on others for support or encouragement. This implies that autonomous persons are self-contained and do not need or respond to others. In fact, those who are impervious to the opinions of others, or uncaring about the effects self-directed choices have on others, are as undesirable as those who rely too heavily on the approval of others (Candy, 1991).

Self-direction is characterized by doubt.
All knowledge, plans and choices are subject to systematic criticism in which
the premises and logic which underlie them
must be reviewed critically to detect error.

It is impossible for most adults to escape the socializing influences of others in determining their own set of beliefs, values and attitudes. The characteristics describing a self-directed person, therefore, represent an ideal which few, if any, are able to invoke in all contexts.

Self-direction should be understood as behaviour which results as much from
interaction between the individual actor and the environment
(characteristics of other persons, groups institutions, etc.) as from a personal trait (Pratt, 1988).

Self-direction can be understood in three ways:

1. as an innate disposition, trait or characteristic one is born with;

2. as an acquired quality developing naturally with increasing age; and/or

3. as a learned characteristic encouraged through educational activities.

As an innate characteristic, we can talk about individuals who have a natural predisposition to doubt and to go their own way. If self-directedness is an innate characteristic, then facilitators will have very little effect in helping individuals develop it. If self-directedness evolves as a natural aspect of human development, then facilitating activities would have little effect in encouraging such development. In both cases, therefore, the best a facilitator can do is to provide opportunities for self-directed persons to do their own thing. However, if self-directedness is a learned characteristic, then it is amenable to the educative process.

Presumably we could develop facilitating activities which would encourage and support the development of self-directed characteristics. It is a mistake, however, to believe that simply providing certain freedoms in the instructional setting will inevitably lead to the exercise of the learners' personal autonomy.

As with all behaviours, the exercise of self-direction is affected as much by personal characteristics of the individual as by the characteristics of the environment.
Self-direction as an outcome, therefore,
is reliant on the self-direction or autonomy of the person and
the absence of external constraints in the environment.

Self-direction as a specific characteristic of adult learners

Self-direction as a specific characteristic of adult learners adds some new dimensions to the discussion. When Candy (1991) reviewed the literature on the skills and competencies required for self-direction in learning, he described the ideal self-directed learner as someone capable of exercising control over the tasks to be mastered in the learning process, and of working independently by:

- ❖ being methodical and disciplined, logical and analytical;
- ❖ being reflective and self-aware;
- ❖ demonstrating curiosity, openness and flexibility;
- ❖ being interdependent and interpersonally competent, independent and self-sufficient;
- ❖ being persistent and responsible, venturesome and creative;
- ❖ showing confidence and having a positive self-concept; and
- ❖ having knowledge about, and skill in, learning generally (knowing how to learn).

This list certainly describes an ideal learner, but it is likely someone who may exist only in the hearts and minds of adult educators. **Lists of this type have been criticized for at least five reasons:**

1. **The list represents the characteristics which are expected of able-bodied, white, middle to upper class males in Euro-American societies** (Walker, 1984). Lists of competencies are rarely developed on the basis of the learners being female, members of racial and cultural minorities, persons with different abilities, members of the working class, or poor. A few of the many questions which could be asked about this list are:

    1. What does being methodical and self-disciplined have to do with being self-directed as a learner?
    2. Could a self-directed learner be analogical and holistic rather than logical and analytical?
    3. Is it possible that self-direction in learning is a consequence of competence and a positive self-esteem, rather than a required, pre-existing competency?
    4. Is learning how to learn the same for those who have sensory or physical disabilities as it is for the able-bodied?
    5. Does the word "responsible" mean the same to men and women, or to members of racial and cultural minority groups?

2. **The manner in which these competencies are used and to what end differs greatly depending on the political philosophy of the educator.** This list seems to fit best with the *liberal orientation* described in Chapter One. Those who espouse the *conservative orientation* might not wish to encourage curiosity, openness, flexibility, venturesomeness, creativity or self-awareness. And within the conservative orientation, it is unlikely that the learner would be allowed to develop criteria for assessing learning.

    Those who espouse the *socialistic or radical orientation* are unlikely to encourage independence since it is through interdependence that learners increase their awareness of the conditions constraining them and that groups can plan and implement social change. Rarely is social change instituted by the actions of a person acting independently.

3. **Adult educators often fail to take into account situational differences** (Pratt, 1988).

    Individuals may be self-directed in learning activities related to their own work but be dependent in learning activities related to knowledge or skills lying outside their expertise. Among the learner characteristics which will affect how individuals behave, are not only their self-directedness but also their level of expertise and general familiarity with the knowledge and skills to be learned (Candy, 1991).

4. **The issue is confounded by our definition of "self" and of "learning".**

    We have already defined learning as a meaning-making process through which each learner develops a personal model of reality centred about the experiences of the developing and evolving "self." This personal model of reality and "self" effectively direct all further learning. According to this definition, all learning is directed by the self, even among learners who are dependent. Their self-concept may not be very strong or very positive, but according to the definition of learning used here, that self is the agent who will do the learning. *To speak of self-directed learning, therefore, is a tautology.*

5. **These competencies are not readily measurable or assessable behaviours.**

    Many attempts have been made to develop a means for assessing individuals in terms of self-directedness. The two most frequently used are the Self-Directed Learning Readiness Scale (SDLRS, Guglielmino, 1977) and Oddi's Continuing Learning Inventory (OCLI, Oddi, 1986). The SDLRS consists of 58 items designed to assess the degree to which individuals perceive themselves as possessing eight competencies usually associated with self-directed learners.

A high total score on the Self-Directed Learning Readiness Scale (Guglielmino, 1977) is perceived as indicating a high degree of readiness to be a self-directed learner.

The OCLI, a self-report instrument with 24 items, identifies clusters of personality characteristics found to relate to initiative and persistence in learning over time:

❖ proactive versus reactive drives;

❖ commitment versus apathy or aversion to learning; and

❖ cognitive openness versus defensiveness.

Criticism of the tests for assessing self-directedness

Both tests (SDLRS and OCLI) have been used in a number of research studies and have a strong following among adult educators. A major problem with both tests is that their supporters claim them to be con-text-free (Candy, 1991).

Both tests are no more context-free or culturally unbiased, than self-directedness can be considered context-free or culturally unbiased. A learner may be self-directed in one context but paralyzed in another.

Learners from a culture which is not Euro-American may have no experience with the idea that they have a choice in what or how things are learned.

A second problem is that both appear to measure self-directed-ness in school-and book-oriented contexts, and as a result, both may be inappropriate from some types of learners. A third problem is that it is unclear what a low score means, particularly on the SDLRS. Bonham (1991) reports that a low SDLRS score means an antipathy to all modes of learning rather than a preference to have others direct learning activities. This implies that a high score on the SDLRS indi-cates a positive attitude toward learning in general rather than a positive attitude toward learning described as self-directed. Bonham questions whether the instrument measures self-motivation to engage in learning or self-management of the learning process.

The development of self-directedness in learning

Finally, we should consider how self-directedness in learning devel-ops. We do know that simply placing adult learners in a context with few constraints and telling them to be self-directed is an inadequate (some would even say unethical and incompetent) way to facilitate the development of self-directedness.

Within the literature on self-directed learners, there is some spec-ulation about how self-direction as a characteristic develops. An underlying assumption of such research is that an individual can have more or less of the characteristic (assuming self-direction is quantifiable) and that an individual acquires more of the necessary components of the characteristics over time (Knowles, 1990). Delahaye, Limerick and Hearn (1994), as well as Grow (1991) and Smith (1989) view self-direction as situation-specific and address changes through using a modified version of situational leadership concepts (Hersey & Blanchard, 1982).

The general tenor of their ideas is that adults change in their need for direction, support and structure over any learning episode.
Most begin with a high need for structure and direction and a low need for support.
Over time the need for support increases, then decreases toward the end of the learning activities; while the need for direction and structure decreases gradually over time.

Pratt (1988) presents similar ideas but sees the need for support as varying over time. Kasworm (1983) addresses the issue through examining qualitative changes in three components of learning:

1. level of skill and behaviour for engaging in learning,
2. cognitive capabilities and competencies, and
3. affective and value orientations focused on the nature of the inquiry process and beliefs about how knowledge is generated.

As an organizing model, the approach taken here integrates Brim's ideas about socialization and self-direction as a specific role related to the self-as-learner, with the components of learning described by Kasworm.

Brim (Brim & Wheeler, 1966) writes that
the purpose of socializing an individual to any new role (in this case, the role of self-directed learner) is to help that person acquire
the necessary knowledge, attain the appropriate skills and develop the essential motives.

Brim goes on to say that the individual must learn the knowledge, skills and motives necessary for the actual performance of the role *and* the knowledge, skills and motives necessary for valuing the role. He tells us that childhood socialization is focused on learning values appropriate for development of later roles, while adult socialization focuses on learning to perform actual roles. His model suggests that if a person reaches adulthood not valuing the role of self-directed learner, then learning to perform the role is very difficult.

While self-direction is rarely described as a role,
many writers imply that all adults value the 'role of self-directed learner'.
This belief has become part of the mythology of adult education; and
as a myth, blinds us to the fact that
some adults cannot, will not, or do not perform as self-directed learners.

Believing in such a myth may also prevent critical examination of its inherent assumptions. Brim would tell us that in order to help an adult perform the role of self-directed learner we must first ensure that he or she values the role.

But if we assume that all persons reach adulthood valuing the role of self-directed learner, then the development of the necessary knowledge, skills and motives to perform this role ought to be relatively easy to accomplish through especially designed activities. Grow (1991), for example, outlines four stages in the development of a self-directed learner. In these stages the learner moves from using dependent behaviours to

1. first being interested in becoming self-directed,
2. then being involved in being self-directed and
3. finally becoming fully self-directed as a learner.

In the process the learner develops competencies in data gathering, organizing and retrieving information, critical thinking and systematic goal setting. This developmental process can be nurtured through facilitating methods which call for the use of these competencies in:

❖ collaborative learning,
❖ discovery learning,
❖ contract-based learning,
❖ individualized instruction,
❖ learner-controlled instruction, and
❖ problem-based learning and independent study.

MATCHING LEARNER CHARACTERISTICS TO FACILITATING BEHAVIOURS

When we apply the B-P-E model first proposed by Lewin (1951) to the learning-facilitating context, the "P" stands for Person (the learner) and can include any characteristic of a learner which affects learning. The "B" stands for Behaviour and can include any outcome (the knowledge, meanings, values, skills, attitudes that are learned, how the learner responds to the learning process, and so on) which occurs during or after the learning-facilitating interaction. The "E" stands for Environment and can include any factor within the learning situation or context which might affect learning including, for example, facilitator behaviours, quality of the physical environment, nature of the learning resources, technologies, and so on.

LEARNING AND FACILITATING PRINCIPLES

❖ Self-direction is an individual personality characteristic or trait which includes: conceiving goals and plans, exercising freedom of choice, using rational reflection, using will power to follow through, assessing plans, choices and outcomes, and exercising self-discipline. These activities are accomplished without depending on others for encouragement and reassurance.

Self-direction in learning is facilitated when opportunities are provided in which learners can: conceive goals and plans, exercise freedom of choice, use rational reflection, follow through on planned activities, assess goals, plans, choices and activities, and exercise self-discipline.

❖ Self-directed plans, choices and assessments are strongly affected by the socializing influences of other persons.

❖ Self-direction may be an innate disposition but it can also be learned.

Self-direction in learning is facilitated when learners are assisted to learn how to learn.

❖ The exercise of self-direction is situation-specific; it can be constrained or enhanced by the learners' environment.

Self-direction in learning is facilitated when the environment is free from any constraints which might impede self-directedness.

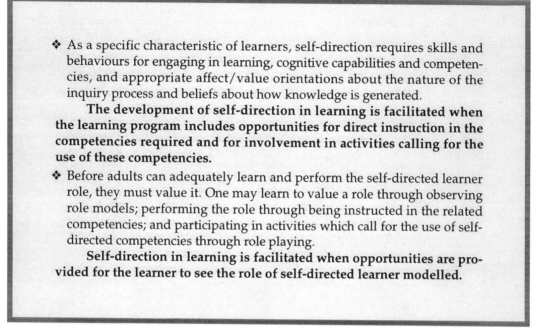

❖ As a specific characteristic of learners, self-direction requires skills and behaviours for engaging in learning, cognitive capabilities and competencies, and appropriate affect/value orientations about the nature of the inquiry process and beliefs about how knowledge is generated.

The development of self-direction in learning is facilitated when the learning program includes opportunities for direct instruction in the competencies required and for involvement in activities calling for the use of these competencies.

❖ Before adults can adequately learn and perform the self-directed learner role, they must value it. One may learn to value a role through observing role models; performing the role through being instructed in the related competencies; and participating in activities which call for the use of self-directed competencies through role playing.

Self-direction in learning is facilitated when opportunities are provided for the learner to see the role of self-directed learner modelled.

The B-P-E model is written as:
$$B \rightarrow f\,(P, E)$$
and is read as:
Behaviour is a function of the interaction between the Person and the Environment.

This is not a mathematical formula which can be tested through research, nor is it a theory. The model postulates a relationship among the three major components of learning-facilitating interactions but does not specify that the characteristics of a learner *cause* certain behaviours, only that there is an as-yet-undetermined relationship among Person, Behaviour and Environment.

Hunt and Sullivan (1974, p.31-32), in an extensive review of the B-P-E model, state that:

> We believe that the person occupies the central role in any psychological theory and that educational planning should begin with the [learner] rather than with objectives or teaching methods.

They distinguish between two kinds of individual differences:

1. contemporaneous characteristics or traits which are relatively stable over time and/or consistent across situations; and

2. developmental characteristics which change over time and/or in response to the perceived environment.

We need to think flexibly about characteristics in terms of this distinction. For example, if on the basis of initial responses in a learning context, we describe an adult learner as using dependent behaviours, we may come to think of that behaviour as a fixed trait. We might treat this learner as a dependent person and not see that the initial behaviour changes as the individual's anxiety goes down or as a sense of personal control is gained in the learning context.

If we continue to treat such learners as dependent, they may resent such treatment, or perceive themselves constrained to continue the dependent behaviours because our facilitating denies them the opportunity to develop as independent learners. For example, we might give them help with an answer if they look puzzled or complete a sentence if they get stuck on a word, instead of giving them time to work it out.

A major difficulty in conceptualizing adult learner characteristics, therefore, is that concepts have a tendency to become fixed labels.

Further evidence of the learner's behaviour contradicting such labels may be discounted or denied, which is a serious disservice to adults. Not much information is available regarding how characteristics change over time in response to developmental changes in the learner or to changes in the environment.

For example, if an adult learner enters a learning program using dependent behaviours, which environmental characteristics or facilitator behaviours would be most likely to help move the individual toward increasing independency or interdependency?

Facilitating concepts developed on the basis of the B-P-E model are thought of as "matching models". That is, the characteristics of learners are matched to the characteristics of learning environments to produce a statement about the most probable learner behaviours associated with any match. This matching, in turn, can yield a series of facilitating principles.

Developing a matching model

To develop a matching model, the concepts used to describe Person, Behaviour and Environment must bear some relationship to each other. Candy (1987) describes research in which learners wanting more direction and those wanting more permissiveness were randomly assigned to facilitators who provided either a more structured environment or more freedom. Diagram 3 outlines this match.

▬▬▬▬▬▬▬

The B-P-E model predicts that a positive match will occur between the want-more-direction learners and the structure-providing facilitator and between the want-more-permissiveness learners and the freedom-providing facilitator.

▬▬▬▬▬▬▬

	E = Environmental Characteristics (Facilitator)	
	Provides structure	Provides freedom
P = Person Characteristics (Learner) Wants more direction	Matched Facilitator assessed in positive terms	Mismatched Facilitators assessed as "never lectured, poorly prepared, couldn't answer questions in straightforward manner"
(Learner) Wants more permissiveness	Mismatched Facilitators assessed as "lectured too much, discouraged viewpoints other than own"	Matched Facilitator assessed in positive terms

3. MATCHING MODEL: DESIRE FOR DIRECTION

Source: Adapted from P. C. Candy (1987) Evolution, revolution or devolution: Increasing learner-control in the instructional setting. In D. Boud & V. Griffin (Eds.) **Appreciating adults learning: From the learners' perspective.** London UK: Kogan Page (p. 163).

Mismatches will occur between the want-more-direction learners and the freedom-providing facilitator and the want-more-permissiveness learners and the structure-providing facilitator. The same facilitators were used for both matching and mismatching conditions and the facilitators were equally competent. The most dissatisfied learners were those who wanted more direction but were mismatched with the freedom-providing facilitator (Candy, 1987).

Such results indicate that adult learners are not homogeneous and will vary widely on any given characteristic. Most learning groups include individuals representing different aspects of any given characteristic. The normal facilitating behaviours of facilitators will match some but rarely all adult learners in a group setting.

Facilitators can address this problem by learning a variety of facilitating behaviours which will match different characteristics. These can be used differentially with individual learners or to add variety when working with groups of learners. A facilitator who tries to match all the behaviours of all the learners in a learning group at the same time is bound to fail or burn out in the attempt.

The idea of matching learner characteristics to facilitating characteristics is complicated by a further issue. Hunt and Sullivan (1974) discuss different matches one might develop when considering developmental characteristics such as cognitive complexity rather than fixed traits. For these characteristics, a "comfort" match would provide facilitating behaviours at a level exactly matching the learner's current level of cognitive complexity. Any other facilitating behaviours would be a mismatch.

For example, learners who think in conceptual categories which have only a minimal connection to other categories (dualistic thinking), need a well-structured environment with clear rules as a comfort match, and an environment with more flexible rules and less structure for a developmental match.

Take some time to consider characteristics described in this chapter in terms of how each might be understood as a range of learner behaviour. Consider whether the characteristic is developmental in nature or a fixed trait, and what facilitating behaviours would match or mismatch the variations within the characteristic. You may want to develop a list of facilitator behaviours and skills to learn in becoming a more effective adult educator.

EMOTIONAL ASPECTS STRESS AND MOTIVES IN LEARNING

3

Learning is much affected by emotions from three sources:
those we bring to the learning process,
those which are generated during the learning process, and
those which we feel when we receive feedback about whether we have succeeded or failed.

The values, beliefs and attitudes which we have learned as part of our personal model of reality are those concepts and meanings which have emotional or affective attached to them and incline us to act in certain ways. If the affective component is positive our tendency is to move toward something or someone; if it is negative, our tendency is to move away from something or someone. The meanings to which I attach positive affect are not necessarily the same as those to which you attach positive affect. Whether we attach positive or negative affect to a certain meaning then, is a result of our personal experiences and our socialization. Sometimes the affect attached to an unquestioned value is of the aversion type — we believe something because to do otherwise would result in something terrible.

The "something terrible" ranges all the way from a physical punishment, to the burning fires of hell, to bringing punishment or disaster to another highly valued person.

We tend to believe that our values constitute some aspect of truth. Anyone who disagrees with us is likely to be viewed as someone who doesn't know "the truth" (meaning our own truth). Our values tend to conform, at least in part, to those espoused by the groups to which we want to belong. Many of our values come to us unquestioned from our parents and favoured social groups.

Our values, beliefs and attitudes can relate to what we know or do, and to the processes by which we learn to know and do. For example, I may value "good writing" but learning how to write well may require that I submit to the assessment and evaluative comments of others. I may not value such a process, perhaps because I don't value the opinions of others or because I don't want to hear negative comments about my own work. So, while I may value good writing, I may never put myself through the process required to learn to write well. Our values, attitudes and beliefs constantly affect what we are willing to learn and how we are willing to learn it.

ENERGY, AROUSAL, EMOTIONS AND STRESS

Learning involves the arousal and energy deployment system of the human body. Minimum, but preferably optimum, levels of arousal and energy are required to create the internal conditions necessary for learning. The arousal and energy systems are also directly linked to emotions and stress.

Emotion is a term used to describe various states which are both desired and not desired, which can make behaviour both more effective and less effective, and which can be both energizing and debilitating.

Emotions have the following features in common (More, 1974):

❖ They are all special states of arousal or motivation.
❖ As arousal increases, so does the emotional level.
❖ As arousal increases, the motivation to act in organized ways increases to a maximum level and continues at this level for some time, depending on the individual and the

situation; then, even though arousal may continue, motivation decreases rapidly, disorganized behaviour ensues and physical collapse becomes a possibility.

❖ Arousal is physiological and is interpreted in the subcortical areas of the brain according to previous experience and the situation involved. The interpretation determines the type of emotion felt (Hebb, 1972).

Stress, as described by Selye (1956), is a non-specific response to a real or perceived threat to the body or the self.

Stress involves a hormonal (adrenaline) reaction, the purpose of which is to

❖ arouse the body to a more effective and efficient level, known as the "fight or flight" response;

❖ enhance sensory reception and mental functioning; and

❖ increase the ability to cope and change.

Excessive arousal may become distress or euphoria depending on how the individual defines the situation (Brammer & Abrego, 1981; Schlossberg, 1984).

If the situation which gives rise to emotions or stress is defined in positive terms, then the emotions are experienced as positive and are felt as excitement, happiness, joy and pleasure, leading eventually to a state of *euphoria* (the opposite of distress). If the situation is defined in negative terms, then the emotions are experienced as negative and are felt as fear, anxiety, anger, and pain, leading eventually to a state of *distress*. Both euphoric and distressed adults may become totally engaged in their own feelings, often to the point of appearing to exclude or ignore others.

---

*Both euphoria and distress involve an
expression of energy
which is consequently not available for learning (Selye, 1956).*

If the threat which causes the distress increases or cannot be terminated by the individual's response, the physiological response continues until exhaustion occurs. The behavioural responses which accompany this are initial alertness and increases in organized and productive mental and physical action. But if the response continues unabated, that initial competence is followed by confusion, disorientation, and distortion of reality; then fatigue, tenseness, anxiety, irritability; and finally withdrawal, depression, and apathy (Wlodkowski, 1985; Hart, 1983; Brammer & Abrego, 1981; Adams, 1980; Brown, 1980; Hopson & Adams, 1976; Selye, 1956).

Anxiety is a non-specific stress response to an unlabelled fear, an unidentified source of danger (Rowe, 1975).

The source of anxiety may be internal to the self but perceived as originating in the external world. Learning situations, schools, teachers, grades, tests, and the threat of failure or exposure of inadequacies represent, for many adults, primary sources to which anxiety becomes attached (Kidd, 1973a).

Adults and emotions

These definitions point out that emotions, stress, and anxiety share a similar physiological arousal process and have similar behavioural outcomes in the presence of continuing and unresolved threats to an individual. Hebb (1972, p. 206) notes that adults and children both experience these arousal reactions, but the level, strength, and duration of the reaction increases with intellectual capacity and with age. Hart (1975, p.227) explains:

> ...change upsets and perhaps deeply disturbs us because it aborts [programmed responses] what used to serve well, and forces in adults the continual revision of the world-as-perceived that has always been normal in children. ...Hebb and others have pointed out that adults are not really less emotional than children, but more. We feel stronger emotions, much longer. With experience, however, we acquire [programmed structures] for handling — and to a large degree in our society, "corking up" — the more visible emotions.

Kidd (1973a) tells us that adults have not fewer, but more emotional associations with material to be learned than do children. We sometimes mistakenly assume that the adult has fewer because the adult's devices of control are more elaborate and more effective. Hebb (1972) continues in the same vein:

[We] are sheltered by what we call a civilized environment, within which we are not much exposed to the causes of emotional disturbance. It offers actual physical protection... [and] also psychological protection from emotional disturbance by reducing the causes to near zero. In a `civilized environment' [an adult] never has to be in strange places in darkness (Hebb 1972, p. 206).

Adults have more to be threatened about in learning situations than children do, because their self-concept is already well organized. They stand to lose much of their previous gains in self-esteem and self-confidence if they try to learn and fail. Many adults would prefer not to try at all, and therefore appear to resist learning. Further, many adults are as apprehensive of appearing to be euphoric as they are about appearing to be distressed.

Effect of emotions and stress on learning

The issue of emotional responses, stress, and anxiety affects adult learning in a number of ways. The energy mobilized through arousal can be channelled equally well into learning and ultimately into success and satisfaction or into increasing anxiety, distress and resistance to learning.

Most adults start new learning experiences under some stress and arousal, and do not generally require further arousal to motivate learning. If the facilitator further stimulates arousal or stress through demands created by

❖ information overload,
❖ competition,
❖ exposure of inadequacies,
❖ discounting personal experience and so on,

the learner may withdraw or become self-defensive and appear to lack motivation. Excessive arousal and distress will negate the early benefits of limited arousal.

Facilitators would be wise to spend some time during the first few learning sessions deliberately lowering anxiety to a manageable level (Knowles, 1990, 1970; Wlodkowski, 1985).

One outcome of a prolonged stress reaction is reduced competency in communicating. Poor communicating can take the form of

- ❖ repeating phrases,
- ❖ not finishing sentences,
- ❖ not listening,
- ❖ excessive talking,
- ❖ omitting details,
- ❖ repeating questions which have already been answered, and so on.

Thistle (1968) indicates that the prospects for effective communication with persons in an angry, fearful or hostile state of mind are mediocre and with those in an apathetic state of mind, very poor. Learning in this condition would be distorted learning at best. Adults who have reached this level of distress tend to appear child-like. They need to have a facilitator who will not misinterpret their behaviour as childish or immature and who will help them reduce their stress level before getting on with the learning activities.

Not only do distressed persons use less verbal communication, which is often disoriented and confused, and use more non-verbal communication, they also hear and see distorted versions of reality.

Since the arousal response can motivate an individual to be a more productive learner as well as a more defensive learner, stress and anxiety show up in both learning and resistance to learning. Presumably learning is more productive when there is an optimum level of arousal. In such cases, learners might appear excited, agitated, curious, restless, and perhaps anxious or frustrated. All these behaviours, as with those in prolonged stress reactions, can be labelled as childish and immature. If the facilitator then proceeds to treat adult learners as if they were childish and immature, any motivation to learn will be diverted into defensiveness and resistance in order to protect the self.

For adults to become fully engaged in learning, they must

- ❖ be aroused,
- ❖ be relatively undefensive, and
- ❖ be willing and able to channel their motives into change processes.

For these reasons, adults need a learning environment which supports and encourages them and does not threaten them. This is facilitated when relationships between the facilitator and learners are built on trust (Combs, 1974; Kidd, 1973a).

Effect of emotions and stress on communicating

Work reported by O'Connor and Seymour (1990), Katz and Kahn (1970), Cropley (1977), and Toffler (1970) indicates that in the presence of excessive amounts of information from the environment (sensory overload, over-stimulation), the adult processes information in ways which delete, distort, oversimplify, and over-generalize. The manner in which the overload is processed can vary from being highly productive (specializing) to highly dysfunctional (omitting, denying). The result is a set of corresponding deletions, distortions, simplifications, and over-generalizations in the individual's personal model of reality. Lack of sufficient information, boredom, under-stimulation, excessive repetition, nonproductive and irrelevant activities will produce the same result as over-stimulation (Wlodkowski, 1985; Hart, 1983; Toffler, 1970).

Effects of emotions and stress on information-processing

Some individuals learn information-processing skills which are functional at all times but particularly so in periods of over-stimulation. These include employing multiple channels for processing information and learning how to learn.

The skill of employing multiple channels[3] requires that an individual avoid using only conscious, verbal modes of thought and use instead subconscious, non-verbal modes of thought.

Verbal thought tends to be based on

- ❖ a high level of mental attention,
- ❖ a low degree of diversion and novelty in the environment, and
- ❖ the use of small amounts of selected and specific information.

Verbal thinking is ordered by sequence of words and the grammar which guides it. The consequences of error early in the sequence tend to be magnified in succeeding steps. Distress and information overload make this mode of thought difficult to maintain for any length of time.

Non-verbal thought requires

❖ the intake of large amounts of information,

❖ a low level of direct attention,

❖ reliance on non-verbal forms of representation,

❖ simultaneous processing of information through multiple channels, and

❖ enough time to permit processing to occur without having to produce an output or reach an answer.

In non-verbal thinking, order emerges as a result of thinking, not as a factor which guides it. When the same information is processed through several different channels, errors in one channel will be corrected by the results from another.

*Several writers, such as Hart (1983), suggest that
the skills involved in employing multiple channels and
in learning how to learn are normal mental activities
which have been deactivated by the process of formal schooling.*

Such schooling places a higher value on conscious, sequential, verbal modes of thought than on subconscious, simultaneous, non-verbal modes of thought. Whether the skills develop normally or are acquired through training is not clear. It is clear, however, that certain conditions increase the capacity of an individual to make use of these skills in certain situations (Smith, 1990; Candy, 1990; Brookfield, 1987; Denis & Richter, 1987; Hart, 1983; Norman, 1973). These conditions include:

❖ the learner's perception of the situation as free from threat;

❖ material which is personally relevant to the learner and/or learning experiences and processes which are perceived as relevant to the learner's life experiences and current needs;

❖ presentation of information through a variety of sensory modes and experiences, with sufficient repetitions and variations on themes to allow fine distinctions in patterns to emerge;

❖ effective two-way communications with primary emphasis on learner talking and self-reflecting and facilitator listening and reflecting; and

❖ individual learning styles or preferences in using learning strategies which support multiple channel learning.

Learning how to learn

*Learning how to learn involves
a set of processes in which individual learners act, in whole or in part, as
managers of their own change, and
their focus needs to be on their own actions, ideas and learning processes.*

This requires that learners recognize and be able to pay some attention to their own learning processes. They must also be willing to trust themselves to manage this process and be able to request help when necessary. Such learning can be carried out more productively in situations which do not threaten the learner (Candy, 1991).

Developing skills in learning to learn can create a challenge to the adequacy of the learner's existing meanings, values, and skills. At the point of change, the learner is likely to

❖ experience internal conflict as old and new meanings or values clash,

❖ feel disconnected from past habits and

❖ feel disoriented as new skills require new behaviours.

It is a point at which stress can increase and the learner might abort the learning process as too risky (Pine & Boy, 1977; More, 1974)

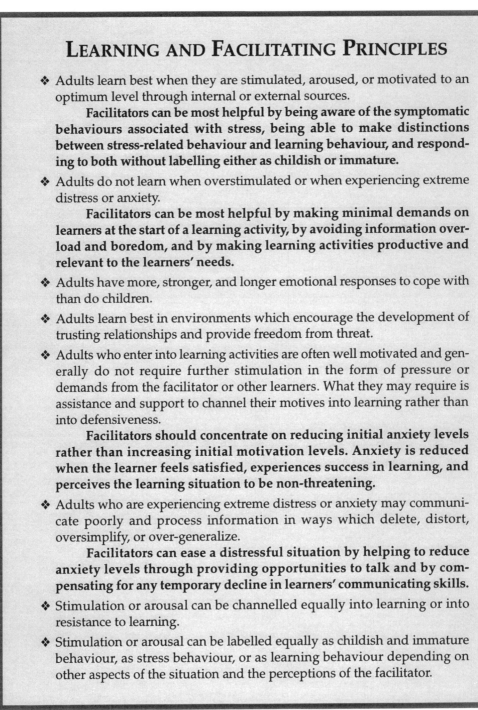

LEARNING AND FACILITATING PRINCIPLES

❖ Adults learn best when they are stimulated, aroused, or motivated to an optimum level through internal or external sources.

Facilitators can be most helpful by being aware of the symptomatic behaviours associated with stress, being able to make distinctions between stress-related behaviour and learning behaviour, and responding to both without labelling either as childish or immature.

❖ Adults do not learn when overstimulated or when experiencing extreme distress or anxiety.

Facilitators can be most helpful by making minimal demands on learners at the start of a learning activity, by avoiding information overload and boredom, and by making learning activities productive and relevant to the learners' needs.

❖ Adults have more, stronger, and longer emotional responses to cope with than do children.

❖ Adults learn best in environments which encourage the development of trusting relationships and provide freedom from threat.

❖ Adults who enter into learning activities are often well motivated and generally do not require further stimulation in the form of pressure or demands from the facilitator or other learners. What they may require is assistance and support to channel their motives into learning rather than into defensiveness.

Facilitators should concentrate on reducing initial anxiety levels rather than increasing initial motivation levels. Anxiety is reduced when the learner feels satisfied, experiences success in learning, and perceives the learning situation to be non-threatening.

❖ Adults who are experiencing extreme distress or anxiety may communicate poorly and process information in ways which delete, distort, oversimplify, or over-generalize.

Facilitators can ease a distressful situation by helping to reduce anxiety levels through providing opportunities to talk and by compensating for any temporary decline in learners' communicating skills.

❖ Stimulation or arousal can be channelled equally into learning or into resistance to learning.

❖ Stimulation or arousal can be labelled equally as childish and immature behaviour, as stress behaviour, or as learning behaviour depending on other aspects of the situation and the perceptions of the facilitator.

❖ Adults who can process information through multiple channels and have learned how to learn are the most productive.

❖ Adults learn best when novel information is presented through a variety of sensory modes and experiences, with sufficient repetitions and variations on themes to allow distinctions in patterns to emerge.

❖ Adults learn best through effective two-way communications emphasizing learner talking and self-reflecting and facilitator listening and reflecting.

❖ Adults have developed well-organized strategies for defending against threat and for covering emotional reactions. These may mask stress or anxiety but rarely completely alleviate it.

❖ The consequences of learning can lead to disorientation and conflict which in turn, can lead to further learning or can lead to increased distress and decreased learning.

Facilitators may need to reassure learners that confusion has a function in the learning process and be prepared to halt learning activities periodically to help learners clarify issues, problems and concerns.

MOTIVES FOR LEARNING

*Motivation is an all-purpose term defined as
a tendency within a person
to produce organized behaviour.*

This organized behaviour allows individuals to respond to their internal or external environment to ensure their own and their communal groups' survival and satisfaction. In biological terms, human behaviour is motivated by five basic tendencies — hunger, pain, sex, maternal, and exploratory motives (Hebb, 1972). In social and psychological terms, human motives are extremely complex because of the number of variables involved. I present the concept of motivation in very simplified terms and as it relates to learning.

*Motivation can be described as
being either a drive to reduce unmet needs or
a drive toward positive growth.*

Reduction of unmet needs describes those motives which arise when something is absent or deficient in the individual's life. Adults who engage in learning to reduce unmet needs may arrive at the learning experience feeling threatened by others (whom they may see as controlling them), and feeling powerless or incompetent to change the conditions of their lives.

They may indeed be threatened, and may be present as non-voluntary learners. Such adults may require structured learning experiences, extensive help in determining their own directions, and prolonged support. They need both feedback and positive reinforcement from the facilitator. Once their initial feelings of threat or anxiety have been resolved or reduced, they can be assisted toward taking increasing responsibility for their own learning.

The drive toward positive growth presupposes, not an aversive set of existing conditions which need to be changed, but a potential positive outcome which will reward the individual as it is sought and obtained. Maslow (1970) suggests that people cannot move toward these positive goals until the aversive conditions have been reduced. He describes these aversive conditions as "deficit needs" and the positive goals as "growth or being needs".

*Deficit needs focus on survival and security tendencies.
Growth needs focus on belongingness, self-esteem, and self-actualizing tendencies.*

Gibb (1964) indicates that the two types of needs are not mutually exclusive and that as one increases in strength and priority, the other decreases. Facilitating strategies can focus on reducing deficit needs first, thus freeing the learner to pursue growth goals that, in turn, would enable dealing with future deficit needs. Facilitating could focus on some combination of these.

*Growth needs relate to such personal goals as
improving job skills, getting a salary increase, developing professionally, meeting new people,
developing trust relationships, learning for the pleasure of learning,
expanding knowledge, extending oneself, and so on.*

Kidd (1973a) suggests that adults who attend learning experiences on the basis of personal growth in the direction of positive goals tend to be relaxed, do not require much structure or direction from facilitators, and are able to negotiate and plan their own structure, directions, feedback, and reinforcement with minimal assistance.

Houle (1961) describes three motives which adult learners give for participating in formal learning activities:

1. **goal-oriented** motives in which the individual sees the learning as a means for accomplishing fairly clear-cut objectives;

2. **learning-oriented** motives in which the individual seeks knowledge for its own sake; and

3. **activity-oriented** motives in which the individual participates in the learning activity for reasons which have no necessary connection to the announced purpose of the activity.

Of these three, only goal-oriented motives seem to address learning related to deficit needs.

Behaviour is organized around action tendencies

*Another way to conceptualize motivation, apart from the deficit and growth needs perspective,
is to see the individual's organizing behaviour as related to two major tendencies:
(i) a tendency to function autonomously or independently in the environment,
and (ii) a tendency to function harmoniously in interdependent relationships
with others in pairs or groups (Jones, 1968).*

In the literature, the tendency to *autonomous, independent behaviour* is variously referred to as

* achievement needs,
* instrumental participation,
* career-oriented learning needs, and
* self-confidence needs, among others.

This tendency is accompanied by the need to reduce threats to autonomous functioning, to reduce feelings of powerlessness and incompetence, to build competent, skilled performance, and to improve self-esteem and self-concept.

The tendency *to interdependent behaviour* is variously referred to as

- ❖ affiliation needs,
- ❖ expressive participation,
- ❖ social-oriented learning needs, and
- ❖ acceptance needs, among others.

This tendency is accompanied by the need to reduce threats to one's secure place within communal groups, to reduce isolation and alienation, to build and improve interpersonal relationships, and to create and maintain communal and collaborative groups.

As we have seen in the section on self-concept, autonomy-seeking motives may be more salient for men, while relationship-seeking motives may be more salient for women.

Adult educators tend to assume that all adults have put dependency needs behind them. In fact, some adults prefer to use *dependent behaviours* rather than independent or interdependent behaviours. Most adults use dependent behaviours in situations which are perceived as novel, emergency, or trauma.

These tendencies include a variety of more specific behaviours. For example, interdependence (Schutz, 1967) includes issues related to inclusion within the group and affection or closeness to others. Each tendency can be thought of as a continuum of behaviours which ranges from too-much-need at one end, to too-little-need at the other. For example, too-much-need for independence is described by Hunt (1971) as *counter-dependency*; and too-little-need for independence, as *unilateral dependence.*

If we understand behaviour to extend across a continuum, then we can perceive adults as using behaviours which range across part of that continuum, with most using behaviours from the middle range (Morstain & Smart, 1977; Schutz, 1967).

Motivation is connected both to success (or failure) in reaching desired outcomes or changing adverse conditions and to feelings of satisfaction (or dissatisfaction) which attend such progress. Satisfaction and success are not separate issues. Both are related to progress away from entry conditions and toward anticipated or desired conditions. The deficit or growth needs or motives with which learners enter a learning program determine their initial participation in the activities. Thereafter, their motives for continuing in the program will depend on whether they feel they are moving toward their anticipated or desired outcomes.

To be able to see their own progress, learners must receive frequent information about changes in their behaviour relative to what they anticipated or desired. Information which describes the results of change is referred to as *feedback*. When feedback is specific in describing changes relative to planned changes, it leads to an awareness of success or failure.

Knowledge of success or failure is accompanied by feelings of satisfaction or dissatisfaction, and it is these feelings which then become powerful motives for further learning or withdrawal (Jones, 1968).

Lam (1976) has shown that satisfaction is derived from group processes and from formal and informal interpersonal interactions and not from increased comprehension or absorption of information. The process of clarifying educational needs which can be met through specific learning activities and for which specific feedback can be provided is essential for eventual satisfaction.

Motivating learning

If, as facilitators, we assume that motivation is based primarily on the learners' knowing where they are now (existing conditions, needs, problems) and where they want or need to be at the end of the learning activities (objectives, goals), then we likely would design activities which rely on initial high motivation levels but pay scant attention to maintaining this level through remaining sessions. When initial motivation is high, the learner may have enough drive to complete the program without further input. Particularly with adult learners who also hold jobs and take care of families, the chances are good that initial motivation levels will drop and new energy must be generated through learning activities.

If, as facilitators, we assume that motivation is based primarily on the learners' knowing the results of their own learning (outcomes in relation to objectives) and on their feelings associated with these results, then we would design learning activities which provide opportunities for feedback to learners about changes in their behaviour. Feedback can come from

- ❖ facilitators,
- ❖ from other learners,
- ❖ from a non-human resource (as in biofeedback), or
- ❖ from learners' observations about their own behaviour and environment.

Feedback which is spread throughout the learning program can assist in maintaining learner motivation levels (Wlodkowski, 1985; Lam, 1976; Bortner, 1974).

What seems clear from the literature on motivation,
*is that the tendencies which are labelled "motives" arise from **within the learner**.*
Despite encouragement from some writers to "motivate learners," facilitators cannot do this directly.

The behaviour of the facilitator must be viewed as contributing either to feedback or to reinforcement and by this route indirectly to further motivation. Motives are not something added on by an external agent or facilitator, although the actions of the facilitator may tend to help or hinder already existing motives.

Wlodkowski, (1985) suggests that the most suitable facilitator functions are:

- ❖ discovering, through consultation, the prime motives and specific learning needs of each learner;
- ❖ assisting the learner to establish specific objectives which can be translated into specific behaviours and hence into specific feedback;
- ❖ providing feedback on the basis of these choices; and
- ❖ allowing the feelings of success and satisfaction from these processes to be the major reinforcers of subsequent learning.

Feedback can only be provided following activities which permit the learner to test out new behaviour. Feelings of success, therefore, are available to the learner only after that point in the learning process. If this point comes early in the session, then the good feelings from success will motivate the remainder of that session. If this point comes at the end of a session, then the good feelings may have dissipated before the next session.

If feedback is delayed from one session to the next, the learner may have trouble connecting it to the behaviour that was tested out previously. As the time lapse between action and feedback increases, the impact and reinforcement from feedback decreases, as does its value for further motivation (Arends, Hersh, & Turner, 1978; Coleman, 1976).

Involving adults in clarifying their own ambiguous needs and in defining clear learning needs is acknowledged as one of the most important aspects of adult learning (Knowles, 1990).

Most adults, however, have little experience in verbalizing their own needs, let alone turning them into learning objectives. They are often embarrassed about expressing their needs in front of others and do not communicate them unless there is some personal crisis or external reason for doing so. If adults are asked to complete a needs assessment instrument, they are likely to respond as an "average adult" rather than as themselves, or to give the answers which they assume the assessor wants to hear. Therefore, adults may need considerable assistance and support in verbalizing, clarifying, and specifying their learning needs (Arends and others, 1978).

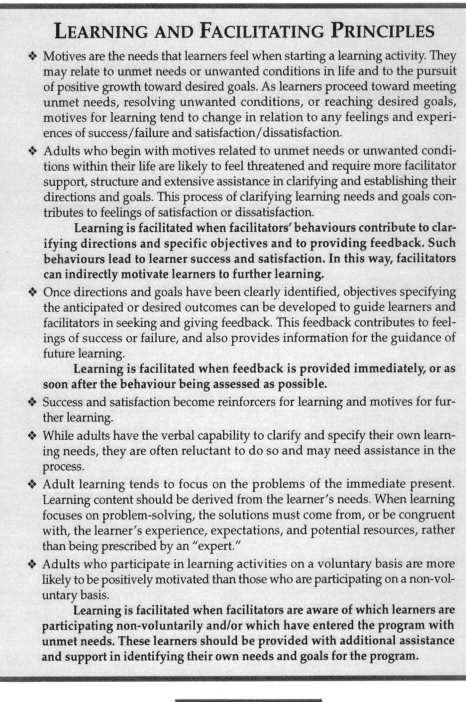

LEARNING AND FACILITATING PRINCIPLES

❖ Motives are the needs that learners feel when starting a learning activity. They may relate to unmet needs or unwanted conditions in life and to the pursuit of positive growth toward desired goals. As learners proceed toward meeting unmet needs, resolving unwanted conditions, or reaching desired goals, motives for learning tend to change in relation to any feelings and experiences of success/failure and satisfaction/dissatisfaction.

❖ Adults who begin with motives related to unmet needs or unwanted conditions within their life are likely to feel threatened and require more facilitator support, structure and extensive assistance in clarifying and establishing their directions and goals. This process of clarifying learning needs and goals contributes to feelings of satisfaction or dissatisfaction.

Learning is facilitated when facilitators' behaviours contribute to clarifying directions and specific objectives and to providing feedback. Such behaviours lead to learner success and satisfaction. In this way, facilitators can indirectly motivate learners to further learning.

❖ Once directions and goals have been clearly identified, objectives specifying the anticipated or desired outcomes can be developed to guide learners and facilitators in seeking and giving feedback. This feedback contributes to feelings of success or failure, and also provides information for the guidance of future learning.

Learning is facilitated when feedback is provided immediately, or as soon after the behaviour being assessed as possible.

❖ Success and satisfaction become reinforcers for learning and motives for further learning.

❖ While adults have the verbal capability to clarify and specify their own learning needs, they are often reluctant to do so and may need assistance in the process.

❖ Adult learning tends to focus on the problems of the immediate present. Learning content should be derived from the learner's needs. When learning focuses on problem-solving, the solutions must come from, or be congruent with, the learner's experience, expectations, and potential resources, rather than being prescribed by an "expert."

❖ Adults who participate in learning activities on a voluntary basis are more likely to be positively motivated than those who are participating on a non-voluntary basis.

Learning is facilitated when facilitators are aware of which learners are participating non-voluntarily and/or which have entered the program with unmet needs. These learners should be provided with additional assistance and support in identifying their own needs and goals for the program.

COGNITIVE ASPECTS: BRAIN AND MIND IN LEARNING

4

To understand learning fully, we need to consider cognitive aspects of learning and explore the relationship between brain and mind. When we speak of *brain*, we are speaking of the physical structure and the physiology of a part of the human body. When we speak of *mind*, we are speaking about the cognitive constructs and the processes that the mind uses for learning, deciding, solving problems, making decisions and so on.

Learning is as much grounded in the physical structure and physiology of the brain as it is in the cognitive constructs and processes of the mind.

Some of the things we know about the relationship between brain and mind are:

❖ Under relaxed conditions, visualizing a physical activity can actually stimulate motor activity in the relevant muscle groups. Visually practising a skill helps both in learning and performing it.

❖ Facial expressions have a strong effect on mental states. If you frown, you'll begin to feel depressed; if you smile, you'll begin to feel better. Adults learn better in a positive mental state. So encourage adult learners to smile.

❖ Both sensory over-stimulation (information overload) and under-stimulation (boredom) can produce stress responses which interfere with learning. Adults who are getting too much or too little information for their current learning task may not be learning (Hart, 1975).

❖ Laughter produces a synchronous response in both cerebral hemispheres making the learning vivid and adding emotion to whatever is being learned. Laughter in the right place makes learning more fun and easier to remember (Wischnewski, 1983).

❖ Learning and a lively environment help reduce the possibility of cognitive decline in old age and greatly improve mental functioning at all ages. Generally, lack of environmental stimulation reduces intelligence. The more a nerve cell is stimulated, the more it develops connecting links (dendrites) to other nerve cells, and the more links, the more efficient thinking becomes. Nerve cells that are not stimulated may develop "stubby dendrites" and lose their links to other dendrites and their contribution to thought processes.

❖ Physical activity, when used alternately with mental activity, enhances learning by providing the brain with time out to process ideas and experiences. When you get tired from your learning activities, take a break with a physical change. Go for a brisk walk, scrub the floor vigorously, go dancing, or do the gardening to give your thought processes time to work things out without interference from the sergeant major in your mind who is constantly at you to work harder.

❖ Intelligence appears to be related to neural efficiency. For example, while learning spatial manipulation tasks on a computer, learners use lots of mental energy at first. After practice, the brain burns less energy even though scores continue to improve. Learners with higher intelligence scores show the greatest drop in energy (Newsweek, April 20, 1992).

I will begin the discussion about cognitive aspects of learning by considering how the central nervous system functions and then move on to consider cognitive styles, intelligence, and cognitive development.

THE CENTRAL NERVOUS SYSTEM

The central nervous system (brain, spinal cord and peripheral nerves) consists of an estimated one trillion brain cells or *neurons* (see Diagram 4. The Central Nervous System). Each neuron is a powerful and complex, microscopic, data-processing and transmitting system. Each consists of a central body, an elongated extension or *axon*, and many small branch-like extensions called *dendrites*. The axon serves as the main exit point for the information transmitted from that cell. Some neurons are specialized to

- ❖ receive sensory information from the external environment (visual, auditory, pain, pressure, temperature, smell, taste);
- ❖ receive sensory impulses from the internal environment (physical balance, chemical balance);
- ❖ transmit impulses from one neuron to another; and
- ❖ transmit nervous impulses to muscles to initiate motor responses.

Each dendrite terminates on a dendrite of another nerve cell and each cell receives dendrites from hundreds of other cells. The minuscule space between any two dendrites is called a synaptic gap. Information is transmitted within the nerve cell as an electrical impulse and across the synaptic gap by chemicals or neurotransmitters. The surge of biochemical information across a synapse (where nerve impulses are transmitted and received) is "awe-inspiring in its volume and complexity" (Buzan & Buzan, 1995).

The combined electrical impulses of the neurons form brain waves:

❖ *Beta waves* are very rapid and dominate most of our waking hours; they are active when the person is consciously thinking and solving problems.

❖ *Alpha waves* are slower and can be recorded when the person is awake but relaxed and not engaged in conscious thought; they are associated with creativity and the use of imagery.

❖ *Theta waves* are very slow and are recorded during sleep.

The brain

The upper part of the central nervous system expands to form the brain (see Diagram 4). Three levels of activity can be distinguished within what is called the *triune brain* (Hart, 1975). The lowest level of the triune brain is the *reptilian brain*, the middle level is the *paleomammalian brain*, and the highest level is the *neomammalian brain* (Ferro, 1993; Hart, 1983).

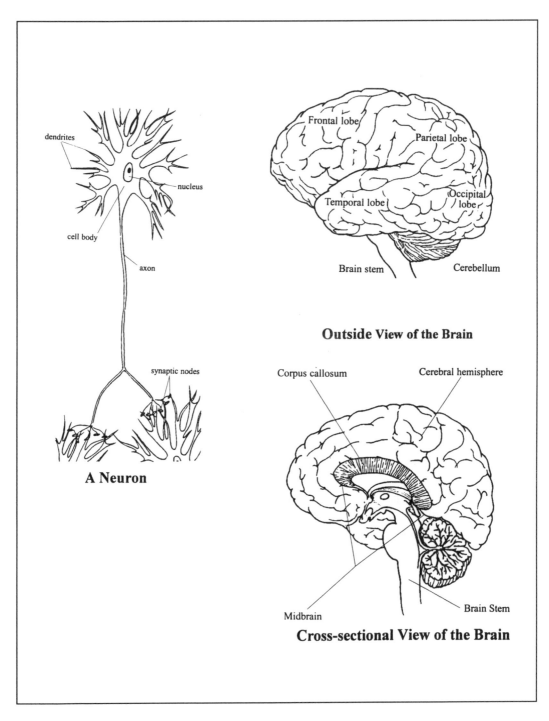

dendrites

nucleus

cell body

axon

synaptic nodes

A Neuron

Frontal lobe

Parietal lobe

Temporal lobe

Occipital lobe

Brain stem

Cerebellum

Outside View of the Brain

Corpus callosum

Cerebral hemisphere

Midbrain

Brain Stem

Cross-sectional View of the Brain

4. THE CENTRAL NERVOUS SYSTEM

Each level of the triune brain has its own form of memory,
its own way of gathering information, its own sense of space and time,
its own intelligence, and its own means for controlling behaviour.

The **reptilian brain** or brain stem consists of the brain structures formed by the swelling of the top of the spinal chord at the point where it enters the skull. It is both the lowermost and innermost part of the brain.

The most important component of the reptilian brain is the reticular activating system,
a relay station between nerves entering and leaving the brain and those within the brain.
It can suppress or augment stimuli moving in both directions on
the basis of specific needs for individual survival, safety and bodily functions.

Bodily functions include feeding, fighting, fleeing, courtship and mating behaviours. When faced with conflicting stimuli, it will always augment those which enhance survival and suppress those which might provoke increased threat. If this relay station does not "turn on" (become activated), the higher brain centres will not be activated (Hart, 1983). The reticular activating system is suppressed in sleep and is affected by biorhythms and the chemical balance of the blood. That is, it is sensitive to changes in the internal environment through blood chemistry, nutrition, hormone level and so on, but not to changes in the external environment. The reptilian brain is programmed through genetic codes and its various functions are instinctive (Ferro, 1993). Its memory relates to survival and threat.

What this part of the brain understands as being a threat may have no connection to what the higher brain centres understand as being a threat. The reptilian brain plays a large role in managing stress responses; it is impervious to learning as we understand it. The reptilian brain is a unitary structure which is not divided laterally (right and left).

The **paleomammalian brain** or midbrain consists of the limbic system (between the brain stem and the cerebral cortex) and is involved in the experience and expression of emotions (Ferro, 1993). "Only those creatures [birds and mammals] which have a limbic system are devoted to the care and raising of their young" (Ferro 1993, p.26). The stimuli for all experience passes through the limbic system first before patterns are identified and meanings developed in the neo-mammalian brain.

That is, the emotional content of experience is processed before meaning and is under the control of a brain structure below those responsible for thinking and reasoning.

The limbic system controls the individual's basic value system and enhances or suppresses the short-term memory (strategies for remembering what happened in the past 24 hours). It also has a marked effect on what we store in long-term memory (Hart, 1975). The limbic system determines how the brain will respond to all information received.

> The memories triggered by any new experience include the memory of the feelings and emotions that accompanied the original experience. If the original experience was one of happiness, delight, joy or pleasure, the response to a current situation that has triggered that memory will be similar. If, on the other hand, the original experience caused anxiety or fear and triggered a fight-or-flight response, the reaction to the current situation will also be anxiety or fear (Ferro 1993, p.26).

The limbic system judges all experience on the basis of pain and pleasure.

When we behave in ways which enhance our self-preservation, the paleomammalian brain registers pleasure; when our self-preservation is threatened, it registers pain. This part of the brain is relatively impervious to change through learning but can be changed through some forms of psychotherapy, particularly those which do not rely on verbal dialogue. New learning is mostly restricted to expanding existing values and registering new experiences. The paleomammalian brain is not divided laterally and has no direct speech functions except for guttural sounds which register pain or pleasure (Hart, 1983).

The **neomammalian brain** or forebrain consists of the *cerebral cortex* which is divided laterally into two cerebral hemispheres joined by the corpus callosum. This part of the brain represents an enormous expansion of the total brain structure, in comparison with other mammals.

Virtually all the learning we are concerned with in formal and informal education occurs in the cerebral cortex.

All verbal speech functions originate within it. It reasons, plans, worries, writes poems, makes lists, invents engines, paints pictures, and programs computers. Its products are foresight, hindsight and insight; it is the "mother of invention" and the "father of abstract thought" (Hart, 1975). It coordinates relationships with the outside world through its centres for vision, hearing, taste, smell, bodily sensations and motor responses. Its memory has kinesthetic components (skin sensations, muscular movements, balance), iconic components (images, sounds, tastes, smells), and words or verbal components (Hart, 1983).

*The **brain as a whole** works through a precarious, constantly changing balance between the three levels. Each level has power within its own area.*

The highest level has control over conscious activity and thought; but this level is dependent on the lower levels to pass on information, yield control over various activities, and keep the entire system activated. Waking activities bring the cerebral cortex into action. Any time sensory stimuli are received, consciously or unconsciously, from the inner or outer environment, implying a threat to the individual, the brain will down-shift, taking away direct control over cognitive functions from the neomammalian brain and giving it to the paleo-mammalian or reptilian brains (Hart, 1983).

When down-shifting occurs, self-preservation becomes more important than learning and the cerebral hemispheres are put on hold. To reactivate the learning process, the lowest two levels must be satisfied that the threat to self has been resolved. In Chapter Three I discussed the effect of stress on learning in terms of emotional responses.

Here we see that stress also has a direct effect on brain functioning.
Distress causes the brain to down-shift,
thereby halting or diminishing normal learning processes.

The cerebral hemispheres

The *cerebral hemispheres* are connected to each other through the *corpus callosum*. Research done on patients in whom this connecting bridge has been severed indicates that, in most humans, the hemispheres are specialized for different mental functions (Bogen, 1977). Being of "two minds" appears to have a physical basis. The left hemisphere controls most of the sensory input and all the motor responses for the right side of the body and the right hemisphere for the left side of the body. This arrangement is reversed in a small percentage of the population.

For most people, the left hemisphere is specialized for language and
the right for non-verbal pattern recognition.

Hemispheric specialization is reversed in some people, particularly those who are left-handed. Specialization, or lateralization, is rarely complete in the majority of normally-functioning humans. The left hemisphere usually retains some capacity to process non-verbal information and the right hemisphere some capacity to process verbal information. Lateralization appears to be somewhat more pronounced and more complete for the average male than for the average female.

Communication between the two hemispheres and the integration
of their functions appears to occur more easily
for the average female than for the average male (Hart, 1983).

Whether mental functions other than those for language and pattern recognition are lateralized to one hemisphere or the other is open to question. Writers in this field do not always agree about which functions are lateralized to which hemisphere and to what extent. Most researchers believe that experience is processed and memories stored somewhat differently in each hemisphere (Springer & Deutsch, 1985; Bogen, 1977).

Diagram 5 lists those functions about which there is some agreement. This list should not be taken to mean that all verbal functions reside in the left hemisphere and all non-verbal functions in the right hemisphere.

The mental functions are distributed across both hemispheres, although one hemisphere tends to dominate in the actual use of specific functions. Further, each hemisphere differs among individuals in terms of abilities and capacities to perform selected functions (Buzan & Buzan, 1995).

The list in Diagram 5 tells us that there is more than one way to process and store experience and that each person's model of reality has both verbal and non-verbal, temporal and spatial components. We also know that normal human functioning requires the coordination and collaboration of both hemispheres.

Language, for example, is a very complex process requiring
  ❖ semantics or words (a left hemisphere specialization),
  ❖ assignment to meaningful patterns (a right hemisphere specialization),
  ❖ syntax or grammatical rules (left hemisphere),
  ❖ the use of metaphor or imagery (right hemisphere), and
  ❖ sensitivity to sound (both hemispheres).

The spoken word requires the use of sub-vocals, facial expressions, motor responses and pronunciation, as well as language. The written word requires the use of motor skills and eye-hand coordination, as well as language.

That is, both spoken and written language require many different mental processes which are not necessarily specialized to the same hemisphere.

LEFT-HEMISPHERE FUNCTIONS	RIGHT-HEMISPHERE FUNCTIONS
Verbal — turns experience into words which name, describe and define it; recognizes language; stores data in linguistic or symbolic form.	**Nonverbal, visual-spatial** — recognizes patterns, keeps data in original form (visual, auditory, kinaesthetic).
Logical, analytical — figures things out sequentially step-by-step and part-by-part; reduces wholes to meaningful parts; uses rules of logic to draw conclusions.	**Gestalt, synthetic** — sees experience or ideas whole rather than in parts; perceives global properties of patterns; integrates parts into meaningful wholes.
Temporal — keeps track of things in time-ordered sequences.	**Spatial** — keeps track of things in spatial arrangements.
Sequential — links ideas in sequences so that one thought directly follows another logically.	**Non-linear** — figures things out simultaneously.
Digital — uses words for cognition.	**Analogical** — uses analogues for cognition.

5. FUNCTIONS OF THE CEREBRAL HEMISPHERES

Adapted from: Springer, S. P. & Deutsch, G. (1985) **Left brain, right brain** (revised edition). New York: W. H. Freeman and Co.; and Edwards, B. (1979) **Drawing on the right side of the brain.** Los Angeles: J. P. Tarcher.

▬▬▬▬▬▬▬▬▬▬▬▬

The current fashion of labelling people as "left brain" or "right brain" is dysfunctional.
Much has been made of the assumption that
formal educational institutions educate only one side of the brain.
This assumption is false (Springer & Deutsch, 1985).

▬▬▬▬▬▬▬▬▬▬▬▬

Sensory information is received by both sides of the brain and motor responses originate from both sides. One reason for believing that formal educational programs educate only one side of the brain is that such programs tend to evaluate, and hence reinforce, the kind of knowing and learning accompanied by language, for which the left hemisphere is specialized. It is more difficult to assess learning outcomes which reside in the mute right hemisphere (Springer & Deutsch, 1985).

Astronomer-biologist Carl Sagan (1977), in describing the role of the two hemispheres in scientific thinking, tells us that one objective is to observe natural phenomena and identify the meaningful patterns which characterize them (right hemisphere thinking). Sagan suggests that many identified patterns do not, in fact, correspond to the data.

Scientists, like all humans, see what they want to see. All identified patterns, therefore, must be subjected to critical analysis (left hemisphere thinking).

The search for patterns without critical analysis, and rigid scepticism without a search for patterns, are the antipodes of incomplete science. The effective pursuit of knowledge requires both functions (Sagan, 1977).

The cerebral hemisphere and gender

Most research indicates that the average male brain and the average female brain show slight differences. In one study, men and women were asked to listen to "Row, row, row your boat" and raise a finger when they heard a four-letter word, as researchers observed brain activity. While men and women did equally well, men used only one hemisphere to do the task while women used both (Newsweek, April 20, 1992).

Most women are more adept than most men at both verbal and nonverbal communication. The average woman's corpus callosum (the brain structure linking the two hemispheres), is larger than that found in the average man. Women therefore, may be better able to integrate the activities of the two hemispheres, thus improving their capabilities in communication tasks.

The average man lacks this cross-talk between his hemispheres; and thus each half of his brain may be better able to concentrate on what it does best. Studies show that when men are confronted with problems dealing with spatial concerns, they tend to use the right hemisphere only. They experience few distracting verbal messages coming in from the left hemisphere.

The research steers clear of suggesting that men's brains are superior to women's; and there is, as yet, no evidence of what causes these gender differences. The entire brain is awash in hormones, including the sex hormones, even before birth. These hormones may have a direct effect on the brain's development. Do not place too much importance on these gender differences. The term "average" means that there are some women whose brain structures and cognitive abilities resemble those of many men, and some men whose brain structure and cognitive abilities resemble those of many women.

▬▬▬▬▬▬▬▬▬

*However, it is more likely that the socialization which occurs after birth
has a stronger effect than actual physical differences by reinforcing communication skills
for girls and spatial skills for boys (Gorman, 1995).*

▬▬▬▬▬▬▬▬▬

Facilitating learning in both hemispheres

Most facilitating activities have an effect on both hemispheres. Some, however, have a stronger effect on one hemisphere than the other. Diagram 6 describes activities which can be used to facilitate activity in each hemisphere. The left hemisphere responds best to activities depending on time-ordered sequences; the use of words and numbers; and organized, analytical thinking. The right hemisphere responds best to activities depending on the use of visual, non-verbal materials and on simultaneous presentations with lots of redundant information.

LEFT HEMISPHERE	RIGHT HEMISPHERE
Note taking, writing outlines, listening for facts.	Making mind maps, drawing, doodling, guided imagery.
Comparing patterns, analyzing information.	Identifying patterns.
Planning, setting priorities, clarifying objectives.	Going with the flow.
Eliminating extraneous ideas.	Being open to new ideas, brainstorming.
Using questions to obtain "right" answers; closed, convergent questions.	Using questions to explore new ideas; open-ended, divergent questions.
- - - - - - - - - - - - - - - - - - - -	- - - - - - - - - - - - - - - - - - - -
Analytical listening	Empathic listening
Crossword puzzles	Jigsaw puzzles
Puns, irony	Cartoons, visual humour
Describing emotions	Feeling emotions
Adopting the attitude of challenging the ideas of others, debating	Adopting the attitude of accepting ideas of others
Making the mind to do mental push-ups	Dreaming; day dreaming
Focus on time, numbers, money	Opening up to "irrelevancies"
Concentrating on the meanings of words	Awareness of colours, odours, space around you
Staying focused on "reality"	Depriving the body of food, sleep and/or sensory stimulation
Staying still	Use of repetitious sounds, rhythms, actions
	Extreme physical comfort, relaxation

6. ACTIVATING THE BRAIN HEMISPHERES

Developed from: Wonder, J. & Donovan, P. (1984) **Whole-brain thinking: Working from both sides of the brain to achieve peak job performance**. New York: Ballantine Books; Edwards, B. (1979) **Drawing on the right side of the brain**. Los Angeles: J. P. Tarcher; and Buzan, T. & Buzan, B. (1995) **The mind map book: Radiant Thinking**. London, UK: BBC Books.

LEARNING AND FACILITATING PRINCIPLES

❖ A learner's personal model of reality is composed of both verbal and non-verbal components and integrates memories stored in both hemispheres. Learning is more effective when ideas, information and knowledge can be learned and stored in both verbal and non-verbal forms.

  Facilitating is most effective when ideas can be presented in both verbal and non-verbal forms.

❖ To function at top efficiency, the brain requires that the individual be in good physical condition This includes being in good health, well rested, well nourished, and physically fit. The brain also requires that learning activities be carried out in a physically supportive environment in which the learner is reasonably comfortable, the temperature and lighting are suitable, and the air quality is good.

  Good facilitators ensure that the physical environment is comfortable and that learners are not overly tired or hungry. Avoid having learners sit for extended periods of time. Plan learning activities which allow learners to move around periodically.

❖ When learners are distressed, control of brain activity down-shifts from the cerebral cortex to the midbrain. When down-shifting occurs, learners become more concerned with self-preservation and self-protection than with learning. Once the brain has down-shifted, learners stop using both logical and analogical thinking processes. Stress affects both cerebral hemispheres equally.

  Good facilitators are aware of signs signifying down-shifting and take time to help learners deal with distress.

❖ Processing information through verbal functions is time consuming but logical and analytical; processing information through non-verbal functions is time conserving but analogical and holistic. Effective learning involves both logical and analogical, analytical and holistic approaches. Effective learners and sound critical thinkers use the functions of both hemispheres to engage in learning and thinking.

  Facilitating activities calling for collaboration and integration of the activities of the two hemispheres are more likely to promote sound learning than activities which draw on the specialized talents of only one hemisphere.

❖ The opposite of logical (left hemisphere) thinking is analogical (right hemi-sphere) thinking not illogical or non-logical thinking. Analogical thinking makes use of pattern recognition through metaphors, images, and the like. Non-verbal, analogical, holistic learning sometimes appears to be non-rational because it is not linear, not sequential, and frequently non-verbal.

Good facilitating activities should include opportunities to engage in non-verbal, analogical, visual activities. The use of humour is a particularly effective way to encourage such activities. Laughter is good for learning.

❖ Part of the time taken to process information while learning involves processing it in both hemispheres, communicating between hemispheres, and integrating the results. If one hemisphere works faster than the other, the learner may accept the first answer which comes to mind, an answer which may not be the best answer. Learners should be encouraged to think twice and think critically before generating final learning responses.

Good facilitators should not be too quick to judge first answers or initial learning attempts.

The Mind and Cognitive Style

The brain represents the physical side of mental functioning; the mind represents the cognitive side. Wilder Penfield, a noted neurosurgeon, once said that he never saw a thought when he opened up the skull to do brain surgery but he believed in the concepts of thought and think-ing. We experience the collective electrical and chemical activity of the brain as cognitive processes. We know about cognitive processes because we are capable of being aware of, and thinking about, our own thinking. The concepts we have developed to describe cognitive processes are many. Here I will address three groups of cognitive processes — those related to perception, memory and thinking. I will begin by considering the differences between cognitive ability and cognitive style, then describe two basic, over-arching cognitive styles, and finally consider how perception, memory and thinking processes subserve these two basic cognitive styles.

Cognitive ability and cognitive style

Cognitive style is different than cognitive ability. The differences between them are important and can be explained in at least four different ways.

1. Cognitive ability refers to the content (what you know) of cognition, while cognitive style refers to the manner or mode (how you know) used to process information.

Two individuals may be equal in ability to solve problems but go about the solving in quite different ways and come up with quite different solutions (Messick, 1976).

2. Cognitive ability reflects one's ability (maximum performance) in completing cognitive tasks; while cognitive style reflects one's preference (generalized habits) in completing cognitive tasks.

Cognitive style has very little to do with intelligence, although traditional means for measuring intelligence tend to favour those who use the analytic cognitive style.

3. Cognitive ability is understood as being unipolar; cognitive style as bipolar.

Cognitive ability is usually conceived as a singular dimension (unipolar) of cognitive behaviour. An individual's ability ranges from low to high on each dimension. A learner cannot be assessed as being both high and low in ability on any given dimension. For example, one can be assessed as high or low on the single dimension of verbal ability.

Writers who promote the use of paired cognitive styles invariably state that both poles of the continuum are equally valuable, each having adaptive qualities in different contexts. The idea that cognitive styles are value-free is hard to sustain in many cases, particularly when the description of one style clearly indicates that it is more preferable and virtuous than the other.

Most cognitive styles are understood as ranging across paired behaviours (bipolar) with opposing styles being perceived as occupying opposite ends of a behavioural continuum. The more one uses of one aspect of the paired behaviours, the less one uses of the other. Individual assessments place a learner at some point along the continuum. The individual can be described as being high on one cognitive style (narrow scanning) or low on its opposing style (broad scanning); and both descriptions would be correct (Miller,1991).

An example of this value problem is provided by the cognitive styles of *field independence* and *field dependence*. In field independence, the individual can clearly distinguish a figure from the ground or perceptual field in which it is embedded and multiple figures can be perceived as separate and distinct from each other. Learners who use the field independent style often have trouble perceiving the ground and finding connections among the different parts of the field.

In field dependence, the learner sees the overall organization of the perceptual field as fused and the figure(s) as almost impossible to distinguish from the ground and from each other. Learners who use the field dependent style often have trouble distinguishing figure from ground and focusing on one part to the field to the exclusion of other parts.

As a field independent person, I never see deer or moose when I am driving across country; I concentrate too hard on the road, thus limiting my perceptual field to the "figure" of the road in front of the car. My field dependent colleagues, whether they are the driver or the passenger, see deer and moose in profuse numbers along the same highways. I'd like to think that my car emits a deer/moose repellent which is why I never see them; I would not like to think that I am missing some very important information which might affect my safety record.

When field dependence-independence (FDI) was originally described by Witkin and Goodenough (1977), the independence pole was imbued with all the virtue and those who were field dependent were described as if they were "dependent" (not self-directed) persons (Miller, 1991). Research indicates that more men than women are field independent and more women than men are field dependent. Eichler (1988), a noted feminist scholar, suggests that this pair of cognitive styles should be renamed "context blindness" and "context awareness."

4. In the fourth explanation of the differences between them, cognitive ability is understood as referring to a specific cognitive domain, while cognitive style refers to behavioural differences akin to personality traits.

Cognitive ability enables specific types of mental performances on such cognitive tasks as verbal comprehension or spatial manipulation.

Cognitive style refers to consistent individual differences in the manner of processing information which are perceived to be "interwoven with other personality structures and which function as general organizing and controlling mechanisms" (Miller 1991, p.31).

Cognitive style is thought of as a higher-order (more general) organizing principle which can recruit lower-order (more specific) cognitive abilities and strategies. In at least some individuals, "styles are embedded in personality in such a way that [learners] may not be able to change their prevailing style even though they may wish to do so" (Miller 1991, p.31).

Cognitive style

Specific cognitive strategies can be understood as contributing to three groups of cognitive processes:

1. perceiving,
2. remembering and
3. thinking.

Miller (1991) suggests that within these three cognitive processes we can distinguish two over-arching cognitive styles — an analytical style and a holistic style (See Diagram 7). An *analytical style* breaks down perceptions, memories and thoughts into their constituent parts

> ...with each part being studied as a discrete entity in isolation from all other parts and their surrounding context. The concern for detail plays an important role in everyday cognition as well as in more specialized tasks such as finding errors or faults in complex systems. Taken to extreme, however, one finds individuals virtually paralyzed by a preoccupation with minutiae, so narrowly focused that they lose touch with a broader reality (Miller 1991, p.32).

The analytical style is also described as articulated, differentiated, rigorous, constrained, convergent, critical, unified, ordering, and so on. The **holistic style** is harder to define and involves a preference to perceive, remember and think by being aware of the whole perception, memory or thought without breaking it into parts.

> The ability and inclination, to see patterns and configurations is a necessary complement to analytical thinking, as well as being at the root of many forms of creativity. Like analysis, however, it too can be taken to extremes. When holistic thinking takes the form of avoidance of detail the individual loses touch with what one might call empirical reality (Miller 1991, p.33).

Most learners are capable of using the cognitive processes which subserve both of these basic styles, but each person tends to prefer one style over the other. If our preferred style does not work, we reluctantly may try the other.

Miller views these two styles as basic aspects of cognition, both of which, in mature cognition, contribute to a higher-order capacity in which "previously differentiated parts are combined with intuitively sensed wholes to form complex patterns, thereby fashioning order out of chaos" (Miller 1991, p.33). Miller calls this higher order, "combined capacity", the synthetic/integrated style, and views it as the epitome of creative thought.

Entwistle (1981) describes cognitive style in similar terms. He reports that most adult learners use one of two basic cognitive styles (analytic or holistic) and refers to the small minority of learners who are able to use the synthetic/integrated style as "reasonable adventurers." He also describes the analytical, holistic, and synthetic/integrated styles as mature cognitive styles and views individuals who fit none of these three styles as "immature" learners. Entwistle's immature learners tend to be passive and dependent, and their learning is largely reproductive (Entwistle, 1981).

The two basic cognitive styles — analytic and holistic— are outlined in Diagram 7. The diagram presents the cognitive strategies which subserve each style as paired opposites organized as perceptual, memory and thinking processes. In the next three sections on Perception, Memory and Thinking, these cognitive strategies are described in greater detail.

I would caution you to try to separate the ideas about cognitive style and the ideas about hemisphere specialization outlined earlier in this chapter. The terms used in discussing hemisphere specialization and cognitive style tend to overlap inadvertently suggesting that the analytic cognitive style is specialized to the left hemisphere and the holistic cognitive style to the right hemisphere.

However, there is still no research which links a particular cognitive style to hemisphere specialization. What we should probably do is develop new terms to describe the two basic cognitive styles. Taking Entwistle's term of the "reasonable adventurer" as the person who can combine the two basic styles , we might call a person who prefers to use the analytic cognitive style, a "determined and directed walker" and a person who prefers to use the holistic cognitive style, a "curious and meandering wanderer."

	ANALYTIC STYLE	HOLISTIC STYLE
Perception		
a. Pattern Recognition	Feature analysis	Prototype matching
b. Attention	Narrow scanning Field independent (articulate)	Broad scanning Field dependent (global)
Memory		
a. Representation	Verbal-analytical memory codes	Visual-analogical memory codes
b. Organization	Narrow categories (differentiated) Analytic/semantic memory	Broad categories (overlapping) Thematic/episodic memory
c. Retrieval	Convergent search strategies	Divergent search strategies
Thinking	Paradigmatic thinking	Narrative thinking
a. Classifying	Sequential, serial	Simultaneous, global
b. Reasoning	Tight analogical reasoning — use of literal analogies — avoids metaphors	Loose analogical reasoning — use of poetic analogies — uses idiosyncratic metaphors
c. Infering	Actuarial judgement — based on hypotheses	Intuitive judgement — based on collection of attributes

7. COGNITIVE STYLES

Sources: Miller, A. (1991) **Personality Types: A modern synthesis.** Calgary: University of Calgary Press; Entwistle, N. (1981) **Styles of learning and teaching: An integrated outline of educational psychology.** Chichester, UK: John Wiley & Sons.

Perception Strategies

Perception is the process by which sensory information is interpreted in the light of one's previous experience and personal model of reality, in preparation for the more complex mental activity of thinking.

Two important aspects of perception are pattern recognition and attention. Whether these two aspects of perception occur in order, if indeed one does occur before the other, is a matter of considerable debate.

Pattern recognition involves comparing incoming sensory stimuli with existing patterns already stored in memory, and consists of two different sub-processes:

1. **Feature analysis** allows us to analyze the distinctive features of the incoming stimuli, one feature at a time, and to compare each feature with known features of existing patterns.
2. **Prototype matching**, on the other hand, involves comparing the incoming stimuli holistically with stored templates or mental copies of patterns.

Feature analysis contributes to an analytical cognitive style, while prototype matching contributes to a holistic cognitive style (Miller, 1991).

Attention involves selecting patterns for further processing. Attention is also usually understood as involving two different sub-processes:

1. If we think of attention as a beam of light, then **scanning** refers to the way the beam moves around the perceptual field. A widely-focused beam of light is called *diffuse scanning* and a narrowly-focused beam is called *limited scanning*. A beam that moves around to examine many different parts of the perceptual field is called *extensive scanning* and a beam that stays focused on one part of the perceptual field is called *intensive scanning* (Miller, 1991). Limited/intensive or narrow scanning is typical of the analytical cognitive style, while diffuse/extensive or broad scanning is typical of the holistic cognitive style.
2. The second sub-process of attention is **field articulation**. Focusing attention on a figure, while screening out background and irrelevant information or "informational noise," is typical of a field independent style. Attending to all the information as if each bit had equal relevance, including "informational noise," is typical of a field dependent style (Miller, 1991). Field independence contributes to the analytical cognitive style and field dependence to the holistic cognitive style.

Memory Strategies

Memory is a cognitive process which allows us to maintain a reasonably complete record of our life experiences.

Information is stored in memory so that it can be easily retrieved when we need it. There are three basic cognitive processes associated with memory:

1. the form in which it is stored or represented,
2. the manner in which it is organized, and
3. the processes involved in retrieving the stored information.

The *analytical cognitive style* is served by verbal-analytical strategies for representing information in memory and the use of narrowly-defined categories for storing information. The analytical style encourages a high degree of differentiation between categories (patterns and concepts), with very little overlap among them.

The *holistic cognitive style* is served by visual-analogical strategies for representing information in memory and the use of broadly defined categories for storing information. The holistic style encourages the development of many different and frequently overlapping categories (Miller, 1991).

In our discussion about brain structure, we have already seen that memories can be stored in kinesthetic (felt sensations), iconic (visual, auditory) or verbal (words) forms.

Tulving (1985) has proposed a different way of understanding how long-term memories are stored through *habituated, episodic and semantic memories.*

Habituated memory stores the knowledge and skills we use in everyday life.

For example, the alphabet is stored in habituated memory as are such daily skills as tying shoelaces and writing. Habituated memory serves both analytic and holistic cognitive styles.

*Episodic memory is a store of life events,
still more or less in their original form as specific impressions.*

Sometimes a familiar smell will trigger a complete scene or episode from your life. For example, the smell of gingerbread baking might recall a scene from childhood in which you can see your mother baking cookies. The memory likely comes complete with sounds, sensations and feelings. Episodic memory stores raw data which has gone through a pattern recognition process but the patterns have not been assigned words or abstract meanings.

Semantic memory is a store of the meanings
we construct as a consequence of our life experiences and our learning.

If I asked you to think of what represents "love" for you, you might tell me one of the symbols is your mother baking cookies — a meaning assigned to the scene stored in episodic memory.

> To give you some idea of how your memory is organized — before your read the next paragraph, think of a home in which you lived as a child, one that you can recall vividly. How many windows were in that home?
>
> If you walked through the home from room to room or around the outside, counting windows as you went, you are probably drawing on your episodic memory. You probably encountered other memories as you did the task. Episodic memory serves the holistic cognitive style.
>
> If you recalled that each room had one window and there were seven rooms, then you are probably drawing on semantic memory and did not recall any other "facts" about your home. You may have had an argument with yourself about whether or not you should include the patio/porch door as a window. Semantic memory serves the analytical cognitive style.

I regularly teach a course in Adult Development. In the past, I have asked course participants to write a partial autobiography or life narrative as one assignment. My instructions to them are to begin the process by recalling their lives using an analytic strategy which involves listing dates and events from birth to the present time and then adding details for each event. Many students find this impossible and switch to a more holistic strategy.

Birren and Deutchman (1991) describe a course on autobiographical writing which begins with a more holistic approach. Participants in their course are asked to identify a "branching point" in their lives and to write everything they can recall of the conditions and events which surround it. The writing does not need to be chronological. In preparing the manuscript for this book, I realized that I could help the students in my course by amending my instructions to include both analytic and holistic strategies as alternative starting points.

Information is assumed to be stored in long-term memory as part of conceptual networks. Any word can become a trigger to call up a network of associated words, images, sounds, and sensations.

Buzan and Buzan (1995) advocate the use of "mind maps" to retrieve information from conceptual networks. Their technique for drawing mind maps includes the use of words and phrases, drawings, icons, and so on (see Diagram 8, for an example). Since mind maps clearly appeal more to learners who are highly visual, we need to think of ways to develop similar techniques which draw on auditory representations through music or poems for example, or kinesthetic representations through dances, games or charades.

8. DOROTHY'S MIND MAP

<hr>

*Stored information can also be understood in terms of
conceptual level or cognitive complexity (Joyce & Weil, 1986; Hunt, 1971; Harvey, Hunt & Schroeder, 1961).
Conceptual complexity ranges from low to high.*

<hr>

A learner who is using *low complexity* understands and stores information in discrete categories (black/white thinking). Two or three categories may be understood in relation to each other (right/wrong, good/bad) but discrimination between paired concepts is minimal.

For example, in low conceptual complexity, all "adults" might be lumped into one category and contrasted with other groups of persons, such as "children," and all assigned the same characteristics such as self-directed. Truth is understood to be absolute and thinking is described as dualistic and unidimensional. A conceptual structure that depends on a single fixed rule reduces the individual's ability to think in terms of relativeness (Joyce & Weil, 1986).

A learner who is using moderate conceptual complexity understands and stores any given concept in various combinations with other concepts (black-grey-white thinking). These combinations allow for several different ways of structuring the world, thus introducing problems of choice and probability.

For example, "adults" and "children" might be understood in terms of selected characteristics based on both similarities and differences. That is, self-directedness might be understood as a characteristic of some children, while some adults might not necessarily be self-directed.

<hr>

*In **moderate conceptual complexity**, truth is understood to be multiplistic.
That is, what I know to be true may not be the same as what you know to be true.
Such thinking is described as multiplistic and multidimensional (Joyce & Weil, 1986).*

<hr>

A learner who is using *high conceptual complexity* greatly increases the number of networks within which a single concept can be understood. In order to determine "truth," the individual must be prepared to select a context and specify under what conditions various versions of the truth are acceptable.

For example, "adultness" might be understood as having different meanings depending on the specific context in which the characteristic is observed. Truth and knowledge are understood to be relativistic — what is true in one context may not be true in another — and thinking is described as relativistic or contextualized.

---

*Loevinger (1976), Hunt (1971) and Perry (1970), among others, define **cognitive complexity** as a developmental characteristic, one which can be modified through appropriate educational experiences. Most of us exhibit at least moderate conceptual complexity within our own area of expertise. and low conceptual complexity in areas in which we are totally unfamiliar.*

The retrieval of information involves searching conceptual networks for the information needed. The search strategies contributing to the analytic cognitive style are convergent in nature, and tend to narrow the search for relevant information by attempting to find the single "correct" bit of information through narrowly defined and sequential strategies. The search strategies contributing to the holistic cognitive style are divergent in nature and tend to broaden the search for relevant information by retrieving a wide range of information, some of which is more relevant than others.

Learners who use divergent strategies like to brainstorm, almost always coming up with many answers to the question being asked, while those who prefer the convergent strategy will brainstorm until they have identified the "right" or "best" answer.

Thinking Strategies

Thinking processes are even harder to differentiate and describe than those related to perception and memory. Cognitive psychologists do not agree on the names of the processes or whether thinking styles are stable over time and contexts (Miller, 1991; Flannery, 1993a).

We can consider thinking as a group of sub-processes (classifying, reasoning, inferring) which allow the individual to give meaning to, describe and explain experience, and to predict what might happen in future similar experiences or circumstances.

These processes can also be described as theory-building processes. Personal construct theory (Candy, 1990; Kelly, 1955) states that individuals build theories to explain past experiences, predict future outcomes and control present activities. Thinking consists of cognitive processes which allow us to build our own theories about our own experience and thereby create our personal model of reality.

The analytical cognitive style involves thinking in which the individual processes bits of information sequentially, in a stepwise fashion. Such thinking is

❖ serial,
❖ systematic,
❖ logical,
❖ generally based on abstract ideas, and
❖ allows the learner to adopt an objective stance toward reality.

Explanations and predictions (hypotheses) are about specific, single attributes based on tight logical reasoning.

---

*The analytic thinker makes 'actuarial judgements' in which
one attribute of a situation is considered at a time, with
irrelevant attributes being eliminated in serial fashion while holding others constant.*

Those who use this strategy "worry away at difficulties until they have been mastered, in preference to leaving loose ends" (Miller 1991, p.58). The analytic thinker prefers literal analogies, rejects metaphors, avoids figurative speech and rarely appreciates how one area of knowledge might be seen as analogous to another.

The holistic cognitive style involves thinking about whole concepts or groups of concepts simultaneously. Such thinking is

❖ global,
❖ redundant,
❖ analogical, and
❖ allows the learner to adopt a subjective stance toward reality.

---

*The holistic thinker develops explanations and predictions based, not on single attributes,
but on collections of attributes, poetic analogies,
idiosyncratic metaphors and intuitive judgements.*

"It follows that [holistic thinkers] seem happy enough juggling several ideas at once, hoping the situation will clarify itself in due course" (Miller 1991, p.59). Holistic thinkers enjoy looking at things from several different points of view at the same time.

Bruner (1986) describes analytical thinkers as using *paradigmatic thinking* and holistic thinkers as using *narrative thinking*.

> [Paradigmatic thinking]...seeks to establish general laws of causal relations between events in the world, laws that are context-free and universal. The verification of ideas is through formal and empirical proof...However, comprehensiveness and richness of ideas are sacrificed in pursuit of rigour; denotation is preferred over connotation. In contrast, the narrative mode is a form of storytelling that seeks to establish, not general laws, but patterns of behaviour, general themes that typify a single human life seen in its full social context (Miller 1991, p.64).

In narrative thinking, truth is based on credibility and rigour is sacrificed in favour of idiographic richness and coherence. Narrative thinking is described in the literature under other labels, such as "personal practical knowledge" (Connelly & Clandinin, 1990). This area is currently being explored by adult educators (Randall, 1995) for a variety of reasons.

Narrative thinking is a useful way to store and describe information for which no clearly defined propositional knowledge is available.

Narratives are used frequently by individuals who are novices in an area of study and provide a useful means for helping adult learners examine their sense of self and self-esteem and their early experiences as learners.

Thinking and Age-related Changes

Thinking strategies, as with all strategies which contribute to cognitive style, are affected by normal age-related changes. Changes in cognition have always been assumed to lead to deficits in thinking. Berg, Klaczynski, Calderone and Strough (1994) view holistic thinking strategies, particularly narrative thinking, as having adaptive functions in relation to age-related changes.

*The **analytic style or paradigmatic thinking**, is concerned with the accuracy of texts and leads to better performance on text-processing tasks, such as recalling stories by remembering factual information.*
*The **holistic style of narrative thinking** is more concerned with metaphorical and psychological interpretations of texts and leads to poorer performance on texts requiring recall of factual or propositional knowledge.*

Berg and others (1994) claim that paradigmatic thinking is more typical of younger adults while narrative thinking is used by many older adults, putting them at a disadvantage when performance tests call for remembering factual content. Narrative thinking, however, may provide older adults with a more efficient means for storing and retrieving information and for transmitting knowledge to younger generations.

LEARNING AND FACILITATING PRINCIPLES

❖ No matter how information is presented to learners, each will process the information by using personal cognitive style. The new information, combined with the individual's personal and unique model of reality, will rarely be interpreted and understood in the same manner as is understood by the facilitator presenting the information.

   Good facilitators will take the time to find out how learners have interpreted and understood the presented information.

❖ Cognitive styles are assumed to be stable characteristics and an integral part of personality. Individuals may have considerable difficulty changing their styles to match those being used by others.

   Good facilitators will deliberately learn other cognitive styles to better understand all learners. In making this effort, each facilitator will develop what Miller (1991) calls "an integrated/synthetic style" and become what Entwistle (1981) calls a "reasonable adventurer."

❖ Misunderstandings among learners or between learner and facilitator are often the result of differences in how a situation or information is processed through different cognitive styles.

   Facilitators must understand other cognitive styles in order to understand the origin of misunderstandings among learners and between themselves and individual learners.

❖ Information needs to be presented to learners in a variety of perceptual modes: visual, auditory, kinesthetic and verbal.

❖ Assessment procedures generally favour analytic cognitive styles. Assessment methods must be designed to support holistic learners in their learning activities. Holistic thinkers would probably do better on essay questions or questions based on case studies than on multiple choice or true-false questions. If true-false questions must be used, holistic thinkers could be asked to explain why an answer is true or false (Flannery, 1993a).

❖ Narratives are stories learners tell which emerge from their personal model of reality, and are stories which relate to their "self."

   Listening emphatically to narratives told by adult learners about their own learning is an excellent way to find out the best way to facilitate their learning and to affirm what they know and who they are.

INTELLIGENCE

For most of us, *intelligence* is represented by a score on an intelligence test, a test which is highly suspect. IQ scores may be statistically reliable but they are also totally irrelevant to normal daily living. However, "intelligent" is also a concept which we draw on to describe the behaviour of others as well as our own. While we may not agree with or approve of IQ tests and IQ scores, most of us have a clear understanding of what we believe constitutes intelligent behaviour and most of us assess potential employees, co-workers, peers and students in terms of their intelligence.

Intelligence is a quality of mind that we use continually in our daily lives. Sternberg (1988) defines intelligence as

> ...mental self-management — the mental management of one's life in a constructive, purposeful way...Mental self-management can be said to have three basic elements: adapting to environments, selecting new environments, and shaping environments (Sternberg 1988, p.11).

Intelligence, even in traditional definitions,
involves the ability to adapt or change
one's behaviour to fit more easily into the environment.

What is adaptive in one setting may not be adaptive in another. When an environment is unsatisfactory for a variety of reasons, it may be maladaptive to adapt, and the intelligent choice is to select a different environment. "Trying again" or "trying harder" may have merit but individuals must also know when to stop banging their heads against the walls of one environment and move on to another.

Sometimes neither adaptation nor selection is possible and environmental shaping becomes the intelligent choice. *Whereas adaptation involves fitting oneself into the environment, shaping involves fitting the environment to oneself.* There is no single set of behaviours which is intelligent for everyone in every situation. What does appear to be common among intelligent people is their ability to capitalize on their strengths and compensate for their weaknesses.

Sternberg's triarchic theory of intelligence

Sternberg (1988) describes his theory of intelligence as a triarchic theory in which intelligence is conceived as having three parts or subtheories:

1. a fundamental or componential part, which forms the basis for learning and reasoning,
2. an experiential part, and
3. a contextual part.

The **componential subtheory** deals with fundamental components of intelligence or underlying cognitive processes. Sternberg (1988) proposes three types of cognitive components or strategies in this subtheory:

1. *Knowledge acquisition or information processing components* are basic cognitive strategies for learning, allowing one to translate sensory input and information from life experiences into a personal, conceptual model of reality.
2. *Metacomponents* are overarching or executive cognitive strategies allowing one to use knowledge and information to reason, plan, decide and evaluate personal actions.
3. *Performance components* are basic cognitive strategies allowing one to turn plans into actions or motor outputs.

*Intelligent behaviour involves an
interactive relationship
between these three fundamental components of cognition.*

The **experiential subtheory** of intelligence underlies an individual's responses to life experiences. This ranges along a continuum from highly novel experiences (never encountered) to highly familiar experiences for which responses have become automatic.

*Intelligence involves the ability to reason and
learn in new experiences
resulting in the development of new knowledge and skills and new executive strategies.*

Novelty can be a function of the context in which tasks are to be carried out or a function of the unfamiliarity of the tasks themselves. Experiential intelligence involves bringing into play fundamental components of intelligence in both novel and routine tasks (Sternberg, 1988).

In adult education, for example, we are concerned about the transition from school to work and the transfer of knowledge from one experience to another. Sternberg would define the ability to make such transitions and transfers successfully, as aspects of experiential intelligence, or one's ability to retain composure in difficult situations.

The **contextual subtheory** of intelligence underlies an individual's ability to

❖ adapt to, select and shape environments in which he or she must function;

❖ know, in the words of the song, "when to hold, when to fold, when to walk away, when to run" and

❖ know, presumably when to challenge other players or change the environment itself (Sternberg, 1988).

Contextual intelligence can be thought of as one's ability to be "street smart."

Individual differences in intelligence are partly a matter of genetic inheritance, partly a matter of personal preference, partly a matter of socialization and other environmental influences, and partly a matter of opportunity.

The cognitive strategies we use are selected on the basis of our personal preferences from a range of potential processes. The more we are able and willing to use alternate cognitive strategies, respond to novel situations, and adapt to and shape environments, the more intelligent we become. Sternberg (1988, p.270) states:

> Levels and patterns of intelligence and their manifestations in intellectual performance, are substantially affected by socialization processes. Because of the vast differences in socialization that occur across cultures and subcultures, intelligence is not quite the same thing for everyone.

However, traditional IQ tests are based on the assumption that intelligence is the same thing for everyone. In some sense, intelligence is consistent across cultures because, for example, adaptation is always required. But what constitutes adaptation varies from one culture to another and what is acceptable as adaptation varies from one person to the next.

Sternberg discusses the many ways in which early socialization in different cultures affects intelligence in children. And if intelligence is strongly affected by socialization, then the intelligence of adults can also be affected by socialization processes in workplaces, families, communities and educational programs. To some extent, one can improve intelligence through learning.

Assessing intelligence

Each of the three aspects of intelligence and the associated knowledge and strategies can and should be assessed differently. Traditional IQ tests measure the knowledge acquisition and executive aspects of componential intelligence. Academic achievement relates closely to such measures. However, when young adults leaves full-time attendance in educational institutions and enter the workplace or start a family, their intelligence should be assessed some other way. Sternberg (1988) has designed a checklist which is used to predict intelligence (see Diagram 9). He reports that the checklist has been found to be a reasonably good predictor of overall intelligent behaviour.

Schaie (1977–78) directs our attention to the fact that as we develop and change our social roles and responsibilities over our lifespan, our need for intelligent behaviour also changes. While we need all three forms of intelligence throughout life, the emphasis changes.

As youth, before entering the workplace and starting families, we need the intelligence necessary to acquire knowledge and skills for future occupational and professional roles. The aspects of intelligence which we use most often in this process would be the *fundamental components.*

As young adults, when we enter the workplace and start families, we need to use *experiential and contextual intelligence* as well as the *fundamental components*. If we have had no opportunities to practice such behaviour, we may have trouble making the necessary transitions. Assessing intelligent behaviour in this stage of development could involve, for example, performance appraisals by supervisors or responses to case studies rather than IQ tests.

As middle-aged adults, many of us assume responsibility for managing the affairs of our families or our workplaces. To do this we need to draw on our creativity and ability to respond to others, behaviours which Sternberg identifies as beyond intelligence (1988, p.240).

Responsiveness involves the ability to coordinate the behaviour and performances of two or more persons as they carry out cooperative activities on behalf of the family or workplace.

Creativity involves developing new ways of understanding or doing things. Assessing intelligent behaviour in this stage of development could focus on performance appraisals from co-workers and peers, responses to case studies and in-basket techniques.

As older adults, we need to draw on wisdom, a form of behaviour which also goes beyond intelligence (Sternberg, 1988). Schaie (1977–78) describes this stage as involving reintegrative intelligence. Assessing intelligence at this stage seems counter-productive unless it is done by colleagues and peers in the same age group and focuses on contextual intelligence and the adaptiveness of behaviours developed to deal with age-related changes in oneself and in the environment.

Rate on a 1 (low) to 9 (high) scale the extent to which each of the following behaviours characterizes the person being assessed.

1. **Practical problem-solving ability**

   ____ Reasons logically and well.
   ____ Identifies connections among ideas.
   ____ Sees all aspects of a problem.
   ____ Gets to the heart of problems.
   ____ Interprets information accurately.
   ____ Responds thoughtfully to others' ideas.
   ____ Goes to original sources for basic information.
   ____ Poses problems in an optimal way.
   ____ Perceives implied assumptions and conclusions.
   ____ Listens to all sides of an argument.
   ____ Deals with problems resourcefully.

   ____ Keeps an open mind.
   ____ Is a good source of ideas.
   ____ Sizes up situations well.
   ____ Makes good decisions.

2. **Verbal ability**

   ____ Is verbally fluent.
   ____ Studies hard.
   ____ Reads with high comprehension.
   ____ Deals effectively with people.
   ____ Sets aside time for reading.
   ____ Speaks clearly and articulately.
   ____ Is knowledgeable about a particular field of knowledge.

   ____ Converses well.
   ____ Reads widely.
   ____ Tries new things.
   ____ Writes without difficulty.
   ____ Displays a good vocabulary.
   ____ Accepts social norms.

3. **Social competence**

   ____ Accepts others for what they are.
   ____ Has social conscience.
   ____ Is on time for appointments.
   ____ Displays interest in the world at large.
   ____ Thinks before speaking and doing.
   ____ Does not make snap judgements.
   ____ Assesses well the relevance of information to a problem at hand.
   ____ Is sensitive to other people's needs and desires.
   ____ Is frank and honest with self and others.
   ____ Displays interest in the immediate environment.

   ____ Admits mistakes.
   ____ Displays curiosity.
   ____ Makes fair judgements.

---

9. STERNBERG'S CHECKLIST OF INTELLIGENT BEHAVIOURS.

Source: Sternberg, R. J. (1988) **The triarchic mind: A new theory of human intelligence.** New York: Penguin Books, (pp. 238-239).

LEARNING AND FACILITATING PRINCIPLES

❖ We have all been socialized to believe that certain behaviours indicate intelligence and other behaviours indicate lack of intelligence. Definitions of what constitutes intelligent behaviour vary by subgroups within each culture. What is viewed as intelligent behaviour for men may be quite different than what is viewed as intelligent behaviour for women. Differences also exist between social classes, racial and linguistic groups, and so on.

What facilitators believe demonstrates lack of intelligence, may be indicative of highly intelligent behaviour in a different culture. Facilitators need to consider carefully what types of behaviour they use to assess an adult learner's intelligence.

COGNITIVE DEVELOPMENT

Until very recently, our understanding of cognitive development was based on the belief that our development was complete by adulthood and that any subsequent changes were age, accident and disease-related and involved declines and deficits. In the past twenty years, psychologists, gerontologists and adult educators have carried out considerable research and written many opinions which refute this. Traditional beliefs held that, by the time individuals reached adulthood, they were capable of

- ❖ performing cognitive operations on internal mental representations of experience,
- ❖ identifying patterns among these representations,
- ❖ assigning meanings in the form of symbols, words and signs to the patterns,
- ❖ using these meanings to think (solve problems and plan actions),
- ❖ identifying patterns among these meanings and assigning increasingly abstract meanings to them,
- ❖ using these abstract meanings to think, and so on.

Mental operations performed on abstract meanings can become highly complex and sophisticated.

*Cognitive development from birth onward results in an organized set of mental constructs, our personal model of reality. This model consists of the **processes of cognition** attending, selecting, representing, storing, retrieving classifying, reasoning, inferring, etc. and the **structured concepts or results of cognition:** stored systems of generalized and specialized dimensions of knowledge, as well as the skills to be activated in specific contexts.*

The development of both the processes and structures of cognition proceeds through two basic processes — *differentiating* (analyzing) and *integrating* (synthesizing) (Kegan, 1982).

❖ When the integrating process results in expanded concepts without changing their essential meaning, the process is called **assimilation**.

❖ When the integration process results in transformed meanings, wholly new meanings, or new cognitive strategies, the process is called **accommodation** (Kegan, 1982) or **transformation** (Mezirow, 1991).

Those transformations which are accompanied by a major shift in the way the individual perceives, remembers and thinks about the world are viewed as marking transitions from one stage of cognitive development to another.

According to Piaget, the developing individual goes through *four stages of cognitive growth:*

1. sensory-motor thought,
2. representational or preoperational thought,
3. concrete operational thought (mental operations converting concrete information into abstract ideas),
4. formal operational thought (mental operational converting abstract ideas into increasingly abstract and complex ideas)

These four stages are necessary to reach the abstract thought perceived as typical of adults (Kegan, 1982). Each new cognitive stage brings a more adequate and more logical set of concepts and processes for knowing the world.

According to Kegan (1982), Piaget viewed "more adequate" cognitive processes and structures as those which would allow the individual to adopt an increasingly less egocentric stance from which to perceive, differentiate and integrate increasingly more complex and inter-related meanings based on accumulated experience.

Adult cognitive development

Piaget's four stages were once thought to be universal, to happen to every human being. It has since been shown that development of formal thought is largely dependent on the influence of secondary and post-secondary educational institutions and therefore, is not universal.

We know that any cognitive development during adulthood must take place in response to some or all of the following conditions and needs:

❖ Adults must transfer knowledge from one context to another, most often from a training context to a practical, applied context. **Transferability** involves the recognition of new instances in which existing knowledge and skills can be applied, a form of *contextual intelligence and learning* not accounted for in formal operational thinking (Kolb, 1984).

❖ Adults are called on to **develop specialized knowledge and skills.** Kolb (1984) describes specialization as a powerful developmental dynamic in which adults are encouraged, through professional, occupational and role socialization, to develop the personal characteristics deemed appropriate and acceptable to their field of specialization and which increasingly becomes an integral part of one's self and one's personal model of reality, As we saw in Chapter Two, when these characteristics are an integral part of personality, they may affect cognition.

❖ While children and adolescents spend much of their time solving problems and answering questions posed by others, adults must be able to **identify and formulate problems before solving them, or invent questions before answering them** (Arlin, 1986; Watzlawick, Weakland, & Fisch, 1974). While these tasks sound simple, many adults, even those in formal educational systems, cannot do them.

❖ Many adults live in work, family and community environments where it is not clear what one's goals should be. Indeterminate situations call for the development of **projective images of future possibilities** of what could be (Schön, 1971). Such situations also require cognitive strategies allowing the individual to move back and forth between this future image and the current situation in order to monitor forward progress and modify actions before implementation.

❖ Adults must be able to **deal with uncertainties, doubts and ambiguities**. Riegel (1973) criticizes the idea that formal operation thinking is the highest stage of cognitive development because uncertainty, doubt and ambiguity cannot always be resolved through formal logic or rational thought. Therefore, it is logical to assume such situations call for cognitive strategies which represent a more advanced stage of cognitive development.

❖ Most adults must live and work within complex systems of roles and relationships and must learn how to **manage the interactions and conflicts** among them (Koplowitz, 1987). *Systems thinking* involves cognitive strategies for managing the complex interactions typifying most places of work and also the complexities of an individual adult's life.

❖ Adults need to be able to **reflect on their own actions and change those actions even in the process of acting** (Argyris & Schön, 1974; Schön, 1987). We have already encountered this concept when we discussed learning to learn (Smith, 1990) in Chapter One. The cognitive strategies required for learning how to learn and for reflective practice involve the development of executive cognitive strategies guiding and controlling other cognitive strategies. Executive cognitive strategies are not accounted for in *formal operational thought*.

❖ Adults need to be able to **identify, through critical thinking, the assumptions which underlie ideas or systems of ideas** (Brookfield, 1987). Critical thinking calls for the use of cognitive processes allowing one to think about or operate on formal thoughts. In every previous stage of cognitive development, similar shifts in cognition are perceived as the beginning of a new stage of development. Many writers view critical thinking as indicative of a fifth stage of cognitive development called, variously, *post-formal or dialectical operational thought*.

❖ Adults need to be able to **deal with paradoxical situations**. Doubt, ambiguity, uncertainty, systems thinking and self-reflective thought tend to give rise to paradoxes. It is reasonable to assume, therefore, that post-formal operational thought must allow the adult to develop strategies for dealing with paradox.

A *paradox* is a conundrum raised when a rule, command or generalization appears to contradict itself. For example, "all generalizations are false," "this statement is false" and "be spontaneous" are examples of paradoxical statements. A paradox can only be resolved by moving outside the frame of reference (or personal model of reality) which contains it and beyond the cognitive strategies which are creating it. This requires moving into a new frame of reference and using new cognitive strategies. This type of learning is called perspective transformation within the field of adult education (Mezirow, 1991).

Development of cognitive complexity

In this chapter we have already encountered a number of ideas offering some insights into the nature of adult cognitive development. The development of increasing cognitive complexity is one such characteristic. In Chapter Two, we saw that cognitive complexity can range from very low, stereotypic thinking to very complex, multidimensional thinking (Loevinger, 1976; Hunt, 1971).

Perry (1970) conducted research with university men to determine whether their cognitive complexity changed over four years of undergraduate study. He found that these men tended to enter post secondary education using dualistic thinking in which truth is viewed as absolute and knowledge is viewed as whatever authorities tell you. By their third year, most had moved to *multiplistic thinking* in which different versions of truth and knowledge are viewed as equally acceptable; and by graduation, many had moved to *relativistic or contextual thinking* in which knowledge and truth are understood as being dependent on the context in which they are used.

Baxter Magolda (1992) conducted similar research with both men and women. She found that both genders moved from dualistic to *individualistic thinking* by the end of their second year and to multiplistic thinking by graduation.

Individualistic thinking is described as a stage between dualistic and multiplistic thinking in which the individual becomes aware of personal ideas in contrast to those presented by authorities.

Baxter Magolda also reports that contextual thinking does not develop until the individual's first year in work, family or community settings.

Sternberg's (1988) triarchic theory of intelligence suggests other ideas about adult cognitive development. Clearly an adult needs to make full use of all three types of intelligence (information processing, experiential and contextual). In North America, cognitive development in early adulthood probably involves the belated development of both contextual and experiential intelligence.

Our current concern in many adult programs for such topics as job readiness, life skills, stress management, problem solving skills, time management skills, and the like, may be a reflection of our formal educational programs which do not necessarily foster the development of contextual or experiential intelligence at an earlier age.

Adult cognitive development probably involves an expansion of experiential and contextual intelligence by increasing the adult's experiential base, expanding the ability to reflect on experience and learn from it, and enlarging the number of contexts one must adapt to, select and shape. Such changes most likely will be accompanied by changes in performance and the metacomponents of fundamental intelligence (reasoning, planning, organizing, deciding, etc.).

Speculatively speaking, Schaie's (1977–78) *reintegrative intelligence* may involve an integration of the three aspects of intelligence into a sort of global intelligence where mental processes may become an integral part of the experience and context within which they are developed and used. Such a process would likely make older adults both more competent in familiar contexts, and less competent in unfamiliar contexts (within which they have no previous experience).

That is, the more the three forms of intelligence are integrated with each other, the more difficult the transfer of knowledge from one context to another.

LEARNING AND FACILITATING PRINCIPLES

❖ Since cognitive complexity is a developmental characteristic, we can facilitate learners best by using a matching model such as was discussed in Chapter Two.

For example, a comfort match for dualistic thinkers would be a facilitating style presenting knowledge as absolute truth, probably through lecturing. A developmental match for a multiplistic thinkers would be a facilitating style encouraging and supporting individualistic thinking, probably through discussions.

❖ **Adults may need assistance in learning skills typifying the post-formal stage of cognitive development such as:**

❖ finding and formulating problems;

❖ asking questions;

❖ recognizing instances in which transfer of knowledge or skills can occur;

❖ developing projective images of future possibilities and working toward them;

❖ dealing with uncertainties, ambiguities and doubts;

❖ thinking critically;

❖ reflecting on action; and

❖ learning to learn.

SOCIAL ASPECTS: GENDER AND CULTURAL BASES IN LEARNING

5

This chapter could address a number of different issues, all related to the social aspects of learning; but because I see learning as a multi-faceted and dynamic interplay of complex factors, many of these issues have already been addressed. In Chapter Two, I considered the socialization of adults into new roles and responsibilities as an important component of adult learning and in the section on "the self", I examined the difficulties women have had in using traditional developmental theories to understand their own self-development.

In the past three decades, female researchers have investigated this problem.
Josselson (1992) comments that the most impressive aspects of these studies is the consistency of findings
that human interconnection and relatedness are a central plot of human development,
certainly as central as the traditional plot which focuses on autonomy and independence.

In Chapter Three, I discussed motives for learning and Houle's (1961) finding that the social activities of group-based learning support one of three major reasons for participating in adult education programs. I also identified the need for connection or belonging as one of two powerful tendencies for organizing human behaviour. I considered the individual's need for support and acceptance as an important contributor to well-being during learning activities.

In this chapter, I could discuss the importance of learning related to social concerns, social understanding, social policies, and the like.

While all of these socially-defined aspects of learning are important, I have chosen to focus on what is becoming known in the literature as "relational learning" and to use the discussion to address gender-based and culture-based differences in learning

---

I will return to social concerns and social learning theory in Chapter Ten.

NEW WAYS TO THINK ABOUT ADULT LEARNING

This chapter introduces three different ways to think about adult learning in the light of new ideas in adult development. First, new ideas about women's development suggests that there are at least **two paths in "normal" development:**

1. *the autonomous, separate or independent path* which typifies the majority of men (and some women)

2. *the relational, connected or interdependent path* which typifies the majority of women (and some men). These two paths are equally valid and important. Advocates of this conception of adult development (Baxter Magolda, 1992) believe educational programs and learning activities should facilitate development along both paths.

Second, some writers suggest *that the two paths diverge in early development but converge as we grow older.* If we view the two paths as two polarities in human development, then in later life individuals who have developed predominantly along one path as young adults become aware of the other path through individuation (Levinson & Associates, 1978; Jung, 1964). With awareness comes a need to distinguish behaviour associated with the other path, to test out these behaviours for oneself, and then integrate them into one's self-system (self-concept, self-esteem, self-ideal) and model of reality.

*Maturity is sometimes conceptualized as occurring when
the individual is capable of both types of behaviour (autonomous and relational).*

For example, in the development of moral reasoning, Gilligan (1982), in contrast to Kohlberg (1973), proposes two paths or orientations:

1. the *rights-justice orientation*
2. the *responsibility-caring orientation*.

Gilligan proposes that mature, post-conventional moral reasoning would incorporate both orientations. Belenky, Clinchy, Goldberger and Tarule (1986) imply a similar pattern in their work on ways of knowing and being. Advocates of this conception of adult development believe educational programs and learning activities should foster personal growth along the non-dominant path of development. When conducted with some groups, such as re-entry women, these provisions tend to be seen as remedial activities (Mezirow, 1975).

*Third, some writers indicate that **human interconnection, relatedness and interdependence** must be conceptualized as **the** central plot of human development with autonomy, separateness and independence as developing within relationships.*

This conception of human development is reciprocal to traditional thought exemplified by Freud, Jung, Erikson, Levinson, Kohlberg, and others. Josselson (1992, p.3) reminds us that

> ...relatedness is central — to physical health, to longevity, to meaningful social life, and to the growth and development of the self.

She urges us to turn our attention to how relatedness develops, how it becomes increasingly differentiated and integrated over the lifespan and how autonomy develops within relationships. Writers and researchers attached to the Stone Center at Wellesley College (Miller, 1986, 1984; Surrey, 1985; Clinchy & Zimmerman, 1985) also direct our thinking along similar lines. Advocates of this conception of development (MacKeracher, 1993) believe that the use of relational concepts to develop educational programs and learning activities can also accommodate learners who are following an autonomous path (or at least will not place barriers in their way); whereas activities which facilitate the autonomous path (those which now dominate our educational activities) place barriers in the way of those following the relational path, and sometimes exclude such learners entirely.

THE AUTONOMOUS AND RELATIONAL SELVES

New ideas emerging from research into women's self development (as compared to men's), indicate that the self-system can develop along two different paths.

One path of development for the self-system is based on the development of autonomy and independent action and on seeing the self as separate from others.

Development along this path is understood as occurring through a predictable sequence of behaviours or stages in which the individual moves from an immature self-system — derived from unequal relationships, feelings of powerlessness and the use of dependent behaviours — toward a mature self-system which supports equality in relationships, feelings of empowerment and the use of independent behaviours (Levinson & Associates, 1978; Erikson, 1978; Vaillant, 1977; Sheehy, 1976).

The second path to self development is based on connectedness to others and interdependent action.

The development of this self-system is viewed as occurring through multi-dimensional and complex processes emerging from life's expected and unexpected events and changes (Schlossberg, 1987). This self-system is defined and discovered through interacting with others around mutual concerns for each other's well-being, and through responsiveness to each other's needs (Lyons, 1988; Caffarella & Olson, 1993; Miller, 1986; Gilligan, 1982).

The two different self-systems are gender-related but not gender-specific. Research indicates that most individuals use a combination of the two self-systems to create their own unique self-system. A smaller number of people use one system almost exclusively and show little or no development in the other.

Lyons (1987) reports that men are more likely than women to rely on the autonomous or separate components of their self-system as their preferred mode of functioning; while women are more likely than men to rely on the connected or relational components of their self-system. Further, those whose self-system is exclusively based on autonomy are men, while those whose self-system is exclusively based on relationships are women.

How individuals perceive themselves in adulthood depends on:

❖ their early socialization,

❖ their accumulated life experiences, and

❖ the adaptations they have made over time.

Lyons (1987) reports that the autonomous self-system is based on self-concepts derived as a result of an individual seeing the self as if through the eyes of significant others, allowing the individual to affirm and reaffirm aspects of the self-system even when those significant others are not present.

---

*In the **autonomous self-system**,
one **internalizes** the opinions of significant others in childhood and early adulthood, and
then acts as if these opinions came from an external source.*

---

*The **relational self-system** is based on self-concepts derived as a result of
engaging in interactive relationships with significant others who must **be present**
if the individual is to feel affirmed and reaffirmed.*

A comparison between the two modes of self definition is provided in Diagram 10.

Conversational style is one behavioural outcome of the two types of self-systems. Tannen (1990) reports on two ways of carrying on a conversation: report-talk and rapport-talk.

Autonomous or Separate Self	Autonomous or Separate Self	Relational or Connected Self
Major focus of self definition	Autonomous in relation to others Focus on independence	Connected in relation to others Focus on interdependence
Basis for self definition	Through seeing self as if through the eyes of another	Through interactive relationships with others
Relationships between self and others	Experienced through reciprocity Others assumed to be more similar than different in comparison with self and each other — making reciprocity possible Maintained through impartiality, objectivity, and increasing distance between self and others	Experienced through interdependence Others are assumed to be more different than similar in comparison with self and each other — making responsiveness necessary. Maintained through responsiveness to differences between self and others, concern for other's well-being, understanding needs and contexts of others, and reducing distance between self and other.
	Based on report-talk	Based on rapport-talk

10. COMPARISON OF SELF-SYSTEMS

Source: MacKeracher, D. (1993) Women as learners. In T. Barer-Stein & J. A. Draper (Eds.), **The craft of teaching adults** (enlarged second edition). Toronto ON: Culture Concepts, Inc.

Report-talk is a means for preserving independence and for negotiating and maintaining status in a hierarchical social order.

It is more typical of the conversational style of men than of women and is used mainly in the public sphere. Report-talk involves exhibiting knowledge and skills and holding centre stage through verbal performance by such means as giving information and telling jokes or stories (Tannen 1990, p. 78).

Rapport-talk is a means for establishing connections and negotiating relationships.

This is more typical of the conversational style of women and is used mainly in the private sphere. Rapport-talk involves sharing and comparing experiences. Women are typically more talkative in private conversations while men are more talkative in public ones. Men often express frustration when women use rapport-talk in the public sphere, complaining that "she takes too long to get to the point" or "she wastes time on personal matters." Women often express frustration when men use report-talk in the private sphere, complaining that "he never talks to me" (Tannen 1990, p.78).

The research which has led to the understanding that two different types of self-systems are possible is paralleled by research into the ways of knowing and being which typify women (Belenky, Clinchy, Goldberger & Tarule, 1986); and the differences between men and women in their ways of learning and reasoning (Baxter Magolda, 1992; Clinchy & Zimmerman, 1985).

Since the self-system provides the frame of reference through which learning occurs, how each individual combines the autonomous and relational aspects of self will have an important effect on how that individual prefers to go about the learning process.

ALTERNATIVE WAYS OF KNOWING

In recent years, research into cognitive development has resulted in an increasing interest in "ways of knowing." The assumption is that there are many ways of knowing and that each is associated with different kinds of cognitive processes. In Chapter Four, we have already seen that Bruner (1986) identifies paradigmatic and narrative ways of knowing or thinking; while Connelly and Clandinin (1990) discuss personal and practical ways of knowing.

In this chapter, we focus on women's ways of knowing as an example of how knowing and learning affect and are affected by the self-system. Women's ways of knowing are described by Belenky, Clinchy, Goldberger and Tarule (1986) and by Clinchy and Zimmerman (1985). They began by investigating whether Perry's (1970) model of cognitive development, derived from research focused on university men, could be applied to women.

The inner and the outer 'voice'

Belenky and her colleagues use the concept of "voice" to describe forms of knowing and attitudes about self. The concept of voice can refer to the "inner voice" or the "outer voice." The inner voice informs us of what we know and think, how we judge ourselves and our environment, and what we value. You may experience this inner voice as something which "talks with you" or "talks to you". The inner voice can "speak" in words, sounds, images, metaphors, sensations, and emotions.

There are two components to the outer voice:

1. One component is the voice we use in sharing what we know with others. We give voice to our ideas through communicating processes such as speech, body language, writing, drawing, dancing, performing, and so on.

2. The second is the voice we hear as if it were emanating from others, such as the strident voice of our conscience, which often sounds like a sergeant-major living somewhere in our mind. This voice is heard as if it comes from an external source. In reality, it is the voice of others which we have internalized in our conscience.

The model proposed by Belenky and her colleagues describes five ways of being in the world (see below), in which each corresponds to a different world view allowing individuals to

❖ understand knowledge and truth,
❖ relate to authority and
❖ understand self.

The authors specifically tell us that the five positions do not necessarily describe a developmental process or sequence of developmental stages, although supporters identify a direct correlation with Perry's (1970) stages of cognitive development, and therefore with an implied developmental sequence. Note that Belenky and her associates did not conduct their research with men, therefore, they are careful not to attribute their ways of knowing to male learners. Conversations with male students, however, have convinced me that men may experience similar ways of knowing.

The five world views and ways of knowing are:
silence, received knowing, subjective knowing,
procedural knowing and constructed knowing (Belenky and others, 1986).

Each of the five "ways of being" corresponds to a "way of knowing." An individual uses one of the five ways of being (or world views) as the base from which to relate to the world and to others. However, some individuals may use more than one way of knowing.

Similarly, some women have access to only one way of knowing while some have access to two or three and some to all five.

The more ways of knowing one can utilize,
the more one can act in flexible, effective and efficient ways.

However, the description of these five ways of knowing provided in the text, *Women's Ways of Knowing* (Belenky & others, 1986) leaves me frustrated because it offers no consistent means for identifying developmental themes. I have come to understand the five ways of knowing as involving two dimensions of behaviour, one describing sources of knowledge and the other describing the information-gathering procedures necessary for knowing and learning.

SOURCES OF KNOWLEDGE

The dimension of knowing which I am describing as "sources of knowledge" varies from received knowledge at one end of the continuum to subjective knowledge at the other.

Subjective knowledge comes from internal sources and
is based on personal experience, feelings and intuitions.
This knowledge frequently remains unarticulated, wordless.

Subjective knowledge leaves one knowing something but not knowing how one knows it. It is sometimes called intuition and is frequently discounted as non-rational, particularly when used by women. Subjective knowledge is problematic in a learning situation because most of it is unarticulated and unassessed.

Those who use subjective knowledge almost exclusively tend to

❖ see authoritative or received knowledge as irrelevant since there are many personal truths, each one equally valid;

❖ value their inner voice and the spontaneous expression of feelings and opinions, believing that truth cannot be reduced to words;

❖ see no need to revise or even assess their ideas; and

❖ appear often to be listening, but may be attending to their own thoughts.

Their self-identity describes a confident person who knows what's what. (Belenky and others, 1986).

Received knowledge comes from external sources such as family members, friends, colleagues, authors, experts, and authorities.

Those who rely almost exclusively on received knowledge tend to assimilate it as their own and to reproduce it without any substantial deviation or correction based on personal experience. These individuals tend to

❖ perceive authorities as powerful and infallible, as the major and only accepted sources of knowledge in the world;

❖ view truth as absolute, factual and concrete;

❖ search for the one right answer, then interpret it literally and use it as a guide for action without assessing it in practical and personal terms; and

❖ be good listeners but have weak outer voices and often cannot find the "right" words.

Their self-identity defines them as "good" persons (as long as they have the right answer) who are trying to live up to expectations (Belenky and others, 1986).

Maturity in learning and knowing increases as the individual is able to integrate the two sources of knowledge. Those who facilitate adult learning need to help all learners

❖ become aware of their subjective knowledge;

❖ find appropriate words to describe and share it with others by finding their own voice;

❖ assess it against received knowledge and reality;

❖ assess received knowledge against both reality and personal experience; and

❖ modify both sources of knowledge.

Sometimes the individual needs assistance in sorting out what part of their knowledge comes from internal sources and what part comes from external sources.

Procedures for knowing and learning

The dimension of knowing which I am describing as "procedures for knowing and learning" varies from separate or autonomous procedures at one end of the continuum to connected or relational procedures at the other. Belenky, Clinchy, Goldberg and Tarule (1986) describe those who are skilled in both separate and connected procedures of knowing and learning as

- ❖ using the "voice of reason",
- ❖ speaking well,
- ❖ using words easily,
- ❖ listening to others carefully, and
- ❖ communicating effectively.

Their self-identity describes them as a confident person who knows how to get things done.

Separate knowing and autonomous learning

Separate knowing (Belenky and others, 1986) and *autonomous learning* (Baxter Magolda, 1992) are a subset of procedural knowing that allows one to learn and communicate autonomously, detached from others.

*Separate knowing encourages the knower to detach what is known from
the person who knows it, or from the experience which generated it.
That is, to generalize ideas so that they become detached from their real-life experiences,
and to decontextualize knowledge
thereby making it readily transferable to other situations.*

Those who rely heavily on separate knowing tend to

- ❖ be concerned with mastering or controlling their environment,
- ❖ adopt a highly critical adversarial stand when disagreeing with another person, and
- ❖ force a choice between opposing versions of truth.

This process is sometimes referred to as the "doubting game" which is described by Clinchy and Zimmerman (1985) as a strategy which allows a learner to doubt the truth of an idea until convinced by the logic of the argument supporting it. Those who doubt exclude ideas from their personal model of reality until the idea becomes a proven truth.

Separate knowers and autonomous learners

❖ are independent,

❖ tend to use analytical thinking styles,

❖ test for truth by looking for consistency and logic in knowledge, and

❖ prefer to hold thoughts and feelings apart from each other (Lyons, 1987; Wingfield & Haste, 1987; Baxter Magolda, 1992).

When separate learners ask 'Why?' they want an answer which will justify the logic or worth of an idea (MacKeracher, 1993).

Connected knowing and relational learning

Connected knowing (Belenky and others, 1986) and relational learning (Baxter Magolda, 1992) are a subset of procedural learning that allows one to

❖ function in ways which connect self to others,

❖ focus on issues related to affection, affiliation and caring, and

❖ include others in the learning process through cooperation and collaboration.

Connected knowing encourages one to connect what
is known to the person who knows it or the experience which generated it;
to keep ideas connected to their real-life experiences,
to keep knowledge contextualized and situation specific,
but not necessarily generalizable or transferable to other contexts and situations.

Connected knowers tend to

❖ be concerned about remaining connected to others within the environment,

❖ adopt a narrative or descriptive stance when they disagree with another person, and

❖ search for ways to incorporate the other's ideas into a larger conceptual scheme.

This process is sometimes referred to as the "believing game" which is described by Clinchy and Zimmerman (1985) as a strategy which allows learners to believe the truth of another's ideas and search for ways of including it, or a variation of it, in their personal model of reality. Knowledge and truth emerge from integrating different perspectives on an idea.

Connected knowers and relational learners

❖ are interdependent,
❖ tend to use holistic thinking styles,
❖ test for truth by looking for believability in knowledge, and
❖ prefer to keep thoughts and feelings integrated (Lyons, 1987; Wingfield & Haste, 1987; Baxter Magolda, 1992).

When connected learners ask 'Why?' they want to know how ideas were developed or constructed, preferably by hearing a description of the specific situation or activities in which the idea emerged (MacKeracher, 1993).

*Maturity in learning and knowing increases as
the learner becomes skilled in using
separate knowing and autonomous learning in conjunction with
connected knowing and relational learning.*

While the two procedural subsets may become integrated, it is more likely that a mature learner would be able to use each subset appropriately in different contexts and situations. One function of facilitators of adult learning is to help separate knowers recognize the need to contextualize some knowledge and evaluate it against personal experience. Another function is to help connected knowers recognize the need to generalize some personal knowledge so that it becomes transferable to other contexts and then to evaluate it against received knowledge.

Silence as a way of knowing

Belenky, Clinchy, Goldberger and Tarule (1986) also describe silence as a way of knowing and report that it is also associated with a personal history of abusive relationships.

*Silence is the experience of having no voice,
of feeling mindless and voiceless and
of being subject to the whims of external authority.*

It is experienced not only as the lack of an outer voice, but also as an inner silence accompanied by feelings of being suppressed, of feeling deaf and dumb. This way of knowing seems to involve a lack of reliance on any source of knowledge, whether internal or external, and an inability to use both separate and connected procedures.

The women who use silence as a way of knowing are rarely able to generalize from experience, but view each experience as separate and unconnected to other experiences.

- ❖ They perceive authority figures as arbitrary and punitive, as all powerful but mute, as sources of punishment but not sources of knowledge.
- ❖ They do not gain knowledge through words since words were often used as weapons in chronic verbal abuse.
- ❖ They experience themselves as having no words.
- ❖ Their self identity describes them as worthless nobodies.
- ❖ Those who use this way of knowing tend to be poor learners who must first regain their ability to communicate and to trust others before they can become effective learners.
- ❖ Some may have poor literacy skills and many are often found in basic education programs.

Facilitators of adult learning need to be able to identify such learners and offer them special and often extensive support services.

Many learners experience silence in the face of arbitrary, ambiguous, and punitive authorities although they do not use silence as a way of being in the world.

*They experience silence when they feel unable to communicate their knowledge either because they do not have the words or because they feel threatened about sharing what they know.
The experience is described as "feeling dumb" and frequently is accompanied by feelings of being depressed (rather than suppressed) and disempowered.*

Constructed knowing

Belenky, Clinchy, Goldberger and Tarule (1986) describe constructed knowing as a mature world view which appears to be the opposite of silence.

▬▬▬▬▬▬▬▬▬▬▬▬

Constructed knowing occurs when the learner relies on and integrates both subjective and received sources of knowledge and is willing to use both separate and connected procedures for knowing and learning.

▬▬▬▬▬▬▬▬▬▬▬▬

These individuals understand that
* ❖ all knowledge is constructed by persons,
* ❖ all knowledge is contextual and based on real experiences,
* ❖ some knowledge can be transferred to alternate contexts,
* ❖ one's own experiences can be used to generate knowledge equally as well as other people's experiences, and
* ❖ knowledge can and should be assessed against reality.

Those who adopt constructed knowing as a world view assume responsibility for examining, assessing and developing systems of thought, for caring about thinking and thinking about caring (Belenky and others, 1986). They are willing to see themselves as authoritative sources able to engage in collegial and collaborative activities rather than subordinating themselves to authority figures. Such knowers are capable of engaging in multiple dialogues. Their self identity describes a person who is confident, integrated, capable of working alone or with others.

LEARNING AND FACILITATING PRINCIPLES

❖ Learners who feel silenced, or who use silence as a way of being, need opportunities to share their feelings and perceptions with others; to share how they perceive themselves and their learning environment and how that environment is silencing them.

Facilitators need to be alert to the possibility that some learners feel silenced. For those who use silence as a way of being, facilitators need to ensure that supportive services are made available. For those who are experiencing temporary silencing, facilitators need to provide opportunities to talk about the personal experiences which have led to feeling silenced.

❖ Some learners attend only to the knowledge coming from authoritative sources.

When an exclusive focus on received knowledge is inappropriate, facilitators need to help learners think critically about such knowledge and assess it against personal life experiences.

❖ Some learners attend only to the knowledge derived from their interpretation of their subjective experiences.

When an exclusive focus on subjective knowledge is inappropriate, facilitators need to help learners think critically about such knowledge and assess it against the shared knowledge of other learners and of experts.

❖ Most adult learners have developed learning strategies supporting either separate procedural knowing or connected procedural knowing.

Facilitators can help adults become more effective learners by encouraging separate procedural knowers to develop skills of connected knowing, and connected procedural knowers to develop skills of separate knowing.

❖ Some adult learners have fully developed skills in using and understanding all ways of knowing.

The best thing facilitators can do is avoid putting obstacles in their way and act as collaborative colleagues in the learning endeavour.

DIFFERENCES AMONG LEARNERS

*Research into differences between separate and connected knowers, autonomous and relational learners,
emerged mainly because female researchers were unhappy about the way
in which human development and human learning were defined.
Too many women did not fit into the categories and patterns advocated as "normal" by
research based on male participants and ideas described by male researchers (Gilligan, 1982).*

Gilligan goes to considerable lengths to assert that male theorists are not wrong about male development; rather they have failed to perceive the essential differences presented by females because they are so thoroughly steeped in the beliefs and values which uphold the way men think and learn. Friere's (1973) concept of false consciousness works as well for gender related concerns as it does for class related and race related ones. When female researchers conducted their studies, they tended to focus mainly on female participants as a means of righting the balance. The interesting results unfortunately could not be generalized to men.

Baxter Magolda's (1992) study is one of the few recently reported studies which has included both men and women as study participants.

*She found that men and women did not differ in what they learned,
only in how they preferred to go about that learning.*

Women more often than men use connected procedures and relational strategies to gather and understand information, while men more often than women, use separate procedures and autonomous strategies to gather and understand information. Baxter Magolda does not say that all men use autonomous strategies or that all women use relational strategies.

We can assume, therefore, that some men prefer relational strategies for their learning, some women prefer autonomous strategies, and some men and women use both strategies. Making distinctions is clearly dysfunctional when one set of distinguishing characteristics is valued more highly than the contrasting set(s).

Making distinctions among learners is a time-honoured tradition among teachers and facilitators, even those working with adult learners. We do it because it helps us classify the many different individual learners we encounter in group settings and reduces the number of different responses we must make.

Beyond elementary grades, the formal educational system tends to favour and reinforce learners using autonomous or separate learning strategies, preferring independent or self-directed activities, and those using the analytic cognitive style (Steinem, 1992; Restack, 1979). Learners who characteristically use relational or connected learning strategies, prefer interdependent or group-based activities and use the holistic cognitive style, may shine in the elementary grades and later find that the educational system actively discourages or even rejects their way of learning.

In Chapter Four we saw that studies in brain lateralization suggest that the two hemispheres of the brain are specialized. The activities ascribed to these hemispheres sound very similar to the analytic and holistic cognitive styles (Miller, 1991; Entwistle, 1981), to separate and connected procedural knowing (Belenky and others, 1986), and to autonomous and relational reasoning (Baxter Magolda, 1992). However, we should not assume that there is an underlying biological factor which causes males to be more likely to develop the analytic/separated/autonomous group of behaviours and women the holistic/connected/relational group.

A careful reading of the literature indicates that, while physiological differences may play a small part in the differences found among learners, by far the greater influence is exerted by childhood socialization which is further reinforced by adult socialization.

We certainly should not assume that the use of one of these two groups of behaviours is a predictor of intelligence. In the discussion of differences between cognitive style and cognitive ability, I noted that cognitive style in no way predicts an individual's cognitive ability. I also noted that traditional methods for assessing intelligence tend to favour individuals using an analytic cognitive style. IQ tests, therefore, tend to discriminate against those using a holistic cognitive style.

Distinctions based on gender or race have failed to prove that either factor makes any difference in cognitive ability or learning capability.

The fact that we find a mixture of behaviours among both males and females, whites and non-whites suggests that stereotypes based on gender or racial factors are likely to have a very adverse effect on learners.

Since the more preferred and valued gender tends to be "male" and the more preferred and valued race tends to be "white," white male children are strongly socialized to adopt the analytic/separated/autonomous behaviours while females and non-white males are generally left to their own devices. The socialization of females tends to encourage the development of relational aspects of self and adoption of holistic/connected/relational behaviours. The socialization of non-white males depends on their culture. For example, those who are aboriginal in origin are socialized in relational/connected terms.

We all try our best to learn the way our culture, society and school system say we should learn, because that way is the most highly rewarded. The learning of those who use the holistic/connected/relational group of behaviours tends to be actively discouraged, even devalued, in secondary schools, colleges and universities. By the time they have reached university, females have either adapted by learning to "think like a man" or have accepted second class status as learners, or may have dropped out of the educational system. Non-white males, particularly those from our aboriginal cultures, adapt by learning to "think like a white man".

Women who have learned to "think like a man" and "talk like a man" often find that they are using one mode of learning, reasoning and conversational style in their roles as wife, mother and daughter but the alternate mode in their roles in the workplace.

As a woman who spent many years getting the two forms of learning, reasoning and conversation mixed up — using separate knowing and report-talk as a wife, autonomous reasoning and more report-talk as a mother, connected learning and rapport-talk as a student and relational reasoning as a researcher — I can testify to the personal problems which result from such confusion.

LEARNING AND FACILITATING PRINCIPLES

Without attributing relational or autonomous strategies to either men or women or to cultural groups, and without judging the value of one set of strategies over the other, I have provided an outline of known or expected distinctions related to these two strategies in Diagram 11. My advice to the reader is to think of the overall distinctions between relational and autonomous learners as polar opposites in behaviour which can range along a continuum between the two poles. An individual might be relational in some contexts, autonomous in others, and demonstrate a mix of behaviours in still others.

Other uses of the term "relational"

The term "relational" is widely used in the adult education literature. For example, Pratt (1988) describes andragogy as a relational construct, while Mezirow (1991) and Thomas (1991) both define learning as a process involving relationships or interactions between people. Indeed, the definition of "learning" provided in Chapter One also defines it in relational terms. In these cases, interactivity or relationships are understood to be an essential aspect of meaning-making processes.

As we read further, we find that writers have assumed a point of separation within the learning process between interacting learners. After they have completed the meaning making phase of the learning process together, it seems they generally separate to engage in autonomous strategies for the thinking phase of learning. The interacting learners may come together again for the planning, deciding and implementing phases.

	Separate/Autonomous Learners	Connected/Relational Learners
Learning concerns	Mastery of content Individual achievement Identifying truth Ask questions to prove truth or worth of ideas	Establishing connections to other learners Identifying differences between ideas and opinions Ask questions to understand situations. contexts and ideas of others
Learning activities	Challenging ideas of others Convincing others through logic Order maintained through explicit agreement to abide by rules Conflicts resolved through detached imposition of rules Involves doubting or excluding ideas until their worth has been proved Attempts to reveal truth that is general, impersonal, grounded in rational, logical thought or generalized perception of reality Prefers self-directed activities; competition in group activities Objectivity maintained through adopting frame of reference of discipline (e.g., biology, social work) or authority (e.g., the instructor) Prefers to hold thought and feeling separate	Listening when knowledge is uncertain Convincing others through sharing particulars of personal experiences Order maintained through implicit agreement to avoid conflict Conflicts resolved through reconciling differences Involves believing other's ideas in order to expand one's own understanding Attempts to create truth that is personal, particular and grounded in firsthand experiences, unique historical/personal events. Prefers collective or collaborative group activities or learning partnerships Objectivity maintained through understanding frame of reference of other person(s) Prefers to keep thought and feeling together
Preferred cognitive styles	Analytical Based on patterns and exemplars	Holistic Based on narratives and metaphors
Nature of truth and knowledge	Truth resides in reliability and validity of knowledge Knowledge understood separate from knower	Truth resides in believability of meaning given to experiences or interpretation of facts Knowledge understood in relation to knower
Nature of evaluation	Opportunity to correct errors in selection of facts and logic used in interpretation Individual accountable for own learning	Opportunity to demonstrate understanding of different sides of an issue Individual accountable to others for learning

11. COMPARISON OF SEPARATE AND CONNECTED LEARNERS

Source: MacKeracher, D. (1993) Women as learners. In T. Barer-Stein and J. A. Draper (Eds.), **The craft of teaching adults** (2nd edition). Toronto ON: Culture Concepts, Inc. (p. 78).

*Taylor (1987) describes a learning process which
specifies that learners will withdraw from others to think things over.
They then return to their learning relationships when they have something to share.*

If an adult learner insisted on engaging in *relational learning* throughout all phases of the learning cycle, that learner would be perceived as very dependent, the antithesis of what we think a good adult learner is supposed to be. One of the things we do not know is how each phase of the learning process would appear in *relational* as opposed to *autonomous* terms. Perhaps each learner alternates strategies at some point in the learning process and these shifts within the learning cycle may be part of individual learning style.

The term "relational learner" has also been used by Seagal and Horne (1991) who describe learners as approaching the learning process according to three basic principles:

1. **the mental, conceptual or structural principle** in which learning is based on ideas, images, values and conceptual structures;

2. **the emotional, relational or organizational principle** in which learning is based on personal relationships and the interactions among people, information and experience; and

3. **the physical, tactile or operational principle** in which learning is based on concrete facts, specific tactics and physical actions.

They claim all learners use all three principles in learning but have a strong preference for one over the other two. In describing their international research, Seagal and Horne report that 85 percent of individuals from Western countries use the emotional or relational principle, 10 percent use the physical principle, and five percent use the mental principle. They do not report on gender differences among learners.

My observations suggest that many instructors in higher education fall into the mentally-oriented group and teach on the same basis as they learn. That is, their teaching strategies focus on ideas and conceptual structures rather than on the relationships preferred by 85 percent, or the actions preferred by 10 percent of Western learners. When mentally-oriented instructors consider relationships (if they consider them at all), they likely focus on relationships among ideas, conceptual structures and generalized life experiences, rather than on specific experiences and personal relationships of individuals.

My conclusions, after all this has been said, are that using facilitating strategies that support and encourage relational learning processes would be helpful for most learners.

At the very least, such strategies would not adversely affect autonomous learners in the same way that facilitating strategies which encourage autonomous learning processes adversely affect relational learners. One can be autonomous within a relational context but it is very difficult to be relational within an autonomous context.

FACILITATING RELATIONAL LEARNING

To understand the facilitating strategies which support relational learning, and at the same time permit autonomous learning, I will turn to the work of Josselson (1992), who describes the characteristics of relational behaviour. She comments that one is more aware of relatedness when it is absent and more aware of autonomy when it is present. She proposes eight types of relational behaviours, six of which seem appropriate for understanding how to encourage relational learning: holding, attachment, eye-to-eye validation, idealization and identification, mutuality, and embeddedness.

Holding

Holding describes the most basic experience of relatedness and represents security and basic trust as a generalized feeling state.

In adulthood, holding may be experienced as a metaphor rather than as a physical fact as it is in infancy.
To be positive in adulthood, the holding function of relationships must be transparent, a sort of taken-for-granted "thereness."

In optimal holding, the self can develop free of external intrusion or attack. Loss of holding is experienced as falling, as being powerless and helpless, or as being annihilated (Josselson, 1992). The holding function provides meaning for life. Meaning systems, as provided by one's culture or other frames of reference (one's personal model of reality), can also serve as holding environments. Loss of meaning is equivalent to loss of holding.

In facilitating terms, the holding environment established early in adult learning activities is vital to ensuring security for the learner and freedom from threat or loss of meaning.

Attachment

Attachment is the second most basic experience of relatedness and involves actively holding onto another person rather than being held passively. In infancy, attachment allows us to overcome our inevitable state of detachment and aloneness once we have been physically detached from the mother who gave birth to us. In adulthood, attachment becomes a need for closeness with other persons and the comfort and care they can provide, and does not represent a regression to an infantile state.

Attachment in adulthood is experienced metaphorically as a sort of togetherness despite the space between us, a space bridged by the eyes and the voice, by someone using our name and recognizing the value of our past experience, knowledge and skills.

In attachment, it is the *responsiveness* of the other person which is crucial, not the strength or quality of their response. Strongly abusive relationships can generate feelings of attachment just as surely as non-abusive relationships (Josselson, 1992). An attachment is more apparent by its absence than by its presence.

Self-reliance occurs more frequently in contexts in which the individual feels secure attachment. The removal of our attachment is experienced as loneliness and loss.

An attachment in learning activities could be to other learners, to the facilitator or to the learning group. **Some ways to facilitate attachment are learning the names of those involved in activities— essential in a small group, desirable but sometimes not possible in a large group— asking individuals to share their experience and acknowledging it as a resource for learning.**

Eye-to-eye validation

Eye-to-eye validation involves being seen and approved by others rather than being held or touched. In discovering that others respond to us, we affirm that we ourselves are really here and truly valued. Validation infuses us with a sense of our selfhood, of being understood.

To the extent that we matter to someone else, we are able to value ourselves; to the extent that we feel understood, we empower ourselves to cope and learn. Validation determines the quality of our self-esteem. Through validation the autonomous and relational aspects of self can converge and integrate.

The negative aspect of validation occurs when the self feels invalidated, unaccepted. The self may fragment and fail to maintain its cohesion. Validation is best done face-to-face. An over-abundance of validation may feel as if one is being "seen through". Josselson (1992) states that validation for men comes from activity; for women, it comes from recognition of personhood.

As facilitators, we need to validate the individuals through accepting and using their experience and through recognizing and accepting their self-concept and self-esteem.

Idealization and identification

Idealization and identification occur when the individual distinguishes between other people and accepts some as better role models than others.

We strive to be like those we want to emulate (Josselson, 1992). Facilitators need to acknowledge, at least to themselves, that they may be serving as role models for some of the learners with whom they work.

If we want learners to learn collaborative behaviours, we need to use collaborative behaviours ourselves; if we want them to learn to use descriptive feedback, we need to use descriptive feedback; and so on.

Mutuality

Mutuality occurs when we

- ❖ experience companionship,
- ❖ work collaboratively with others whether as facilitator or learner, and
- ❖ stand with another in harmony, thereby creating a bond of friendship between us (Josselson, 1992).

Mutuality is the relational behaviour we need to cultivate particularly when learners are engaged in applied activities such as field placements. The associated learning requires that learners first do something and then reflect on how they did it.

---

*To work relationally during the reflective component,
the need for mutuality suggests a metaphor in which
the facilitator and learner would work beside each other and
look back on the experience together.*

Kennard (1993), a cooperating field placement teacher, reported a conversation with her student teacher:

> She asserted that had I placed our chairs side by side in the room and looked with her instead of looking at her, watching, her experience would not have felt so threatening. `We need to be looking on together,' she said....[This] metaphor of looking on together... was a perfect way to express the feeling of collaboration.

Supervising as a facilitating behaviour is much better conducted side by side, looking on together and talking about experience, rather than metaphorically standing face-to-face.

Embeddedness

Embeddedness occurs as we become aware of differing groups and seek to embed ourselves in selected ones. Within the group we can both differentiate ourselves as autonomous individuals and seek commonality and connection (Josselson, 1992). Embeddedness provides a holding environment (Kegan, 1982) as well as a context or set of conditions from which we may want to differentiate ourselves. Each person must find an acceptable balance between individuality and inclusion in the context. As adults we are free to choose some of the environments in which we want to be embedded, while others are not of our choosing.

Without embeddedness however, we yearn to belong.
We become aware of our embeddedness only when we are out of our normal groups.
Too much embeddedness results in blind conformity; too little, in marginality.

The facilitator's function is to provide an environment within which an adult learner would want to become embedded.

LEARNING AND FACILITATING PRINCIPLES

❖ Adults learn best in environments supporting both relational and autonomous learning strategies.

❖ Adults learn best when their experience and sense of self are validated.

❖ Both relational and autonomous learners are capable of learning the same things, but how they go about doing the learning differs.

❖ Adults learn best in environments fostering the development of trust, attachment, validation and mutuality. That is, most adults respond better to environments supporting relational learning than those supporting only autonomous learning

A relational learning environment utilizes small groups to foster the development of trust, attachment, validation and mutuality, allowing learners to share experience and knowledge comfortably; and to connect with other learners and with the facilitator.

❖ Adults learn best in environments which support the use of both holistic and analytic cognitive styles.

Holistic approaches to facilitating can support both holistic and analytic approaches to learning, and involves focusing first on the global aspects of a subject before examining its various parts, then moving back and forth between the whole and its parts. Unlike analytic approaches, these approaches provide opportunities for learners to integrate thoughts and feelings, theory and practice, to bring together and find connections between specific, concrete experiences and generalized, abstract representations of experiences (Burge, 1993).

Strategies facilitating the holistic cognitive style include: consciousness-raising, journal-keeping, group discussions, case studies, experiments, simulations, field placements, and the like. These strategies also support the use of the analytic cognitive style.

❖ Some adults learn by modelling their learning-related behaviour on that used by the facilitator.

As a facilitator, take stock of how you are behaving in relation to the values you espouse. If nothing else, at least be consistent and congruent. Don't espouse behaviours which you cannot or will not use yourself.

❖ Other strategies which facilitate both the analytic/separate/autonomous and the holistic/connected/relational groups of behaviours include:

  ❖ cooperative and collaborative learning structures such as small groups and learning partnerships help to equalize power relationships among learners and between learners and facilitator.

  ❖ cooperative evaluation techniques encourage all learners in a small group to account for their own learning and for the learning of others.

  ❖ cooperative communication styles occur when each speaker recognizes and builds on contributions made by other speakers.

  ❖ shared leadership includes sharing responsibilities for listening, validating experiences, synthesizing ideas, facilitating interpersonal interactions, and so on.

Physical Aspects: Learning Skilled Performance

6

On the whole, there is not much written in the adult education literature about learning which is physical.
So we need to consult other literature sources, for example those found in rehabilitation, fitness and body training, sports and recreation, arts and crafts, home and workplace skill training, aging, and the use of technological devices.

The lack of adult education literature on this topic suggests that adult educators may view physical learning as relatively unimportant in adulthood. This is not an apt conclusion given the range of skill training opportunities offered for the purposes of occupational and workplace training and for personal development through such things as hobbies, the arts, and physical fitness.

I will address some practical questions in this chapter since there is very little theoretical information:

❖ What is involved in physical learning?
❖ Who is engaged in physical learning and why?

❖ What are the characteristics of physical learning?

❖ How can we facilitate physical learning?

WHAT IS INVOLVED IN PHYSICAL LEARNING?

We can categorize the physical aspects of learning as involving:

❖ general body coordination,

❖ spatial orientation and the effective use of physical resources, particularly in rehabilitating physical skills lost through serious injuries and strokes;

❖ improving muscular strength and flexibility,

❖ improving body-image and general physical conditioning;

❖ learning new or improving existing skills in sports and recreational activities, and in arts and crafts activities;

❖ maintaining and improving eye-hand coordination and fine muscle control, particularly in relation to the use of tools and technological devices;

❖ learning new skills or improving existing skills related to home maintenance and workplace activities; and

❖ adapting existing skills as the need arises in response to age-related and other changes.

All skill learning does not necessarily involve physical learning since the term "skill" is also used to describe cognitive and interpersonal behaviours.

Physical learning involves the coordination of sensory information and physical movement, as well as body image.

Sensory information is derived from specialized neurons which transmit information from receptors outside the body (in the eyes, ears, tongue and mouth, and skin receptors for pain, pressure and temperature) and from receptors *inside* the body (balance receptors in the inner ear; movement and pain receptors in muscles and connective tissue).

Physical learning involves that part of your self-system which is commonly called the body image. Your body image develops in the same way as your self-concept and provides a sense of

❖ how your body will respond when called upon to learn physically,

❖ how you feel about your physical self,

❖ your awareness of your physical sensations and emotions,

❖ your physical experience of anxiety or stress,

❖ how you occupy physical space,

❖ what you think others see when they look at you,

❖ what you see when you look at yourself, and so on.

Most of us have a body image which is very distorted. In part this is because we receive information about our body in ways which automatically distort our body perceptions. For example, if you look down at yourself, what you see is a foreshortened image of your body which may over-emphasize physical attributes you do not like. If you look at yourself in a mirror, you are likely to see not your body as it actually exists — but the body-image you expect to see, an image built up over a lifetime of scrutinizing for minor blemishes and defects. Few of us perceive our body exactly as it is.

Our body-image is a cognitive construct and is as likely to be based on distortions as any other set of concepts.

For example, we hear our own voice as it is transmitted through the bones of the head and as our ears hear it. Since the bones do not transfer vocal quality and the ears are placed at the side of the head and behind the mouth, we do not hear the sound of our voice the same way others do. Body-image can be modified in the same ways that we modify other components of the self-system — through transformative learning.

WHO IS ENGAGED IN PHYSICAL LEARNING AND WHY?

Adults of all ages, all sizes and shapes, all races and cultures, and both genders, regularly engage in physical learning. Some examples of different types of physical learning are provided below. Many of these activities also include cognitive aspects of learning, as well as emotional, social and spiritual aspects. This list does not include all the various types of physical learning by any means; add your own ideas to the following list:

1. General body coordination and the effective use of physical resources:
    ❖ reactivating following stroke or serious injury
    ❖ speech therapy following a stroke
    ❖ learning to read Braille and use other devices to assist with vision impairments
    ❖ sex therapy
    ❖ using crutches or a cane
    ❖ assisting someone into and out of bed

2. Improved muscular strength and flexibility, improved body-image and general physical conditioning:
    ❖ fitness training
    ❖ body building
    ❖ weight training
    ❖ relaxation (tai chi, progressive relaxation)

3. Learning or improving skills in sports and recreational activities;
    ❖ swimming, scuba diving
    ❖ ice skating, roller skating
    ❖ downhill skiing, cross-country skiing, snow-boarding, water skiing
    ❖ golf, tennis, squash, badminton
    ❖ sailing, rowing, kayaking, wind surfing, canoeing
    ❖ running, jogging cycling mountain climbing, hiking, hang gliding

4. Learning or improving skills in arts and crafts activities:
    ❖ woodworking
    ❖ needlework
    ❖ metal working
    ❖ calligraphy
    ❖ playing a musical instrument, singing
    ❖ dancing, acting

5. Eye-hand coordination and fine muscle control, particularly in relation to the use of tools and technological devices:
    ❖ driving a car, bus, truck, motorcycle
    ❖ keyboarding
    ❖ using tools to augment movement of the hand and arm

6. Learning or improving skills related to home maintenance and the workplace such as:
    ❖ plastering, painting, paper hanging
    ❖ heavy cleaning, snow shovelling
    ❖ baking, cooking, sewing, mending
7. Adapting existing skills because of age-related and other changes:
    ❖ adjusting to bifocal glasses
    ❖ walking with painful arthritic or rheumatic conditions
    ❖ walking on ice
    ❖ learning to stay warm in blizzards

Examples of physical learning

Three examples might help to understand the links between the physical aspects of learning and other aspects. In the first example, an adult education student, who recently completed a study of the adoption of high technology by forestry workers, took time to help them develop a curriculum for training workers to use new wood harvesters. The forestry workers with whom she worked insisted that one of the essential skills in which new workers should receive training was "being able to drive on a one-lane dirt road for 20 or 30 miles without breaking down and being able to get off the road very quickly when a fully-loaded pulp truck comes barrelling along from the other direction." The truck cannot stop, so the driver must be skilled enough to get the car out of the way by driving into the bush.

In the second example, I co-facilitate two sessions on teaching skills with graduate students who are working toward a certificate in university teaching. My colleague puts us through voice training before we try out facilitating strategies. We make our voices go up and down the scale, well beyond our normal range and power, while we chant nonsense syllables and tongue twisters.

In the third example, one of my recent classes benefited from the presence of a t'ai chi instructor as a class member. For 15 minutes before the class started, we lined up along the hallway and followed her through traditional t'ai chi movements. I have often thought that we should have exercise breaks rather than having coffee breaks during lengthy learning activities. Line dancing for 10 or 15 minutes would be a good way to relieve tension and increase energy levels. Many research studies report that individuals who participate regularly in physical activities learn more efficiently in cognitive activities.

WHAT ARE THE CHARACTERISTICS OF PHYSICAL LEARNING?

Highly skilled physical performance has five characteristics:

1. fluency of movement,
2. speed of performance,
3. smoothly automated physical actions,
4. ability to do several different physical actions simultaneously, and
5. knowledge about when to use specific actions (Sloboda, 1993).

Fluency of movement

> *Sloboda (1993) indicates that an action is fluent if
> its various sub-components run together in
> an integrated and uninterrupted manner.*

For example, a fluent typist is one who can maintain a relatively even and continuous output of key strokes with a minimum of mistakes. Two things are involved in fluency:

1. a continual performance of one activity, while preparing to perform the next in sequence. That is, in fluent performance, the individual does not have to stop and think about each activity before doing it.
2. several action sequences appear to be chunked into one global sequence, reducing the number of actions to be remembered. Fluency of movement can be severely curtailed by delaying feedback and by nervousness.

For example, when an audience in a baseball stadium is being led in singing the national anthem, the leader will experience a time delay between singing a phrase and the sound of the audience singing the same phrase. Inexperienced leaders sometimes slow down as if this will allow the feedback to "catch up," and sometimes their pace slows so much that the process becomes painful. Delaying auditory feedback can cause stuttering.

Similarly, a delayed feedback occurs when I try to do work on the Internet. I expect that the letters I type on my keyboard will appear on my computer screen at the same rate they are typed; but the system is frequently so slow that I have typed well ahead of the computer's capability to keep up. Then I get frustrated and hit the enter key which just makes everything worse, a sort of "computer stuttering".

Speed of performance

Many physical skills rely on speed of performance or the ability to make quick responses. Skilled tennis players must be able to hit the ball smoothly and effectively, then move where the returned ball will arrive. All these actions must be made within seconds.

Experts and novices differ in the speed with which they can perform a physical action and anticipate the next one. Both speed and fluency are adversely affected by the introduction of randomly occurring conditions which do not follow the anticipated pattern.

For example, in a baseball game, if a spectator suddenly threw a few extra balls onto the field in the middle of a play, the players would become confused and probably stop the play.

Smoothly automated actions

Another characteristic of an expert's skill is that it appears easy because the performer has smoothly automated the required physical actions. You may recall that when we discussed experiential intelligence (Sternberg, 1988) in Chapter Four, one aspect of intelligent behaviour is the ability to respond quickly to novel situations and later to automate such responses for frequently encountered situations.

Automated responses are important in physical learning. For example, as a car driver, think of how you respond to an amber light when approaching an intersection. The automatic response should be to put your foot on the brake. If you don't automatically make this choice, you may find that your foot seems to hesitate and doesn't "know" whether to step on the gas or come down on the brake pedal.

One means for testing whether a skill is automatic is to observe whether the individual can deal appropriately with an unexpected but not abnormal situation.

If you are driving along the highway and see a deer standing on the side of the road, the automatic response ought to be to slow down since deer have a tendency to bolt in unexpected directions. Sloboda (1993) describes a study in a laboratory setting where experienced taxi drivers were asked to describe the shortest route between points A and B. When asked to drive the researcher from A to B by the shortest route, most did not take the route described earlier. They took alternative routes depending on flow of traffic and road conditions. The researchers concluded that the taxi drivers were capable of making on-the-spot choices without appearing to consciously think about them.

Performing multiple skills simultaneously

A skilled expert seems to be able to do two or three things simultaneously. If you learned how to drive a car with a standard gear shift, you will recall that you had to be able to take your foot off the clutch pedal while pressing down on the gas pedal; and when stopping and then starting the car going up a steep hill, you had to ease off the clutch pedal, ease slowly off the brake pedal and then step on the gas pedal before the car stalled or started to roll downhill.

If you are now an expert driver, you no longer have to think about the detailed sequences of driving a car. However, if you were to suddenly find yourself driving in a country where traffic keeps to the "wrong" side of the road, you would have to think very carefully each time you changed direction or turned a corner. Or conversely, you may have become so skilled that you can fasten your seat belt, watch for traffic in front and behind, even while your feet are dancing on the pedals.

Knowledge about actions

*Skilled performance includes the knowledge about **when** to use specific actions. This knowledge must be available when needed, in response to situations demanding its use (Sloboda, 1993).*

It is no use knowing that an amber light means "slow down and stop" unless this knowledge is also an integral part of skilled actions. For example, when I first acquired bifocal glasses, it took me several days not to think deliberately each time I came to a curb while walking. The first day I had trouble seeing the curb and tripped on a few. I found myself walking along partly bent over so that I could see my feet clearly, and it took several days to stop this behaviour and return to walking normally. Learning skilled behaviour takes practice.

We know that practice sessions should be spaced.
It is almost useless to spend a number of hours continually practising a new skill
Rather, practice sessions should be spaced out, making each session short but intense.

All the research indicates that there are diminishing returns from practice sessions over a period of time. Initial improvement is rapid but then levels off to a point where improvements are minimal. For this reason, learning a skill takes determination and continuing motivation. It takes a long time to become an expert in most skilled behaviours.

HOW CAN WE FACILITATE PHYSICAL LEARNING?

There are at least three basic methods for facilitating physical learning:

1. We can let learners figure it out for themselves, by providing opportunities for trying the skill with the necessary resources and giving feedback about results or possible alternative actions.

2. We can tell learners how to perform the skill, by demonstrating and providing specific instructions which, if followed should lead to skilled performance. Then by observing the learners' performance, we can provide feedback to correct improper actions.

Neither of these two options, however, is viable for learning skills in situations where the consequences of performance may be potentially dangerous (a medical student learning surgery; an electrician learning to wire a house). Therefore, we need a process in which learners can perform the skill under supervision.

3. Such a process, called *cognitive apprenticeship*, is described by Brandt, Farmer and Buckmaster (1993) and also by West,

Farmer & Wolff (1991). This process can be used when learners are engaged in learning physical, cognitive or social skills (Collins, Brown & Newman, 1989).

The process of cognitive apprenticeship
Cognitive apprenticeship is described as having five phases.

1. The modelling phase:
The process begins by the **facilitator modelling the skill** to be learned, and commenting or articulating what is being done and why. Such commentary can also be given before beginning the skill or after completion if commentary interferes with performance. The commentary can include tricks of the trade and helpful hints for performing the skill more easily. Learners listen and observe.

2. The approximating phase:
Next, the **learner tries to approximate the skill** by doing it with the facilitator observing. While doing the skill the learner describes what is being done and why. As the facilitator listens to each learner's commentary on thoughts, actions and feelings, problems can be corrected and helpful suggestions provided.

If the facilitator is working with a group, one learner performs the skill while others observe. The facilitator can ask individuals among the observing group to describe what the person must do next and why. This serves to assist the performer and to keep observers alert. The commentary can reflect on differences between the learner's performance and the facilitator's during the modelling phase, or between this performance and previous ones.

The approximating phase can be done several times until each learner seems comfortable. In a small group setting, one or two can perform the task with commentary from observers.

3. The fading phase:
Next, each learner tries the skill alone, in a safe but realistic environment. The facilitator observes and occasionally asks for out-loud commentary if the skill does not seem to be working. In large groups, learners can work in pairs with one performing and the other asking for the learner's commentary at various points in the process.

The facilitator's role in this phase is to circulate and ask observing partners to comment on what is happening in their role of surrogate facilitator. The facilitator can provide checklists to guide partners as they work or learners can develop and revise their own.

4. Solo performance:

The fourth phase involves self-directed learning in which learners perform the skill alone. The performance can be in simulated or real situations within specified acceptable limitations and with supervision available whenever necessary. In this phase the learner assumes responsibility for requesting assistance if the skill performance is not working.

5. Discussing the skill learning:

The fifth phase involves facilitator and learners discussing the learning and generalizing about using the skill in different settings or with acceptable variations. This phase is essential if learners are to understand how and when the skill could be used appropriately in other contexts.

Cognitive apprenticeship provides access to knowledge that traditional forms of instruction cannot offer. This is tacit knowledge about performing in the real world.
By asking people with real-world experience to state their thoughts aloud while performing the skill, much tacit knowledge is made explicit (Brandt, Farmer & Buckmaster, 1993).

The facilitator modelling the skill and providing commentary about what is happening, needs to think through the nature of the skills ahead of time, describing rather than prescribing, and "telling it like it is" not "like it ought to be." Choices made by the facilitator in planning and implementing cognitive apprenticeship should make it likely that learners will

❖ quickly succeed in approximating the skill;
❖ pay attention to critical components and knowledge; and
❖ learn how to recognize and overcome flaws in their own thinking.

Cognitive apprenticeship can be used to help learners modify existing skills which are not working well or to improve existing skills.

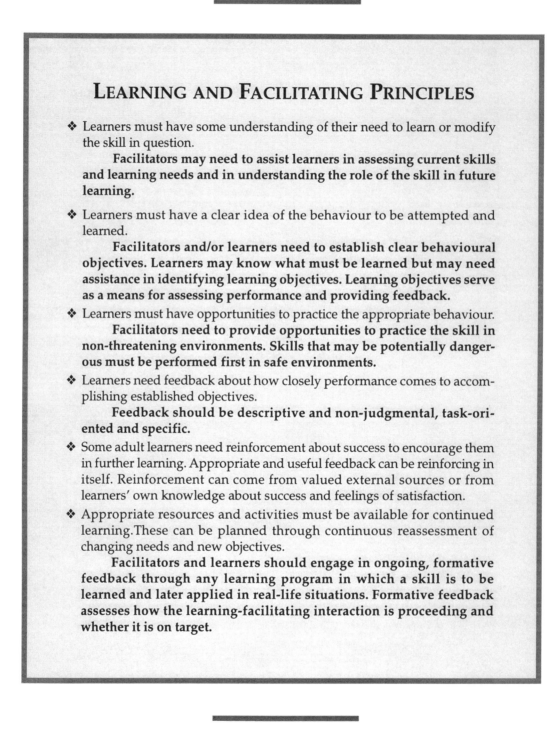

LEARNING AND FACILITATING PRINCIPLES

❖ Learners must have some understanding of their need to learn or modify the skill in question.

Facilitators may need to assist learners in assessing current skills and learning needs and in understanding the role of the skill in future learning.

❖ Learners must have a clear idea of the behaviour to be attempted and learned.

Facilitators and/or learners need to establish clear behavioural objectives. Learners may know what must be learned but may need assistance in identifying learning objectives. Learning objectives serve as a means for assessing performance and providing feedback.

❖ Learners must have opportunities to practice the appropriate behaviour.

Facilitators need to provide opportunities to practice the skill in non-threatening environments. Skills that may be potentially danger-ous must be performed first in safe environments.

❖ Learners need feedback about how closely performance comes to accom-plishing established objectives.

Feedback should be descriptive and non-judgmental, task-ori-ented and specific.

❖ Some adult learners need reinforcement about success to encourage them in further learning. Appropriate and useful feedback can be reinforcing in itself. Reinforcement can come from valued external sources or from learners' own knowledge about success and feelings of satisfaction.

❖ Appropriate resources and activities must be available for continued learning.These can be planned through continuous reassessment of changing needs and new objectives.

Facilitators and learners should engage in ongoing, formative feedback through any learning program in which a skill is to be learned and later applied in real-life situations. Formative feedback assesses how the learning-facilitating interaction is proceeding and whether it is on target.

Spiritual Aspects: Learning beyond Body and Mind

7

I understand spirituality to be the highly individualistic,
internal experience of expanding beyond the limits of my body and mind,
feeling connected to aspects of the external world which are important to me
— to others, to the world, and to a greater cosmic being, and
of feeling connected to all aspects of myself.

An understanding of spirituality can come in many forms and through many experiences:

* seeing tigers burning bright while reading the poetry of William Blake;
* experiencing transubstantiation when receiving the Eucharist;
* walking in woods that are lovely, dark and deep;
* watching kittens being born;
* contemplating the sun going down with flaming rays;
* cuddling a newly-washed baby;
* soaring with the eagles to the sound of your favourite music.

All of these, and more, help us feel a greater connectedness to the larger scheme of things and to feel that we are individual but not alone. Spirituality gives our lives purpose and meaning. It grows out of our sense of self; without a strong sense of self, we would have little inclination to move out into the world.

The noted adult educator, Roby Kidd (1973, p.4), describes learning for "being-becoming-belonging" in terms similar to those I have used to describe spiritual learning. Such learning involves ...

> ...the celebration, the affirmation, the enlargement of the full consciousness; the search for that part of the individual that is truly human, a part of the general condition of the human family, and yet is uniquely me, uniquely I.

Kidd (1973b, p.7) goes on to say that such learning "must be the heart and central goal of education". He tells us that learning for being-becoming-belonging involves both affective and cognitive components; and happens, not only through acquiring knowledge and skills, but also through self-discovery, self-expression and self-fulfilment.

Spiritual aspects of learning are generally understood as encompassing learning which occurs during an altered or higher state of consciousness, helping us to expand our knowing beyond the previous limits of our self-system or model of reality and to connect with some new aspect of our inner or outer world.

Spiritual learning helps us to:

- ❖ connect with a higher consciousness or cosmic being is referred to as "transcendent" learning (Wilber, 1986);
- ❖ move beyond the limits of our model of reality is referred to as "transformative" learning (Mezirow, 1991);
- ❖ move beyond the limits of our self-system to touch others in meaningful ways is referred to as "transpersonal" learning (Roberts & Clark, 1975).

These are not the only forms of spiritual learning but are the most common ones I have encountered in the literature. Out-of-body and near-death experiences are also forms of spirituality which may involve learning.

Writing about spiritual learning is rather like nailing jelly to the wall. Some writers choose to analyze it, and in the process lose the holistic aspects in the detail; others speak about it as a sort of divine revelation. Denis and Richter (1987) recommend that we circle it until we can close in on it indirectly.

I have chosen to use this latter approach, (or Denis and Richter's moose-hunting technique) by sharing a story about one of my experiences with the spiritual aspects of my learning. The story was part of an unfinished and unpublished narrative; I have reproduced an edited version of the narrative here and will use it to examine the nature of spiritual learning.

A STORY ABOUT A STORY ABOUT A DREAM

Early in 1995, I was invited to speak to a Feminist Studies group at a university in northern Sweden. The more I thought about speaking to a group of women in another country, the more anxious I became about finding the right topic and about appearing as someone who knew something profound about women's issues. I was to make two presentations and to identify my topics two or three months ahead of time. I could identify one topic but not the second. After several weeks of ignoring an urgent message from the organizer of the event, I turned to a colleague for advice. She suggested I talk about women and biographies. The topic seemed timely because, on my return from Sweden, I was to present a talk at a symposium on Biography and the Progress of Lives, at which my task was to present biography as a research method. At the time my knowledge about biography was limited to using it to gather research data about learning and aging. I knew very little about biography and narratives in a theoretical way.

I struggled with the biography topic, trying vainly to wrestle it into shape as a result of my anxiety about speaking in front of large groups. I sought out every book in our library system which dealt with autobiographies, life narratives, biographies and women. I could not see how I could turn all that received knowledge into something intelligible to me, let alone talk about it to others. I became more and more anxious.

Then one night I found myself thrashing about in bed, unable to sleep. At five o'clock in the morning I finally got up, sat down in my kitchen at my computer and wrote the following story…

> The heroine of my narrative has always known that she is intelligent and competent. She is successful as an academic and is regarded by her students as a caring person. But she is acutely aware of her shortcomings. She never quite allows herself to excel to the extent to which she secretly aspires. She always feels held back by someone or something or some responsibility. She sloughs it off by convincing herself that she'd rather be good than great, rather be caring that creatively brilliant; anyway, no one would like me if I were too great or too brilliant. So, I

remain intelligent, competent and caring, and above all responsible —
and I dream. Last week I dreamed…

> *It is a cold, crisp winter evening. I am in a horse-drawn hansom cab
> on my way to have dinner with the president. The driver is a man. I
> am accompanied by two other men. One is my father. I don't recognize
> the other man. My father insists on sitting on the roof of the cab. I don't
> ask why. I am afraid he will fall off so I stand on the seat and hold onto
> him through the retractable roof.*
>
> *We arrive at the president's house. His wife greets us at the door. She
> is very kind and gracious but I can tell she wasn't expecting us. The
> president is away at a meeting. It's not clear whether he is coming back
> for dinner although I am sure this is the right night.*
>
> *My father is too cold to walk, so I carry him into the house, into the
> front parlour. It is a cold, cheerless room. My father is now shivering
> and seems quite ill. I carry him upstairs to the family room where there
> is a fire and comfortable, over-stuffed furniture. I lower him onto a sofa
> and wrap a blanket around him. I sit beside him to keep him com-
> pany while the others go off to dinner.*
>
> *Suddenly I am aware that the horses are free of the hansom cab and
> are running around and around the house, running closer and closer to
> the house. One runs at the front door trying to get in. I rush to stop him
> but am pushed aside and bowled over by his size and power.*

*I wake up feeling burdened. "Why," I wonder, "am I carrying my father
around?" "And why would a horse want to get into a house?" Sadness
cascades over me. I can hardly move. I find myself repeating over and over
—Why am I carrying <u>my father</u> around? <u>Why am I</u> carrying my father
around? The answering machine in my brain only provides a busy signal.
So I record my dream and let my questions go unanswered with the hope
that the dream will make sense another day.*

And now, two weeks later, sitting in my kitchen, I am trying to write a
frame of reference for my story. I believe in the Jungian approach to dreaming which holds that all aspects of the dream are aspects of my self (Garfield,
1974). I can now identify some of the metaphors in my dream.

The Father seems to represent the theoretical or academic knowledge
which dominates traditional thinking in adult education, so much of which
does not fit my life experiences. Women have carried their mythical fathers
around with them as conceptual burdens since the dawn of patriarchy — why
should I be any different? Although I don't know why I would go to such

lengths to keep this metaphoric burden from falling off the top of the Cab. Perhaps the Cab is my mind and I don't want to lose it.

The Horse running around the house seems to be a metaphor for power and seems to be my self, trying to get in. I have made the Horse male. I know the masculine side of my psyche to be powerful, to loom larger than life and to dwarf me. I cherish that feeling of power but I cannot claim it every day and in every setting. It is as much a part of me as the conceptual burden represented by the Father.

The President's Wife is kind and caring but wasn't expecting us — certainly she wasn't expecting a female academic carrying her father around as a conceptual burden and bringing power in the form of a horse barging in at the door. Nor was I expecting to discover that male-defined concepts were an academic burden for me or that my power frequently overpowers me. The President's Wife seems to be some uninformed aspect of the feminine side of my psyche.

The dark feelings recede. I know with absolute certainty that I don't want to go to Sweden because I feel inadequate as a representative of the academic community. I don't want to have to live up to any advanced billing. So I find myself dragging my feet and worrying about the topics I have chosen, especially the one about women and biographies. My anxiety does not go away. Maybe I should cancel the trip to Sweden.

I begin to make excuses for myself. I am not an experienced traveller. I have no idea what kind of clothes to pack. I have grown comfortable in my own home, grown attached to my sense of being at home. I like dressing informally. Dressing up makes my knees ache. So does travelling by air. I don't want to go. I recognize that, in some way, I don't want to appear competent to anyone but myself — as if my competence were some great secret. And I recognize this thought as my retreat from my own power. My verbal outpouring, self-rejection and whining end at daybreak. I am not tired so I get on with the work of the day. No doubt I'll be exhausted by evening.

Later, when I am back home washing dishes in the evening, the light finally dawns. I return to my dream and know that I feel burdened, inadequate and incompetent because I have not made my feelings and behaviours — represented in my dream by the Father, the Cab, the Horse, the House and the President's Wife — an integral part of myself.

I have been worrying in my head. When I wrote the story about the dream I had to place myself at the centre of the action; I was forced to go back inside to connect the essential me to my turmoil, anger and anxiety. I recognize that the person who is feeling burdened, inadequate and incompetent is not some object who can be understood by examining her rationally in the cold light of reason which was how I began my story.

I can only understand myself when my feelings are firmly connected to my thoughts and I can only make sense of my life when I allow my feelings and inside thoughts to connect to my outside behaviour. I must be both subject and object in any story of my life; and when I cannot be both, or will not let myself be both, I cannot make sense of what is happening to me. My competence as an academic is only as great and as creatively brilliant as the strength of the connections among my mind, my physical body, my feelings, my caring and my spirit. When I stop myself from making these connections, when I don't fully respect myself, my thinking becomes disorganized.

This is a lesson I learned first when I was writing my thesis, but I never seem to remember it. I seem to need to relearn it over and over again. Perhaps wisdom will come when the lesson has become an integral part of my knowing. Maybe I can talk about writing an autobiography or life narrative as a means for integrating the inner and outer aspects of my life experiences.

POSTSCRIPTS: UNINTEGRATED IDEAS TOO GOOD TO THROW AWAY

I'm back from Sweden and surprise of surprises — I survived. I travelled to Sweden in the company of a feminist educator with an interest in autobiographical memory and decided I would invite her to join me in a discussion with the Feminist Studies group. We talked about women and life narratives and why story-telling is so important to women. I told my story. We encouraged the women who attended to talk about their stories and experiences with narratives. I came away feeling good about the discussion.

Since then, some ideas have occurred to me which I want to record as postscripts to my story. At this moment I'm not sure how everything fits together but I'm convinced that everything is connected to everything else.

> *PS1. Before I went off to Sweden, I did an activity with the students in the Women and Education course, in which I asked them to develop an image to describe themselves when they feel really positive about themselves and their self-esteem is high. I also completed the activity and came up with the "Queen" as an image. I promptly rejected this image as one I did not like for myself. Then I had to ask myself how come I was rejecting the very image which helps me feel really positive about myself? Maybe I need to learn to love the Queen in my soul. She seems to be a very powerful part of me — sort of like the President's Wife should have been but wasn't in my dream.*

PS2. *In my readings about biographies and narratives, I came across the following quote:*

> *Memory is where the self is held captive. Telling one's story is a means of becoming. (Josselson & Lieblich, 1993)*

To have no story to tell is tantamount to having no self and to have no self is to have no voice. I wonder which comes first and how one gets a story. I have very few clear memories of my child-hood. Am I saying that my self from that time is also nonexistent? Or that the self I was then is a self I now do not like or cannot accept? Neither of those ideas seems quite right.

PS3. *Telling a story is a process which objectifies whatever is happening or has happened. My story starts with the objective "she," then moves to the subjective "I." The story becomes objectified once it is down on paper. And once it is on paper, the story seems less threatening and more manageable. At the very least, the story is worth a laugh once it is written down and shared with friends.*

PS4. *Just after my father died, when I was having trouble writing my thesis, I was asked by a counsellor to visualize my thesis already completed, bound and sitting on a shelf. She asked me to report whose name, besides mine, was on the binding. I said that my father's name would be there. I did some excellent writing just after he died. I guess his name was ghost-written on all those works. Now I feel a strong need to write something for my mother. Perhaps this narrative is for my mother. Perhaps this book is for my mother.*

PS5. *The day before the presentation on Women and Autobiography, I had a sort of waking dream just before I fell asleep. I found myself becoming aware of a great Mother who is part of my soul and spirit. She seems to have been taking care of my "becoming" all my life. I once described my image of myself in the role of Learner as someone who collects odd bits of information and pieces of paper on which I have written miscellaneous ideas and as-yet-unconnected experiences. I collect these bits of paper until I have such a muddle of odds and ends that I must tidy up.*

Tidying up seems to involve finding connections among the bits and pieces and integrating them into a coherent whole which can then be connected to already existing larger chunks — and so on.

The Mother of my soul seems to be one of the many role-based figures who populate my psyche. The Mother has assumed responsibility for keeping all the bits and pieces corralled in one place in my mind so that none are lost, so that eventually the Learner can do the connecting and integrating. The Mother seems to act as a shepherd who is always there, freeing the Worker and the Learner to get on with other concerns.

I like this idea — the Mother of my soul has been watching over me all my life and I have only just discovered her and the way she has tended me all this time. I know that my own mother always kept track of my spelling and my grammar but the Mother of my soul seems to have done much more than that. Maybe she has been keeping track of the bits and pieces of my life all this time and she helps me build connections among the ideas in my mind and between my ideas and reality.

PS6. *So this brings me back to the issue I started with — why are narratives so important, especially to women? The more I learn about narratives the more I am convinced that the narrative represents a learning process which is crucial to women. Perhaps, it is just that women know themselves on the basis of the narrative form.*

When I asked one of my students to read this paper, she wrote in the margin:

> *Narratives are important to women because they can be told even when a woman is up to her elbows in bread dough. It's never been a tradition to go to the pump to wash the bread dough off your hands in order to jot down an essay or a sonnet or two.*

PS7. *Narratives include both teller and listener; that is, a narrative implies relational aspects. This would make narratives a natural strategy for supporting women's development and learning.*

PS8. *My title for this section — "Unintegrated Ideas Too Good to Throw Away" — reminds me of the title of an assignment a student once wrote for me entitled — "Bits of String Too Short to Keep". The postscripts I have been writing seem at the moment to be "Ideas Too Small to Matter." But they do matter.*

> **Maybe that is something women do — conclude that their experiences and knowledge are too small to matter. And if ideas are too small to matter, then they never get shared and never get used.**

SPIRITUAL LEARNING RE-VISITED

Now I'll return to the issue of spiritual learning and try to develop an explanation about how my story and paper illustrate such learning.

Spiritual learning involves an altered state of consciousness.

In Chapter Three, I described normal waking brain activity, or normal consciousness, as involving short, rapid *Beta* waves. Both *alpha* waves, which characterize a state of relaxation or meditation, and *theta* waves, which characterize sleep, are indicative of an altered state of consciousness.

To achieve an altered state of consciousness while we are awake, we must engage in activities which will allow the *alpha* waves to emerge by dampening the *Beta* waves. Beta waves are indicative of logical, sequential and analytical cognitive activities, those in which the left hemisphere of the brain is specialized. So another way to induce an altered state of consciousness would be to trick the left hemisphere into taking a rest thus giving the spatial, analogical, holistic and simultaneous specialties of the right hemisphere an opportunity to take over.

An altered state of consciousness of this type can be achieved through relaxing, meditating, day dreaming, and some forms of personal psychotherapy.

Strategies which facilitate an altered state of consciousness include: guided imagery, focused attention, visualizing, dream sharing, creativity (mental play), humour and metaphors. Altered states of consciousness also occur during sleep, during severe trauma accompanied by near-death experiences, just as one is falling asleep in what is called a *hypnagogic state*, and under hypnosis. Altered states can also be induced through the use of mind-altering drugs and sensory deprivation.

In all these activities, individuals must turn their attention inward and allow themselves to become aware of thoughts, images, metaphors, analogies, feelings, physical sensations and other experiences. The facilitator can help by providing a comfortable, non-threatening quiet environment and by guiding such activities in a quiet, leisurely, almost-monotone voice. Once learners have completed the activity, the facilitator must then bring them back to reality and encourage them to share what has happened. During the altered state of consciousness or during the sharing process, an individual may experience the ah-ha of insight, an understanding or meaning which seems to pop into full consciousness unbidden.

An insight may help the individual transcend previously existing boundaries of self thereby permitting feelings of being in touch with a higher consciousness or cosmic being (Wilber, 1986). Or an insight might allow the individual to feel able to reach out to others in new and expanded ways (Roberts & Clark, 1975). Or an insight might provide the transformative knowledge necessary to induce an extensive reorganization of the individual's personal model of reality (Mezirow, 1991).

All of these possibilities, among others, are thought of as spiritual learning.

The terms used to describe such processes are many and include:
transcendent learning, transpersonal learning, transformative learning, holistic learning,
peak experiences, self-actualization, self-transcendence and transconceptual thinking.

Spiritual learning occurs most readily to learners who:
- ❖ are open to new experiences and new ideas;
- ❖ are aware of their own state of consciousness;
- ❖ avoid judging their thoughts or experiences;
- ❖ reflect on their thoughts and experiences;
- ❖ revisit their reflections;
- ❖ share their experiences; and
- ❖ look for connections in unlikely places, between apparently unconnected and disparate ideas and experiences.

Openness to new experiences

We know that spiritual learning happens to those who are open to new ideas and new experiences and who are willing to take a risk in trying learning activities which are, in outward appearance, the antithesis of everything many people think tradition education should be. The activities are non-verbal, non-logical, non-rational, and potentially threatening. They include activities which are frequently labelled as "crazy" by those who do not understand holistic learning.

Awareness of consciousness

We know that spiritual learning happens to persons aware of their state of consciousness and alert to thoughts, images, metaphors, analogies, physical sensations and other experiences which might occur while in a momentary altered state. In other words, learners have to keep track of their dreams and day dreams in some way. When the mind returns to normal waking consciousness and the beta waves reclaim control of the mind, then the thoughts, images and experiences which occurred during the altered state of consciousness will very quickly be forgotten.

It takes practice to develop an awareness of your own consciousness.
If you start now and record your altered state experiences,
in six months you will have expanded your awareness considerably.

Avoid judgments

We know that to learn anything from the thoughts, images and experiences which occur during an altered state of consciousness, the learner must never judge the rightness or wrongness, goodness or badness of the thought, image, feeling or experience. Everything is grist for the learning mill but it must never be judged or the learning will cease immediately. Surprisingly, agreeing or approving of a thought, image, feeling or experience before it is recorded is also a form of judgment. In my dream, I woke up with depressed feelings and a question but when the imagery didn't make immediate sense, I just recorded the dream in my journal with the idea that I would come back to it another day.

Engage in reflection

Once thoughts, images and experiences have been recorded in some objective fashion, the learner can re-visit them at a later time in order to understand and assign meaning to them. Records could include journal writing, drawing, writing poetry, writing stories, and so on. Re-visiting the thoughts, images and experiences often seems spontaneous — as if the mind had been mulling them over and had finally come up with meanings which the conscious mind could understand. This brings spiritual learning into the realm of cognitive learning which I discussed in Chapter Four.

Revisit reflections

Even after the thoughts, images and experiences have been given meaning, it sometimes takes time before the learner can understand how the new meanings could be used in practical ways in work, family or community settings. Even after I figured out the meaning of the metaphors in my dream, I could not see any practical use for the meanings until I talked to someone else who had an interest in biographies and narratives. In fact, I did not really understand what all the activity was about until I sat down to write this chapter and realized that my opening definition of spiritual learning was insufficient and very ineffective, but that my story could serve as an example of spiritual learning.

Share experiences and connections

The expansive feelings accompanying spiritual learning are difficult to share. Almost without fail, learners' enthusiasm for reaching out to touch a higher cosmic being or for transcending themselves, is heard by unbelieving listeners as palpable nonsense. So when you come to share your newfound knowledge, pick carefully with whom you will share your insights.

You will want to talk to someone who is very good at validating your experiences, at listening empathetically and non-judgmentally, and at engaging in mutual, side-by-side, "looking on together" activities of the type I discussed in Chapter Five.

Since I had the dream and wrote the initial story outlined earlier in this chapter, I have shared both story and insights with a number of people. Their favourable responses and the insights they shared with me, gave me the courage to write this chapter as you find it. And each time I share my ideas, my feelings of having expanded in some way and connected to others in a new way, return again.

Look for unlikely connections

The process of revisiting altered-state experiences usually involves connecting their meanings to other concerns, ideas and thoughts from other sources. Sometimes there is no apparent, direct link between the central meaning of the altered-state experience and the ideas which become connected to it. But the connection is there, however well obscured it may be. The meanings of the connections will emerge as time passes.

In my story, the dream itself seems to have nothing to do with the frame I have put around it. On the one hand, the dream is about my reaction to male-defined knowledge and my feelings of power. On the other hand, the frame has two other themes:

1. biographies and life narratives, particularly those of women, and

2. my anxiety about travelling abroad to make an academic presentation.

Ah-ha! As I write, I am seeing a new connection which goes something like this:

> I am supposed to be competent using traditional (male-defined) acade-
> mic knowledge about adult education and women; but my personal
> knowledge is very much woman-defined, often in narrative form, (par-
> ticularly my knowledge about women). I sometimes have trouble
> turning my narrative knowing into acceptable academic knowing. So I
> become anxious when I must speak to a group which I assume wants to
> hear my academic knowledge. Come to think of it, this assumption is
> probably the cause of my anxiety in the first place. In the process of
> going to Sweden, learning about life narratives, and writing this chap-
> ter, I have come to know myself better. I haven't touched a cosmic being
> but I feel I have touched on an essential part of women's experiences and
> this knowledge brings me into closer contact with other women and
> their learning.

CONCEPTS OF SPIRITUAL LEARNING

There are few discussions in the literature about what is involved in spiritual learning. A few authors address some aspects of spiritual learning. Two of these authors have helped me understand spiritual learning in the larger context of adult learning — the work of Carl Jung describes some of the processes which must characterize spiritual learning while the work of Ken Wilber describes the outcomes.

Jung on individuation

To understand how Jung's ideas relate to spiritual learning, I need to provide some background on the *process of individuation*. Jung (Hall & Nordby, 1973) believed that development was not complete by the beginning of adulthood, as postulated by earlier theorists such as Freud. He saw childhood, adolescence and early adulthood as those periods in which an individual learned a set of basic strategies and concepts for coping and adapting to life experiences.

He viewed each strategy as paired with an alternative strategy. For example, Jung paired thinking and feeling as two modes of judging the reality of perceptions and of making decisions. In early development, each individual learns a preference for one of these two strategies and to use the preferred strategy effectively in daily life.

That is, some learn to prefer thinking strategies which
assess the facts of perceptions and their consistency and logic of information.
Others learn to prefer feeling strategies which assess the value of perceptions and
accept or reject them on the basis of whether the information
is pleasing or displeasing, supportive or threatening.

As an individual moves into mid-life, the undeveloped or unpreferred strategy becomes more important and salient to mature behaviour. Through a process Jung called **individuation**, the individual

- ❖ becomes aware of and tries out the alternative strategy;
- ❖ integrates these new behaviours into existing behaviours; and
- ❖ over time, develops the ability to use both strategies.

Jung describes other paired behaviours, such as *sensation and intuition, extroversion* and *introversion, masculine* and *feminine.* He believed that each individual has the capacity to use both masculine and feminine sides of the psyche, and that maturity involves the full use and integration of both sides of each pair of behaviours.

Early socialization, however, encourages the young man to develop some parts of the masculine side of his psyche and to submerge, into the *Shadow of his unconsciousness mind*, those masculine behaviours and feelings which are not acceptable to him. At the same time, he integrates a few behaviours and feelings he defines as "feminine" with his conscious being or self but submerges most into the *Anima of his unconscious mind.*

For a young woman, unacceptable aspects of her feminine side are submerged into her *Shadow* and much of those behaviours defined as "masculine" are submerged into her *Animus.* What aspects of behaviour and feelings are acceptable and what gets submerged is a matter of individual definition and social expectations.

At about age 35, the submerged aspects of the psyche begin to press for attention as if demanding an opportunity to become part of the conscious mind.

Individuation involves becoming aware of these submerged parts of the psyche; bringing them to consciousness through altered states, particularly through dreaming; examining their meaning and implications; integrating those parts found acceptable and useful; and as a result, expanding the self beyond its previous limitations.

In my story, the Horse and the Father both seem to be part of my Animus, one a source of power and the other a source of knowledge. The Queen, the President's Wife and the Mother seem to be part of the feminine side which I have submerged in my Shadow. The Queen represents feminine power and the Mother feminine tending and care. The President's Wife seems to represent my feminine unwillingness to recognize how I have allowed my perceptions of the world to limit my knowing and behaving, perceptions which are largely based on a male-defined reality. **Now I must integrate all of these parts of me into my conscious being. Individuation allows a person to know themselves better, to reach out to others through a greater understanding of human nature, and perhaps, to touch something greater than us all.**

Wilber on spiritual development

Wilber (1986) describes nine levels of human development which occur before a person reaches the tenth or Ultimate level of oneness with the Universe. Wilber's first six levels are similar to those proposed by Jean Piaget. I will not provide an extensive description of the first six levels because the first three seem to be self-explanatory and the second three have already been discussed in Chapter Four.

Levels one through three are part of pre-personal development. These levels are

1. sensory-physical,
2. the image mind,
3. the representational mind.

They describe cognitive development to the level of the ability to represent events, objects and people in the mind as symbols, words and concepts.

Levels four through six are part of personal development. These levels are

4. the rule/role mind,
5. the formal-reflexive mind,
6   the vision-logic mind.

They describe cognitive development through the concrete, formal and post-formal cognitive operational thought discussed in Chapter Four.

Levels seven through nine are part of transpersonal development. The seventh or *Psychic level* involves the development of the "third eye" in which the individual's cognitive and perceptual capacities become so pluralistic and universal that they begin to reach beyond any narrowly defined personal or individual perspectives and concerns. The individual learns to subtly inspect the mind's cognitive and perceptual capacities and thus to transcend them.

At the eighth or *Subtle level*, the individual comes to fully understand Jung's nature of *masculine and feminine behaviours (the Anima and Animus)* and to transcend insight. This level, in Wilber's opinion, is where we form our ideas of a personal deity (Wilber, 1986).

At the ninth or *Causal level*, the centralized sense of self becomes subordinated, lost in the largeness of being and is finally abolished, replaced by a feeling of a boundless universal self, an unlimited consciousness of unity which pervades everything and everywhere.

Wilber (1986) seems to imply that transpersonal development occurs only after one has developed post-formal cognitive skills. However, the description of spiritual learning I have provided in this chapter suggests that it can occur at earlier stages of cognitive development. That is, the activities described in this chapter could occur at Wilber's three levels of personal development as well as at the three levels of transpersonal development.

In my story I seem to have been subtly inspecting my mind's cognitive and perceptual capacities (Psychic level) and to have made a brief and impermanent foray into the Subtle level. Certainly I have the sense that I have expanded beyond my narrowly defined sense of self to connect to a wider group of persons, mostly women, thereby engaging in transpersonal, transformative and transcendent learning (Roberts & Clark, 1975; Mezirow, 1991; Wilber, 1986).

LEARNING AND FACILITATING PRINCIPLES

To engage in spiritual learning, adults need:

❖ to be fully open to new ideas and new experiences.

Facilitators need to provide very safe, supportive environments in which openness to new ideas will not result in feelings of being discounted or devalued.

❖ to be aware of their own state of consciousness.

Facilitators need to provide a variety of activities in which learners can become aware of and identify different states of consciousness. Some useful activities are: deep relaxation, guided imagery, keeping a dream journal, sharing dreams, using humour, meditating, creativity, mental play.

❖ to avoid judging their thoughts or experiences.

In the same vein, facilitators need to avoid judging the ideas, thoughts and feelings proposed by learners as a result of their spiritual learning. This includes avoiding agreement, approval, or rejection of negative ideas and feelings. For example, it is inappropriate to try to talk learners out of thoughts and feelings which are based on a negative view of self. One way to avoid making such judgments is to ask the learner if there is another way to interpret experiences.

❖ to reflect on their thoughts and experiences, revisit their reflections and share their experiences.

Facilitators need to provide opportunities and lots of time to reflect on and share thoughts and experiences following activities which involve an altered state of consciousness. This part of the process cannot be rushed and may take more time than can be provided within a formal class structure and timetable.

❖ to look for connections in unlikely places, between apparently unconnected and disparate ideas and experiences.

Facilitators need to encourage learners to look for connections in unlikely places. This is not easy since many learners insist that insights from one experience bear no relationship whatsoever to other experiences and activities. This part of the process cannot be forced.

CYCLES AND STYLES IN LEARNING

8

In Chapter One, I described learning as a cyclical process of four basic phases with the learner:

1. participating in experiences and activities resulting in the intake of coded and uncoded information from internal and external sources as input to learning;

2. making sense of experience by giving it meaning and value using pattern-recognition, affective processes and meaning-making cognitive processes;

3. using meanings in problem-solving and decision-making cognitive processes to make choices and develop plans for acting to achieve those choices; and

4. implementing action plans which, in turn, generate feedback as new information for the learner.

In this chapter I will discuss other cycles of learning and then move on to address the concept of learning styles.

KOLB'S LEARNING CYCLE

Kolb (1984) proposed a cycle to describe experiential learning (see Diagram 12) which is very similar to the one proposed in Chapter One.

1. The cycle begins when the learner is involved in a specific experience (**Concrete Experience or CE**).

2. The learner reflects on this experience from different points of view to give it meaning (**Reflective Observation or RO**).

3. The learner integrates the meanings from this experience with those from other personal experiences to develop personal explanations, concepts or "theories," or with concepts and theories proposed by others, to draw conclusions (**Abstract Conceptualization or AC**).

4. These conclusions are used to guide decision-making and planning of related actions which are then implemented (**Active Experimentation or AE**) leading to new concrete experiences.

Kolb's experiential learning cycle is grounded in the work of Kurt Lewin (1951) who experimented with learning based on the experience of participating in small training groups (Benne, 1964).

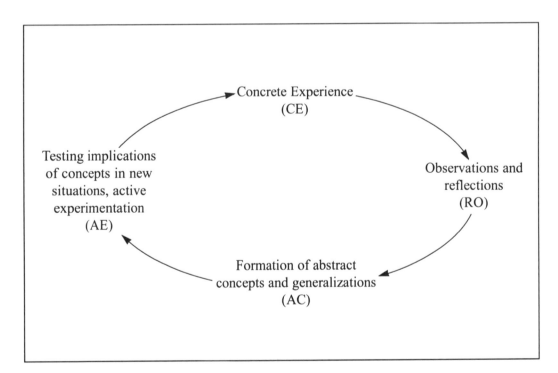

12. KOLB'S EXPERIENTIAL LEARNING CYCLE

Source: Kolb, D. A. (1984) Experiential learning: Experience as the source of learning and development. Englewood Cliffs, NJ: Prentice-Hall (p. 21).

HUNT'S MUTUAL ADAPTATION MODEL FROM THE FACILITATOR'S VIEWPOINT

Hunt (1987) uses another aspect of Lewin's work, the B-P-E paradigm discussed in Chapter Two, to develop a model of the adaptation process which occurs in the learning-facilitating interaction. The mutual adaptation model describes both learner and facilitator behaviour as they "read" or perceive each other's behaviour and "flex" or adapt to each other on the basis of their perceptions.

Only the facilitator's side of this process is shown in Diagram 13. The "reading" part of the cycle includes receiving feedback and perceiving; the "flexing" part of the cycle includes developing intentions and taking action. Links between reading and flexing are made through the individual's implicit theories or personal model of reality. Hunt describes the model as including the following components:

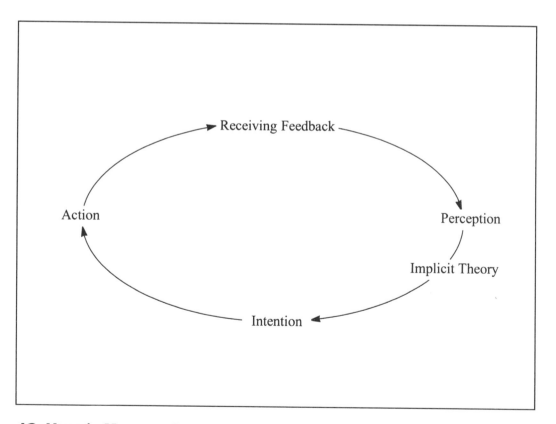

13. HUNT'S MUTUAL ADAPTATION MODEL (FACILITATOR'S VIEWPOINT)

Source: Hunt, D. E. (1987) **Beginning with ourselves: In practice, theory and human affairs.** Toronto ON: OISE Press (p.148)

❖ **Perception** is equated with Person characteristics in the B-P-E model and is similar to Kolb's reflective observation (RO). For the facilitator, perception involves becoming aware of learner characteristics.

❖ **Implicit theory** is equated with the matching models derived by a facilitator using the B-P-E Model and involves searching memory (or one's personal model of reality) for likely matches between learner characteristics and facilitator responses.

❖ **Intention** is the desired outcome or the Behaviour component in the B-P-E model. The facilitator's intention involves deciding which behaviours could or should be elicited from the learner and which actions are best suited to this intention. This aspect of mutual adaptation is equated with Kolb's abstract conceptualization (AC).

❖ **Action** by the facilitator produces Environmental characteristics in the B-P-E model. Actions should be congruent with intentions and with the matching model selected from one's implicit theories. Action is equated with Kolb's active experimentation (AE).

❖ The action of the instructor becomes **Feedback** or new input to the learner's cycle. Feedback is equated with Kolb's concrete experience (CE).

Interacting Cycles of Facilitator and Learner

The learner goes through a similar cycle:

1. perceiving what the learning tasks are and what is being asked by the facilitator;
2. searching memory for an implicit theory or likely response,
3. forming an intention to act and
4. acting;
5. the learner's action generates "feedback" or new input to the facilitator's cycle as well as new input to the learner's cycle.

In Hunt's model, he equates receiving feedback with Kolb's concrete experience (CE). The interaction between the learner's and the facilitator's cycles are shown Diagram 14.

In both models, the most private part of the cycle occurs between Perception (RO) and Intention (AC) (lower right-hand segment). During this part, the facilitator is effectively shut out from what the

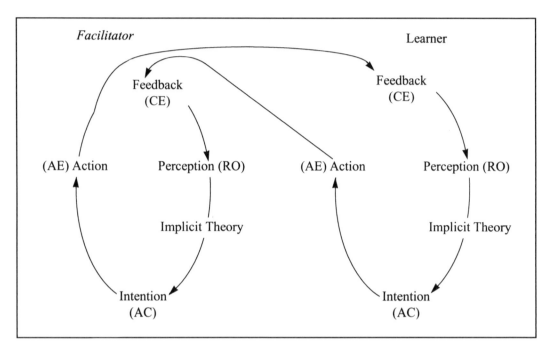

14. INTERACTING CYCLES OF FACILITATOR AND LEARNER

Source: Hunt, D. A. (1987) **Beginning with ourselves: In practice, theory and human affairs.** Toronto ON: OISE Press.

learners are thinking unless they are encouraged to think out loud. As we saw in cognitive apprenticeship (Chapter Six), additional feedback can be provided if learners describe out loud what they are thinking and why. The most public part of the cycle occurs between **Action** (AE) and **Feedback** (CE) (upper left-hand segment). During this part, the facilitator can see what the learner is doing and can provide feedback.

VARIATIONS ON THE LEARNING CYCLE

Kolb (1984) and Hunt (1987) both describe the learning cycle as proceeding in one direction only. Some learners, however, do not make full use of one or two of the learning phases. Abbey, Hunt and Weiser (1985, p.485) describe four types of unbalanced learners:

  1. Those who by-pass abstract conceptualization by moving directly from reflective observation to active experimentation are called "northerners" (because they by-pass the "south pole" of the model). They may have trouble conceptualizing

or making meaning from their experiences and their reflections remain unconsolidated.

2. Those who by-pass reflective observations and move directly from concrete experience to abstract conceptualization are called "westerners". They are likely to develop unclear conceptual frameworks because their ideas remain uncorrected without reflection.

3. Those who by-pass concrete experience and move directly from active experiementation to reflective observation are called "southerners". They may reflect on the mechanics of their actions without benefit of emotional feedback resulting in mechanical and sterile revisions of knowledge.

4. Those who by-pass active experimentation and move directly from abstract conceptualization to concrete experience are called "easterners". They have trouble putting plans into actions and spend much time buried in thought. Their ideas, therefore, are not corrected or rejuvenated through experimentation.

Abbey, Hunt and Weiser (1985) also describe learners who make full use of only two of the four learning phases. They describe these learners as "stuck" and as persons who are likely to enter counselling or psychotherapy sessions. Such learners may move back and forth between two phases so quickly that their learning appears to violate the unidirectional aspect of the learning cycle. However, such truncated learning can also be understood as moving in the direction predicted by the model but as bringing the learner too quickly through the two skipped phases.The authors also speculate that a very few, maladaptive learners may be stuck in one phase of learning.

LEARNING AND FACILITATING PRINCIPLES

❖ Learning is a cyclical process, a sequence of activities. Under normal circumstances, the activities proceed in one direction; to defy this order may reduce the productivity of learning.

An effective facilitator plans activities supporting each phase of the experiential learning cycle and uses these activities in the same order suggested by the learning cycle. For example:

❖ A concrete experience can be an activity structured to illustrate a particular issue or to ensure that learners have a specific type of experience to draw on in subsequent activities. Concrete experience also can provide opportunities for learners to recall and share a personal experience occurring outside the learning environment.

❖ A concrete experience is best followed by an activity in which learners reflect on their experience. Reflective activities should help learners distinguish various aspects of their experience and develop meanings for them.

❖ These meanings can be related to, or integrated with, other meanings to expand the overall meaning of the experience and to develop ideas and plans for testing them.

❖ Active experimentation involves actively testing ideas or putting plans into action. Such activities might include:
— sharing ideas so others can comment on them through oral or written feedback;
— actively testing a hypothesis through research;
— implementing a plan of action to see how it works;
— trying something new or really different which has an element of risk to it; and
— transferring ideas found useful in one setting or context to a new setting or context.

The facilitation of testing or experimenting requires the provision of a "safe" environment in which it is OK to make mistakes without experiencing a sense of failure.

❖ Feedback becomes new information to begin a new cycle of learning and can occur only after the learner has acted overtly. Feedback contributes most to learners' satisfaction and success when it closely follows an action.

Never arrange facilitating activities so that active experimentation activities come at the end of a learning session when there is no time for feedback or debriefing. Always complete any active experimentation activities with plenty of time to give feedback to learners. Cut the AE activity short if necessary.

Never send learners away from a session feeling anxious, threatened or angry, particularly if the feedback is likely to be negative. Between sessions, either learners will forget what happened and any subsequent feedback will be useless, or their negative feelings will escalate, bringing conflict and dissatisfied learners to the beginning of the next session.

❖ Facilitator also go through a learning cycle in learning how to respond (flex) to learners. The facilitator's learning cycle is fuelled by feedback from the learner(s).

Give yourself time to reflect on how you are responding to learners. Don't judge your responses until you have had time to reflect on them and develop alternative plans for the future.

TAYLOR'S LEARNING CYCLE

Another four phase model of the learning process has been proposed by Marilyn Taylor (1987; 1979) and is shown in Diagram 15. Taylor's model focuses on learning which is self-directed (self-managed) and involves a personal concern. While Taylor does not claim that the model is generalizable to all adult populations, the experience of many adult educators suggests that the model is useful, particularly in programs which use a humanistic approach to teaching and learning. Her model encompasses four phases of learning and four transitions (Taylor 1987, 183-191).

The disorientation phase

Taylor's learning cycle begins with a disconfirming event or destabilizing experience. This transition may occur because the individual encounters change and experiences its consequences as involving a major discrepancy between expectations and reality.

Some learners deliberately seek out change, but more often changes occur which are not anticipated. For example, a young mother may go out to work full-time, bringing change into her life and that of her family. While she is adapting to these changes, her children may become difficult to handle because they don't want their mother away from home. The first set of changes which have been deliberately sought may not result in a disconfirming experience, but the second set might. Other possibilities include:

- ❖ other persons may change, or develop in ways demanding a response from the learner;
- ❖ new technologies may be introduced into the workplace;
- ❖ new ideas may surface in the popular media;
- ❖ physiological changes (from aging, stress, illness or accident) may occur which demand an adaptive response; and so on.

If the change is experienced as disconfirming, that is, one which disconfirms the self-system or personal model of reality then the individual is thrown into a Disorientation phase in which confusion, anxiety and tension increase and the learner experiences a crisis of self-confidence.

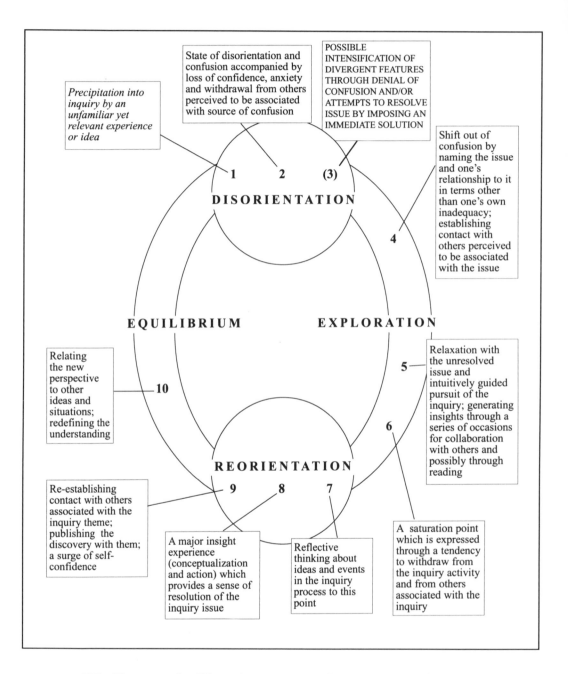

State of disorientation and confusion accompanied by loss of confidence, anxiety and withdrawal from others perceived to be associated with source of confusion

POSSIBLE INTENSIFICATION OF DIVERGENT FEATURES THROUGH DENIAL OF CONFUSION AND/OR ATTEMPTS TO RESOLVE ISSUE BY IMPOSING AN IMMEDIATE SOLUTION

Precipitation into inquiry by an unfamiliar yet relevant experience or idea

Shift out of confusion by naming the issue and one's relationship to it in terms other than one's own inadequacy; establishing contact with others perceived to be associated with the issue

1 2 (3)

DISORIENTATION

4

EQUILIBRIUM   **EXPLORATION**

Relating the new perspective to other ideas and situations; redefining the understanding

10

5 — Relaxation with the unresolved issue and intuitively guided pursuit of the inquiry; generating insights through a series of occasions for collaboration with others and possibly through reading

6

REORIENTATION

9 8 7

Re-establishing contact with others associated with the inquiry theme; publishing the discovery with them; a surge of self-confidence

A major insight experience (conceptualization and action) which provides a sense of resolution of the inquiry issue

Reflective thinking about ideas and events in the inquiry process to this point

A saturation point which is expressed through a tendency to withdraw from the inquiry activity and from others associated with the inquiry

15. TAYLOR'S MODEL OF THE LEARNING CYCLE:

Source: Modified from Taylor, M. (1979) "Adult learning in an emergent learning group: Toward a theory of learning from the learner's perspective." Unpublished doctoral dissertation, University of Toronto, Toronto, ON; and Taylor, M.(1987) Self-directed learning: More than meets the observer's eye. In D. Boud & V. Griffin (Eds.), **Appreciating adults learning: From the learners' perspective. London, UK: Kogan Page.**

At this time, the individual may withdraw from others because of feelings of inadequacy or because others are blamed as the cause of the confusion. In formal learning programs, the person most frequently blamed is the facilitator for such reasons as:

- ❖ not providing enough direction,
- ❖ not being clear about instructions,
- ❖ or the facilitator not being helpful.

By withdrawing from others, the learner may disengage from the relationships most likely to offer the support necessary to make sense of the disconfirming event.

The transition out of the Disorientation phase occurs when the learner is able to name the central issue, problem or source of confusion in relation to themselves, through interactions with others.

In Taylor's opinion, those who cannot do this may become locked into a period of expanded and intensified confusion in which they seek a quick, prescriptive solution which frequently leads to more confusion. For example:

- ❖ some learners try to become more organized on the assumption that their problem has to do with lack of control;
- ❖ some learners ask others to name their problem and accept prescribed solutions;
- ❖ others simply deny they have a problem and suppress the disconfirming information as if it had never happened.

Gavin and Taylor (1990) describe these learners as engaging in a **decremental cycle of learning**; we will discuss this cycle at the end of this section.

The exploration phase

Those who can name the central issue and make contact with others enter the Exploration phase, in which the individual becomes engaged in searching for information or ideas which could assist in resolving the identified problem.

The search leads to intensive and extensive inquiry activities in which new information and ideas are gathered from other individuals or from resources such as books or films; and new ways of doing things are tested. These activities usually involve interactions with others. In this phase the individual is working to identify relevant information and find alternative solutions rather than imposing a quick and prescriptive solution. When individuals have gathered enough information, they **withdraw to reflect** and think things over.

The reorientation phase

Following the reflective transition, the individual enters a Reorientation phase.

In this phase, the individual comes up with a major synthesis which integrates ideas and experience to provide a new understanding of the issue which caused the disconfirming event. The learner consciously acknowledges that learning is a process in which he or she is the agent. This process can be facilitated by others, but the learner is where the learning happens and the learner's own views and judgments are centrally involved.

The transition out of the reorientation phase and into the equilibrium phase is marked by sharing the major insight with others.

The learner does not need the self-affirmation which closes the disorientation phase but does need affirmation of the intelligibility and practicality of the new perspective or insight.

The equilibrium phase
The **Equilibrium phase** is characterized by consolidating and elaborating, refining and applying the new perspective. This phase involves a much reduced emotional intensity. The new perspective may be shared with individuals in other contexts or tested out as new behaviour in new settings. These new activities will eventually lead to new discomfiting experiences.

Decremental cycle of learning

Gavin and Taylor (1990; Gavin, 1992) describe a decremental cycle of learning engaged in by learners who enter a protracted disorientation phase and deny they have a problem or blame others for their current situation. This decremental cycle also encompasses four phases, the first being disorientation.

These learners then enter the second or *construction phase* with their feelings of blame intact, intent on "building a case" for their perception of the situation:

- ❖ They close off open information-gathering in favour of biased inquiries designed to support their point of view.
- ❖ They engage in relationships in which others are used to confirm predetermined opinions.
- ❖ Satisfaction in other areas of life may be imported to mask underlying negative and depressive feelings.

The construction phase replaces the exploration phase of the more positive cycle of learning. Movement out of the construction phase is a private affair leading to the third or *consolidation phase* in which the learner closes off all exploratory options and returns to existing ideas and behaviours. The fourth phase, *decremental equilibrium*, does not involve a comfortable and positive stability but is unsettled. The learner may experience a new disorientation phase without a new disconfirming event and with very little warning.

General comments on Taylor's model

Taylor makes no statement about the amount of time required to move through the entire cycle. It is useful to view Hunt's model as occurring almost instantly as facilitator and learner flex to each other, and to view Kolb's model as occurring over a slightly longer period of time, but still of short duration. Taylor's model probably occurs over several days or weeks or even months if the problem is complex and the inquiry difficult. Kolb's model can be thought of as contributing short cycles which drive the longer cycle proposed by Taylor.

Taylor's model includes the period of confusion, anxiety and tension often associated with learning into the learning cycle, thus making it a "normal" and expected part of learning.

The models proposed by Kolb and Hunt do not include this highly emotional phase and some learners could believe that confusion or anxiety should not occur during the learning process or that they must get over their emotional responses before the 'real learning' can take place. Taylor also includes a phase in the cycle which describes the integration of what has been learned into one's personal model of reality and self-system and the transfer of this learning into different contexts. Both Kolb and Hunt seem to be describing learning which takes place in one context only; transfer would be seen as an entirely new cycle of learning.

When I introduce students to Taylor's model, I get two types of responses. The most frequent response is:

"Why didn't you tell us this would happen? I thought I was the only one who was confused and anxious. I thought I was crazy (or stupid)."

I sometimes introduce Taylor's model in a course when I sense that many learners have become confused and are convinced they are not smart enough to be in the class. By introducing the model, I provide them with an easy way to re-enter dialogue with others and share their concerns.

The second response is:

"Don't try to predict what I'd do next!"

Fortunately, this response does not occur too often. I suspect that learners who respond this way are very self-directed and confident and can't imagine that they will ever become confused or anxious as learners.

LEARNING AND FACILITATING PRINCIPLES

❖ Learning which is related to personal concerns proceeds more effectively when learners define the problem, establish goals and conduct the inquiry process for themselves, providing their own personal meaning to experiences.

If learning relates to personal concerns, encourage learners to set their own learning agenda and provide opportunities for them to discuss their confusion and anxiety, and to share their meanings and insights.

❖ The learning cycle includes periods of high emotionality, particularly at the start.

Assure learners that an emotional phase is a normal part of learning, provide opportunities for them to talk about their feelings, whether positive or negative.

Gavin and Taylor (1990) describe several facilitating strategies which support Taylor's model of learning:

❖ **The disorientation phase calls for supportive relationships and opportunities to talk through the "problem," for encouraging learners to talk about their negative feelings, and for avoiding attempts to cheer them up.**

❖ **To help name the problem, facilitators need to serve as credible, affirming others by accepting learners irrespective of their problems and by avoiding a premature leap into problem solving.**

❖ **In the exploration phase, facilitators can provide information and learning resources, and encourage the development of learning partnerships.**

❖ **In the reflective transition, facilitators should be available to serve as an attentive, empathetic and reflective listeners.**

❖ **In the reorientation phase and the transition which follows, facilitators can be most helpful by providing opportunities for sharing insights and their possible application, and by assisting in the development of ways and means for applying these insights in the learners' workplace, family or community.**

LEARNING STYLES

Learning style is sometimes defined as
the characteristic cognitive, affective, social, and physiological behaviours that
serve as relatively stable indicators of how learners
perceive, interact with and respond to the learning environment (Keefe, 1987).

The terms "learning style" and "cognitive style" are often used interchangeably although they are not exactly the same. Learning style is seen as a broader and more inclusive term than cognitive style.

1. The concept of learning style tends to be used by educators because it is more practical in applied terms than cognitive style.
2. The concept of cognitive style tends to be used by psychologists because each style is usually a more clearly defined and measured personal trait compared to a learning style.
3. The concept of learning style tends to include interpersonal components which are missing from the concept of cognitive style.

The literature on adult learning provides extensive investigations into characteristic ways in which adults

❖ take in information;
❖ select certain information for further processing;
❖ use meanings, values, skills, strategies to solve problems, make decisions, and create new meanings; and
❖ change any or all of the processes or structures described in this list.

*Consistent individual differences in the **ways of organizing***
*experiences into meanings, values, skills, and strategies are called **cognitive styles***
*Consistent individual differences in the **ways of changing***
*meanings, values, skills, and strategies are called **learning styles**.*

Style is distinct from performance level or ability and is viewed as a relatively stable trait which affects everything the individual does. There is some evidence that cognitive styles and learning styles are closely related to personality structure, and at least one theory (Harvey, Hunt, & Schroder, 1961) is used to investigate both cognitive complexity and personality.

Ability generally refers to the content of thought or to what we know; style refers to how we know it (Messick, 1976).

We have seen in Chapter Four, that a variety of cognitive strategies can be understood as contributing to two overall cognitive styles: analytic and holistic, and that some writers see a combined form of these two styles — a synthetic/integrated style — as typifying maturity in cognition. The term "learning style" includes not only cognitive style, but also affective, social and physiological styles of responding to learning tasks or learning environments.

It is very difficult to combine a number of learning strategies to identify just a few overarching learning styles; rather each learning style seems to describe a different quality of Person, Behaviour or Environment. Diagram 16 sets out the variety of strategies thought to contribute to adults' learning styles. We have already discussed various cognitive styles in Chapter Four and social styles in Chapter Five.

Affective styles encompass those aspects of personality which have to do with attention, emotion, and valuing.
Attention components of affective style relate to what the adult learner is most likely to attend to and what will affect that attention.

Optimal attention lies somewhere between boredom and excitement. Motivational components relate to expectancy and importance. Expectancy is the relative certainty that desired outcomes will follow certain actions. Importance relates to the extent to which the learner desires certain outcomes. We discussed some aspects of affective styles in Chapter Three.

Cognitive Styles	Cognitive styles related to receiving information	Cognitive styles related to forming and retaining information
	Perceptual modality preferences — visual, auditory, kinesthetic, gustatory, digital Field dependence vs. independence Scanning — broad vs. narrow Tolerance for incongruous or uncertain experiences Processing styles — discrete/sequential vs. global/simultaneous	Conceptual tempo — impulsivity vs. reflectivity Conceptualizing styles — analytic vs. holistic Breadth of categorizing broad vs. narrow Cognitive complexity vs. cognitive simplicity Levelling/over-generalizing vs. sharpening/over-discriminating
Affective Styles	**Affective styles related to attention in learning** Exploratory behaviour — high vs. low Persistence/perseverence — high vs. low Level of anxiety — high vs. low Tolerance for frustration — high vs. low	**Affective styles related to motives for learning** Locus of control — inner-directed vs. other-directed Achievement vs. affiliation Imitation/role modelling Risk-taking vs. cautiousness Competition vs. cooperation Self-as-learner — high optimism vs. high pessimism Reasons for participating — goal-related, learning, social
Physiological Styles	**Learning behaviours related to physical *or* physiological factors** Sex-related behaviour Healfh reflected behaviour Time-of-day rhythms Need for mobility Responses to variations in light, sound, temperature Age-related changes	
Interpersonal Styles	**Learning behaviours related to social or relational factors** Autonomous vs. Relational Separate vs. Connected	

16. ADULT'S LEARNING STYLES

Source: Keefe, J.W. (1987) **Learning style theory and practice.** Reston, VA: National Association of Secondary School Principals.

Physiological styles are biologically-based modes for responding to learning that are grounded in personal health and nutrition, age-related factors, and accustomed reactions to characteristics of the physical environment.

Sex-related responses to learning are sometimes included under physiological styles. However, the position presented in Chapter Five is that sex-related responses are more appropriately considered as being a gender-related interpersonal or social style of learning.

Learning style instruments

James and Blank (1993) reviewed 20 learning style instruments and identify ten as highly useable. The five most widely used are:

1. **Gregorc's Style Delineator:** a self-report instrument based on four learning styles: abstract sequential, concrete sequential, abstract random, concrete random (Gregorc, 1982).

2. **Hemispheric Mode Indicator:** assesses right or left hemisphere preferences (McCarthy, 1986). McCarthy has also developed the 4MAT System, a complex system which combines hemispheric mode with Kolb's learning styles to develop a set of facilitating styles (McCarthy, 1985).

3. **Kolb's Learning Style Inventory:** a self-report instrument based on four learning styles — converger, accommodator, diverger, assimilator (Kolb, 1985).

4. **Witkin's Group Embedded Figures Test:** assesses field dependence and field independence (Oltman, Raskin, & Witkin, 1970).

5. **Keirsey Temperament Sorter:** assesses preferences on four dimensions: sensing/intuiting, thinking/feeling, introversion/extraversion, perception/judgment. The Sorter is based on the Myers-Briggs Type Indicator which, in turn, is based on Jungian personality dimensions (Keirsey & Bates, 1984).[5]

GENERAL IDEAS ABOUT LEARNING STYLE

❖ Each adult has personally preferred strategies for processing information and for learning, as well as personal traits and levels of ability.

❖ Each adult is both similar to and different from every other adult in ways which vary for preferred learning strategies, types and levels of ability.

❖ Every group of adult learners therefore, will be heterogeneous in nature.

❖ Each individual within the group will be a complex mixture of style and ability.

---

*Adult learning facilitators should **not** assume that a group of adults of the same gender and age with similar social, economic, occupational and educational characteristics will share common learning styles or abilities.*
(Curry, 1983; Even, 1978; Cawley & others, 1976; Messick, 1976; McKenney & Keen, 1974)

Learning styles yield different patterns of meaning for the learners

The literature does not predict how individual adults develop their learning styles. Yet it has a good deal to say about how each style results in differing yet meaningful patterns created from the same experiences by learners with differing learning styles.

For example, *field independent learners* approach learning using analytical strategies resulting in figures which are clearly distinct both from their contexts and from each other. Such differentiated figures become discrete concepts having little overlap with other concepts. Because these differentiated figures can be detached from their embedding concepts, they are perceived as generalizable and transferable from one context to another.

Field independent learners prefer task-focused, flexible activities which allow them to be independent and impersonal and to maintain an acceptable distance between emotions and ideas.

Field dependent learners, on the other hand, approach learning using global strategies resulting in figures which are often undifferentiated from their contexts and from each other. Such undifferentiated figures become broad concepts often overlapping other concepts. Because these undifferentiated figures are rarely detached from their embedding contexts, they are perceived as context-specific and not easily transferable from one context to another.

Field dependent learners prefer highly interactive activities which allow them to be interdependent, interpersonal, and to emphasize the connections between emotions and ideas. (Messick, 1976; Witkin & Goodenough, 1977; Huff, Snider & Stephenson, 1985; Miller, 1991)

In general, field independent learners demonstrate greater competency in analytical cognitive functioning, while field dependent learners demonstrate greater competency in global interpersonal functioning.

If learners of both styles participate in the same learning activity, each will perceive the experience differently and develop different interpretations based on individual perceptions.

One way to help adults learn how to learn more effectively, is to direct their attention to their own characteristic ways of perceiving and point out those aspects of experience they are overlooking.

Some dilemmas for the facilitator

Those who facilitate adult learning, therefore, are faced with dilemmas.

1. In preparing learning material or experiences, how does a facilitator's learning style favour one learning style over another?
2. How can one avoid favouring one style over another?
3. How can two opposing styles by accommodated simultaneously?

Effective facilitators need to be aware of their own style,

❖ how this style affects their preferred facilitating strategies, and

❖ how individuals with similar or different learning styles are affected by these facilitating strategies.

For example, when field-independent facilitators are assisting field-dependent learners to make sense of their own experiences, facilitators need to be aware that they and the learners are using different styles, Further, that *each style is addressing different sources of information*. During the first class session, for example:

❖ Field independent learners may be clearly hearing information about assignments but may not understand that they are expected to learn from fellow students.

❖ Field dependent learners may be figuring out fellow students to interact with and learn from, but may not hear much information about specific assignments.

Learning styles are value-neutral

Cognitive styles and learning styles are theoretically value-neutral. There is no "one best way to learn." Adults with differing styles manage to learn quite productively. Each style is adaptive in some situations and for some learning tasks, but not adaptive in others.

Individual facilitators and institutions, however, may favour one style over another (Even, 1978). Sometimes the less favoured style is perceived by the facilitator or institution as a "disability" and the learners who use such styles may become labelled as slow or disabled learners. There are learning problems which can be traced to difficulties in the way sensory or conceptual inputs to learning are transformed by the learner into cognitive and motor outputs.

Difficulties which can be traced to devalued styles and strategies,
should not be interpreted as disabilities, but rather understood as differences.
Such differences should be celebrated as alternative ways of perceiving and making sense of experience.

An example might help illustrate this. Suessmuth (1985) has developed a learning style inventory which assesses a learner's preference for reporting learning through written or oral styles. In most formal educational institutions, the preferred style for reporting is in writing so that a facilitator would have concrete evidence on which to base an assessment should anyone question it. Learners registered in formal classes who prefer the oral reporting style are frequently out of luck. If they have difficulty reporting their learning in written form, they are sometimes perceived, — and may even perceive themselves — as "learning disabled". I tell such learners to "tell their paper" into a tape recorder and then transcribe the tape.

Suessmuth identifies three general types of personal learning style preferences:

1. **Language learners** prefer to hear (auditory) language or see (visual) language. They are best at remembering and using information in word forms.
2. **Numerical learners** prefer to hear (auditory) or see (visual) numbers. They are best at remembering and using information in a numerical form.
3. **Auditory-visual-kinesthetic (AVK) learners** prefer to learn through personal experiencing and need   combined stimuli. They need to manipulate material and be totally involved or they may not be able to keep their minds on the learning task.

In an educational system which views language as the most important medium for learning, numerical and AVK learners will be at a disadvantage. AVK learners, in particular, are likely to be perceived as unmotivated or learning disabled when asked to do learning tasks involving words.

We can choose to define such differences as "disabilities" when those differences deviate from the expectations of educational institutions or we can choose to celebrate learning styles as differences which demonstrate the range of unique ways in which adults learn.

Adults tend to self-select learning situations and learning-facilitating relationships which enhance their own learning style. They appear to be proficient at knowing intuitively which facilitators and which learning situations are not for them.

Learning style and self-direction

In adult education, very little research has addressed the relationship between self-direction and independence in learning, and specific cognitive and learning styles. It seems reasonable to assume that field-independent adults will more likely be self-directed and independent than field-dependent adults. If this is true, then the major thrust of adult education — supporting self-directedness and independence

— may be ignoring the needs of field-dependent learners. And if theories suggesting that these traits or styles are relatively immune to change are also true, then, as facilitators, we may experience considerable difficulty in helping all adults to become self-directed.

The literature also suggests that warm, caring, supportive, friendly, and non-judgmental facilitators are the best for self-directed (field -independent) learners. Yet these characteristics are more often found in field-dependent adults!

Some writers, therefore, may be recommending a mismatch between facilitating and learning styles possibly leading to dissatisfaction. More research needs to be done in this area (Even, 1978).

Other theorists in learning style research (Taylor, 1987; Kolb, 1984) indicate that, while adults do enter learning experiences with preferred styles, they also use other styles throughout the learning process although less often and perhaps less productively (Abbey, Hunt, & Weiser, 1985).

LEARNING AND FACILITATING PRINCIPLES

❖ Adult learners have individual learning styles, cognitive styles and mental abilities.

Facilitators can assist adult learners to learn how to learn by helping them become aware of their own learning styles and how to develop the skills of the styles they tend to avoid.

❖ A group of adult learners will be heterogeneous in terms of learning styles, cognitive styles and mental abilities.

Facilitators should not try to match styles of all individual learners in a learning group. A better plan is for them to become aware of their own learning styles and develop skills in those they tend to avoid. Also to develop activities offering all learners some opportunities to use their own preferred learning styles.

❖ When a mismatch occurs between the learning/cognitive style of learners and facilitators, the result will be mutually unsatisfactory.

Facilitators must be willing and able to respond to each style and must be aware of their own styles and how these affect processes they use to assist individual learners.

❖ Cognitive styles and learning styles are value-neutral. There is no "one best way to learn." Each cognitive/learning style is adaptive in some situations and not adaptive in others.

In discussing learning styles with learners, facilitators should discuss the strengths and weaknesses of all styles. They should avoid the constant use of their own learning style as the starting point for facilitating activities and definitely avoid any implication that a specific learning style is inadequate.

❖ Adults tend to be proficient at selecting learning situations and learning-facilitating interactions which enhance their own learning/cognitive styles.

❖ Adult learners prefer to start with the learning activities they are most comfortable with and to avoid those they see as difficult or which they like least.

Facilitators tend to start facilitating activities with activities typifying their own learning style. The starting activity determines the focus of preparation for facilitating and what subsequent facilitating activities will look like.

❖ Cognitive/learning styles are not related to intelligence, mental ability, or actual performance.

KOLB'S LEARNING STYLE MODEL

Because there is so much literature on the topic, I have chosen to focus on general issues related to learning styles and to limit the discussion of specific learning styles to the model proposed by Kolb (1984). If we reconsider Kolb's cyclical model of learning and this time view the four activities as representing two dimensions of learning, then

❖ one dimension (AE-RO) allows the learner to move between learning through acting and observing and

❖ the second dimension (CE-AC) allows the learner to understand experience by moving between specific involvement and abstract detachment (Kolb, 1984).

When the two opposing poles are joined, as in Diagram 17, the model is divided into four quadrants which represent four different learning styles.

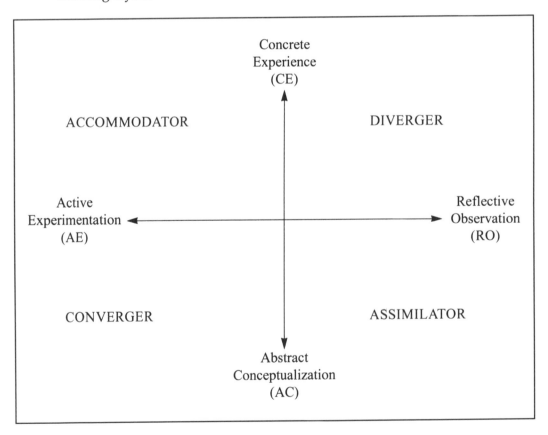

17. KOLB'S LEARNING STYLES

Source: Kolb, D. A. (1984) Experiential learning: Experience as the source of learning and development (p. 42). Englewood Cliffs, NJ: Prentice-Hall.

In Diagram 17, each dimension represents two opposing but related adaptive orientations:

1. **The abstract-concrete dimension** deals with grasping experience and understanding it, either through reliance on conceptual interpretation and symbolic representation; or through reliance on the tangible felt and sensed qualities of immediate experience.

2. The **active-reflective dimension** deals with two opposing ways for converting what has been grasped and understood either through internal reflection or active external manipulation.

Learning, and therefore knowing, requires both a means for grasping and understanding experience through representation of that experience in the mind as concepts or felt sensations, as well as some transformation of that representation.

"Simple perception is not sufficient for learning; something must be done with it" (Kolb 1984, p.42). *Kolb points out that, while both poles of each dimension are necessary for complete, mature learning, all learners are not equally skilled in using all four types of activities.*

Each of the four learning styles — **divergent, assimilative, convergent, accommodative** — represent strengths in one aspect of each of the above two dimensions of learning. Kolb (1985) has developed a Learning Style Inventory allowing individuals to assess their own learning style. I recommend that you obtain a copy of Kolb's Inventory and assess your learning style using his well-validated instrument. Since this test cannot be reproduced here, we will use a less formal process.

First, consider the descriptions of the behaviour which typify the opposing means for grasping and understanding experience, the concrete-abstract dimension.

Concrete experience (CE) emphasizes the use of information derived from personal experiences. Learners who are skilled in concrete experience rely on feelings and sensations rather than thoughts, are concerned about the uniqueness of each new experience, and avoid comparing new experiences with previous ones.

Abstract conceptualization (AC) emphasizes the use of logic, ideas and concepts. Learners who are skilled in abstract conceptualization rely on thoughts rather than feelings or sensations, compare new experiences to old ones to discover similarities and differences, and develop abstract concepts to describe ideas about these comparisons.

Consider yourself and your preferred approach to learning in terms of these opposing means for understanding experiences, and place an X on the vertical axis in Diagram 17 to indicate where you perceive yourself as a learner on this dimension. If you prefer information derived from personal experiences place your X close to the CE end of the axis; if you prefer ideas and concepts, place your X close to the AC end; if you prefer images and metaphors place your X closer to the centre depending on whether your images and metaphors are more concrete or more abstract (your choice).

Next consider the behaviours which typify the opposing means for transforming your understanding of experiences, active-reflective dimension.

Reflective observation (RO) involves understanding the meaning of experiences and situations by observing and describing them. Learners who are skilled in reflective observation transform knowledge through reflective thinking, by understanding why things happen rather than how they work, observing others before trying things out, and developing several different meanings for an experience.

Active experimentation (AC) involves actively influencing people and changing situations. Learners who are skilled in active experimentation transform knowledge through practical applications, by understanding what works rather than why, trying things out first, and learning through trial and error.

Consider yourself and your preferred approach to learning in terms of these opposing means for transforming knowledge, and place an X on the horizontal axis in Diagram 17 to indicate where you perceive yourself as a learner on this dimension. If you have a strong preference for contemplating experience, place your X close to the RO end of the axis; if you have a strong preference for getting on with doing something, place your X close to the AE end; if you do both but tend to think first before acting, place your X near the centre on the RO side; if you do both but tend to act first and think about it later, place your X near the centre on the AE side.

Your learning style is now identified as the quadrant bordered by the two arms of the vertical and horizontal axes on which you have placed your X's. Compare the descriptions of the four styles with your awareness about how you learn — did you end up in the right quadrant?

If your X's are on the CE and RO ends of the axes, you may be divergent as a learner. The greatest strength in this style lies in imaginative ability and awareness of meaning and values; in viewing concrete experiences from many different perspectives; and organizing many relationships into meaningful wholes. The weakness of this style is that, taken to extremes, learners can become paralyzed by perceiving too many alternatives, yet be unable to choose among them.

If your X's are on the AC and RO ends of the axes, you may be assimilative as a learner. The greatest strength in this style lies in the ability to put together many different ideas to form concepts, models or theories which are logically sound, and in combining disparate ideas into an integrated whole. The weakness of this style is that, taken to extremes, learners may build "castles in the air" without understanding the experiences on which they are built and/or without considering their practical application.

If your X's are on the AC and AE ends of the axes, you may be convergent as a learner. The greatest strength in this style lies in problem solving, decision making, and the practical application of ideas. The weakness of this style is that, taken to extremes, learners may end up solving the wrong problem because they did not consider all alternatives and because they did not want to waste time chewing things over.

If your X's are on the CE and AE ends of the axes, you may be accommodative as a learner. The greatest strength in this style lies in doing things, in carrying out plans and tasks, and taking risks by getting involved in new experiences. The weakness of this style is that, taken to extremes, learners may solve problems in an intuitive trial-and-error manner without understanding why they have made certain choices, or they may engage in meaningless activity and make trivial improvements in how things get done.

You can see from these descriptions that each learning style has both strengths and weaknesses. The useful part of Kolb's model is that you do not have to feel pigeon-holed; you can become a more well-rounded, all-purpose learner, by improving the skills associated with the learning styles you do not prefer. For most learners, this will be the style diagonally opposite your own.

Kolb (1984) tells us that divergent learners usually need to improve their deciding skills (decision making, goal setting); assimilative learners, their acting skills (seeking and exploring opportunities, risk taking); convergent learners, their valuing skills (listening with an open mind, imaging the implications of situations); and accommodative learners, their thinking skills (organizing information, developing concepts based on personal experience).

LEARNING AND FACILITATING PRINCIPLES

❖ Learning activities are seen as orderly, cyclical and as moving in one general direction. Several writers note, for example, that it is easier to move from abstract ideas to concrete instances through actively trying the ideas out in real (or simulated) activities. It is much more difficult to move from abstract ideas to concrete instances through the use of reflective activities (Coleman, 1976).

❖ Adult learners generally prefer to start their learning with activities which typify their learning style. For example:

  ❖ Divergent learners like to begin by talking things over with other learners in order to "get the big picture."

  ❖ Assimilative learners like to begin by finding a book and reading about the topic in order to understand where they might go next.

  ❖ Convergent learners like to begin by defining the learning task and setting some clear goals.

  ❖ Accommodative learners like to begin by doing something that will allow them to actively "get on with it."

❖ Each learning style sets up obstacles and frustrations for learners who prefer other styles.

  However, mature learning groups function best when different individuals can take leadership for different aspects of the learning cycle.

  Facilitators tend to start with the activities which represent their preferred learning style on the assumption that this is the "best way to learn" and the best way to "get things off on the right foot". The activity chosen as a starting point will have a profound effect on the remainder of the process.

  ❖ Assimilative learners like to start facilitating activities with readings or lecture-style presentations of concepts, theories or models. Facilitators tend to prepare for facilitating sessions by focusing on what information will be presented first, rarely beginning by asking learners to participate in an experience.

  ❖ Convergent learners like to start facilitating activities by defining the learning task, outlining learning objectives and then letting learners get on with things for themselves. Facilitators tend to prepare for facilitating sessions by setting out goals, objectives, and expectations for a learning program. They rarely begin by having learners identify alternative tasks or objectives.

❖ Accommodative learners like to start facilitating activities by getting learners to do something, often a structured experience in which all learners can participate. Facilitators tend to prepare for facilitating sessions by selecting an activity or experience which illustrates what they want the learners to learn. They rarely begin by giving a lecture.

❖ Divergent learners like to start facilitating activities by sharing experiences in order to generate ideas, for example, through brainstorming activities. Facilitators tend to prepare for facilitating sessions by setting up a metaphor which they can use to bring in a variety of different ideas, or by establishing questions or issues around which brainstorming activities can be conducted. They rarely begin by setting goals or defining the learning task.

❖ Who provides the input, who directs the activity, where the learning process starts, and where it is expected to go are determined by separate decisions. **Learners, facilitators, or both acting collaboratively can take responsibility for these activities or decisions.**

❖ Feedback can occur only when learners use overt behaviour, which occurs only between active experimentation and concrete experience. Learners preferring reflective observation may have trouble getting enough feedback to guide future learning if they avoid overt actions which can be assessed by others. Facilitators who prefer reflective observation may not provide enough activities in which learners can actually test out ideas and get feedback.

❖ Learners avoiding reflective learning tend to repeat mistakes. **Such learners must be assisted in taking the time to reflect on what has happened and what has led to the mistakes.** Learners can then develop plans designed to avoid repeating the same mistakes.

❖ Learners who avoid active experimental learning also avoid having their ideas or actions exposed to the scrutiny of others. In order to correct or modify their ideas and actions, **such learners need to be encouraged to take risks and try something different.**

❖ Learners who avoid developing abstract ideas are often afraid that their ideas will be "carved in marble". They like ideas that are flexible. Often such learners are afraid that their ideas will be discounted or ignored. **They need assistance in proposing tentative or "half-baked" ideas just for the fun of it.**

❖ Learners who avoid concrete experiences are often afraid to emerge from the protection of the super-rational "ivory tower." They don't like the chaotic, disorganized aspects of reality, preferring to impose order on reality in terms of their concepts and theories. **They need assistance to "get their feet wet" just for the fun of it.**

Learning style and the environment

Another aspect of Kolb's model is that each of the four activities is supported by a different facilitative style and learning environment.

Fry (1978) and Fry & Kolb (1979) report that **concrete experience is best supported by an affectively complex environment.** Here the primary purpose is to:

- ❖ participate in actual experience;
- ❖ use these experiences to generate insights and feelings;
- ❖ receive feedback related to personal needs and goals.

In an affectively complex environment, the facilitator is most helpful by serving as a role model and relating to learners on a personal basis, as a colleague rather than authority. Facilitating techniques which seem to support concrete experience include: group projects, demonstrations, visualizations, field trips, case studies and critical incident reports, structured or laboratory method activities which are then discussed.

Reflective observation is best supported by a perceptually complex environment. (Fry, 1978; Fry & Kolb, 1979). Here the primary purpose is to:

- ❖ understand something,
- ❖ identify relationships among ideas,
- ❖ collect relevant information,
- ❖ engage in research activities.

A perceptually complex environment provides access to lots of different types of information in a variety of perceptual modes (books, films, arts and crafts), from both personal and impersonal (expert) sources, and provides many opportunities to discuss ideas with colleagues.

In this environment, the facilitator is most helpful by serving as a mediator, discussion leader, or process facilitator and by providing feedback about the processes being used. Facilitating techniques which seem to support reflective observation include: discussion groups, buzz groups, journal writing, interviewing, creativity activities, puzzles, quiet meetings or talking circles, inquiry projects, brainstorming, and consciousness raising.

Abstract conceptualization is best supported by a symbolically complex environment (Fry, 1978; Fry & Kolb, 1979).

Here the primary purpose is to use knowledge to solve problems or identify solutions and answers. Information is provided in symbolic form through books, research data, and so on.

In this environment, the facilitator is most helpful by acting as the "content expert," as a representative of the body of knowledge being learned and by providing feedback about the aptness of proposed solutions or the logic of proposed concepts, theories and models. Facilitating techniques which seem to support abstract conceptualization include: lectures, reading papers, individual projects, problem-solving activities, forums and panels, debates, seminars, model building, and proposal writing.

Active experimentation is best supported by a behaviourally complex environment (Fry, 1978; Fry & Kolb, 1979). Here the emphasis is on providing opportunities to apply knowledge or skills in practical situations. The information brought to the situation has been abstracted by the learner from previous experiences and is compared with information which can be extracted from the immediate situation.

In this environment, the facilitator can be most helpful be serving as a coach or advisor and by providing feedback about how the learner's behaviours are affecting the overall situation or the task to be completed. Facilitating techniques which seem to support active experimentation include: hands-on activities, games, simulations, field placements or internships, mentoring, drill and practice, role playing, action research, and learning contracts.

Variations on Kolb's model

Kolb's model has been used by other writers to expand on his central ideas. McCarthy (1985) combines each of Kolb's learning styles with left and right hemisphere functions to generate eight styles of learning. She also reports on the likes and dislikes of each learning style with regard to facilitating techniques and assessing procedures. For example, Huff, Snider and Stephenson (1986) report McCarthy's ideas as follows:

❖ **Divergent learners** like group work, group grading, pass/fail grading, self-evaluation, unobtrusive observation, participation grading, and time to reflect. They dislike timed tests, computer-assisted instruction, debates, and "just do it".

❖ **Assimilative learners** like comments on papers and tests, written tests and essays, multiple choice tests, and collecting data. They dislike role playing, pass/fail grading, subjective tests, and group grades.

❖ **Convergent learners** like field trips and labs, hands-on activities, mobility, and skill oriented evaluation. They dislike memorizing, written assignments, group work and group grading, peer evaluations which involve "feelings," and being given the answers by others.

❖ **Accommodative learners** like interdisciplinary approaches, open-ended questions and activities, flexible assignments, and self-discovery projects. They dislike assignments without options, repetition and drills, reflecting, and inactivity.

STRATEGIES AND MODELS IN FACILITATING

9

This chapter is only indirectly about learning. In Chapter One, I described the learner-centred approach used in this book as one in which the learning process is assumed to be of paramount importance, while facilitating is regarded as a responsive activity adapting to the learner's activities and the natural learning process.

In this chapter, I will describe the facilitating models in terms of how each follows a set of assumptions about learning.

I will look at two different ways to understand facilitating and see how each corresponds to learning, then examine three basic strategies or methods for facilitating synthesized from the literature on working with adult learners:

1. *directing,*
2. *enabling and*
3. *collaborating.*

Then I will conclude with a glance at some basic theoretical models of facilitating:

* *behavioural,*
* *information-processing,*
* *humanistic and*
* *dialectical.*

BASIC STRATEGIES OF FACILITATING

As facilitators, we can improve our facilitating strategies by becoming more aware of our own beliefs, intentions and actions. Only when we understand both sides of the learning-facilitating interactions in which we participate, can we determine ways for improving and applying sound facilitating beliefs, implicit theories, intentions and actions about learning.

Each mode must be considered both as part of a continuum of facilitating behaviours, and as unique by itself; each mode has advantages and disadvantages. Good facilitators are able to use all three modes in varying combinations depending on the material, the learners, and the setting of the learning activities.

Directing

The directing mode calls for facilitators to:

* define and structure content;
* structure activities which will constitute the learning process;
* provide feedback and reinforcement to learners;
* provide support, encouragement, and guidance as necessary.

The responsibility for these functions rests with facilitators, but can be negotiated and shared with learners. The time required to complete the learning tasks will increase as the amount of negotiating and sharing increases.

The directing mode:

* helps learners acquire specific skills and knowledge relevant and essential to specific tasks and performance (driving a car, speaking a foreign language, becoming a certified plumber).
* works best with material which, by social convention, professional supervision, or law, is prescribed for certain roles and/or certification.

❖ works best with material which can be segmented into manageable parts and then organized into sequences or hierarchies to form complex units of knowledge and skill.

❖ is the best method when learners are constrained to learn specific material within a short period of time.

❖ requires that someone (an "expert," the facilitator and/or the learner) set objectives, define materials, divide the materials into segments, organize it into sequences and hierarchies, and provide it in a ready-to-use form for learners.

❖ requires facilitators to provide immediate feedback and periodic reinforcement. The type and focus of feedback can be negotiated between facilitator and learner but is generally built into the program. Rewards or reinforcement can also be built into the programmed material, but most adults also require additional support and encouragement from the facilitator or other learners.

❖ can be implemented in situations varying from a "facilitator-less" learning module to a training program combined with other facilitating modes such as micro-teaching programs. Programmed modules provide direction through the design of the material and can be self-paced.

❖ must involve the learner, either explicitly or implicitly, in two critical aspects of the learning process. First, the learner must be willing to make a commitment to the objectives of the program and to the learning processes involved. Second, the learner must be willing and able to learn from the feedback and reinforcement provided.

❖ is relatively non-threatening to facilitators provided they are expert in both content and processes involved in the learning activities. Directing functions, however, may provide little opportunity for interpersonal involvement with the individual learners.

❖ allows learners to acquire material in a relatively short period of time without having to discover it for themselves. There may be few opportunities for facilitator-learner or peer interactions. There is a potential threat to learners at two points; first, if the objectives and processes do not meet the learners' real needs and they cannot exit from the program; and second, if feedback is somehow threatening to each learner's self-system.

❖ is most relevant for mastery learning and achievement needs and for enhancing self-esteem.

Enabling
The enabling mode calls for facilitators to
- ❖ act as a catalyst,
- ❖ provide content and process resources,
- ❖ serve as a reflective mirror or alter ego,
- ❖ act as a co-inquirer with learners, and
- ❖ provide support, guidance, and encouragement.

The responsibility for these functions can rest with the facilitator or can be shared among facilitator and learners. The structure, objectives, and direction of the learning activities are negotiated; the content, in the form of personal meanings, comes from the learner.

The enabling mode:
- ❖ proceeds through dialogue involving statement-making, clarifying, probing, developing analogies and metaphors, and reflecting, among other activities. The dialogue is complete only when learners are satisfied with their own personal understanding of meanings. Reinforcement is a normal part of the dialogue between two persons; and feedback is provided through reflecting, summarizing, and paraphrasing rather than through judging or evaluating.
- ❖ helps learners discover personal meanings within knowledge and skills already learned; discover new meanings within experience; create new meanings, values and strategies from integrating new and old learning , for example, through self-discovery, consciousness-raising, transformative learning.
- ❖ works best with material which does not need to be learned as a logical sequence of parts in order to understand the whole. Allows learners to develop personal perceptions about the parts and about the relationships among them.
- ❖ works best when learners have few time constraints on the learning process.
- ❖ requires that someone (the facilitator, learner, or external resource) provide structured experiences which can be shared by learners and from which knowledge can be gained; a communication process through personal experiences can be shared with others; or a resource such as films, books, art objects, pictures, artifacts and the like, through which experience can be described for the learners.

❖ can be implemented through activities which vary from group experiential processes, to demonstrations and use of media, to one-on-one counselling processes.

❖ is relatively non-threatening for facilitators providing they don't interfere with the content to be learned (the learner's meanings) and become involved only through their own process skills, as a manager of the learning process or as co-inquirer.

❖ is relatively threatening for learners since their personal meanings and self-systems are vulnerable to disconfirmation. For this reason, enabling activities require that time be spent in building a trusting relationship between facilitator and learners.

❖ is most relevant to belongingness and affiliation needs, to mastery learning which requires a sense of personal commitment to a set of values such as those found in professional development, and to improvement of the self-system.

Collaborating

The collaborating mode requires that learners and facilitators share as co-learners in the discovery and creation of meanings and values.

The collaborating mode:

❖ works best with material in which all learners have a stake and through which they can grow individually and as members of a team through, for example, community problem-solving, professional development of a work team.

❖ works best with material which is defined by learners, and through processes, structures, and directions which are negotiated by them. Negotiating processes should result in a group consensus.

❖ is the best method for building "a community of learners," but requires considerable expenditure of time and energy.

❖ requires that learners divide tasks on some mutually acceptable basis and that all contribute to leadership functions in both tasks and interpersonal relationships. The learners are required to act interdependently.

❖ requires that facilitators participate as co-learners with the same responsibilities and rights as other learners and with full membership in the group.

❖ is relatively threatening and high-risk to both facilitator and learners because all are vulnerable within the process.

❖ requires a high level of trust.

❖ is most relevant to belongingness and affiliation needs.

Collaborating could be used for almost any learning need, but this would require that learners be willing to temporarily shift to the enabling or directing mode to learn in relation to specific needs. For example, if a work team needs to develop computer skills, they may need to shift to the directing mode to meet this particular goal.

There is considerable debate among adult educators about which mode of teaching is best suited to the needs of adult learners.

In keeping with Lewin's B-P-E formulation,
each mode is functional for some adult learners, in some learning contexts, and for some content; and that
no single mode will serve all purposes (Pratt, 1992; Thomas, 1991; Smith, 1990;
Knowles, 1990; Joyce & Weil, 1986; Cross, 1976; Hunt & Sullivan, 1974).

MODELS OF FACILITATING

The literature on adult education yields a wide variety of methods and strategies for designing the processes through which a learner can be assisted to learn.

Joyce and Weil (1986) define a model of facilitating as a plan or pattern that can be used to
design face-to-face activities and resources for use in formal, informal or individual settings.

Each model is based on theoretical assumptions about the nature of learning and facilitating, and about the nature and characteristics of adult learners. Each model has direct instructional and indirect nurturant effects. Here, I will discuss four models of facilitating: behavioural, information processing, humanistic, and dialectical models.

These four models are by no means inclusive of all possibilities:

❖ each encompasses a wide range of possible designs;

❖ each tends to overlap with other models;

❖ each serves one part of the learning process very effectively;

❖ each can be used in combination with other models; and

❖ each can be adapted for group or individual learning.

If you wish to know more about models of facilitating, I recommend that you read, *Models of Teaching*, by Joyce and Weil (1986).

Behavioural Models

Behavioural models (sometimes called *operant conditioning*) assume that what learners think and how they manipulate information are less important than how successful they are in achieving behavioural objectives, coping with the environment, or changing their behaviour (Joyce & Weil, 1986; Boshier, 1975; Hoyer, 1974; Skinner, 1971).

Behavioural models assume that learning can be controlled from outside the learner by the application of the correct stimulus for the desired response and by the appropriate reinforcement of that response to encourage its continued use.

A pictorial representation of the behavioural model is shown in Diagram 18. Facilitating strategies are concerned with:

❖ identifying the behaviour which is to be changed;
❖ establishing objectives which state the desired responses;
❖ setting up learning activities through which the learner will have opportunities to use this behaviour;

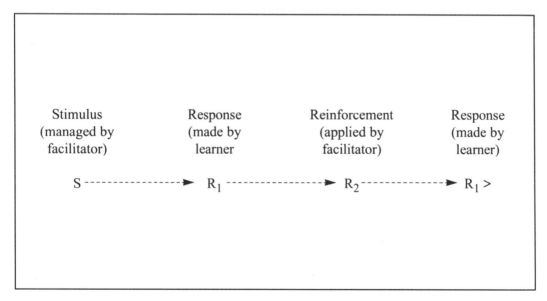

| Stimulus (managed by facilitator) | Response (made by learner | Reinforcement (applied by facilitator) | Response (made by learner) |

$$S \dashrightarrow R_1 \dashrightarrow R_2 \dashrightarrow R_1 >$$

18. BEHAVIOURAL LEARNING MODEL

* identifying the conditions which will govern reinforcement; and
* monitoring and reinforcing behaviour on the basis of this contingency program.

━━━━━━━━━━━━━━━━

The facilitator must have special knowledge about which stimuli elicit desired responses and which reinforcers are appropriate for encouraging further use of the response.
The learner is perceived as a more or less passive respondent; and not much concern is wasted on what, if anything, might be going on inside the learner.

━━━━━━━━━━━━━━━━

The reinforcement or feedback can include:
* describing the learner's performance or results without assessing or judging (here's what you did);
* judging the learner's progress toward established objectives or criteria (you succeeded — or failed);
* advising the learner about ways to modify, improve or augment the next response without actually commenting on the previous response (next time do this);
* rewarding the learner by providing something extra that the learner likes or wants (called positive reinforcement) or removing an undesired condition (called negative reinforcement); and/or punishing the learner by providing something extra that the learner does not like (called aversive reinforcement).

Positive reinforcement makes the response occur more often (smiling, giving the learner a "pat" on the back, administering a "reward" such as grades or money). Negative reinforcement makes the undesired response occur less frequently (in biofeedback an aggravating sound is reduced as blood pressure is reduced). Aversive reinforcement has the same outcome as negative reinforcement but is less pleasant (docking pay). Positive and negative reinforcements are usually more productive than aversive reinforcements.

When working with adult learners, an appropriate approach is to have the learner cooperate in establishing the desired goal, the reinforcement schedule, and to take over the reinforcement process until it can be eliminated. The adult learner must value both feedback and reinforcement, or neither will be effective. In many instances, the act of receiving reinforcement tends be more rewarding than the actual value of the reinforcement itself (Boshier, 1975).

I find that behavioural approaches, while they look rather impersonal, help me understand the most appropriate way to design learning resources (the stimuli), the importance of feedback, and the nature of reinforcement. Behavioural approaches are most appropriate when the learner is trying to learn physical or cognitive skills or modify inappropriate existing behaviour. The facilitator's role in these models is best understood as that of "coach."

Adult educators have a tendency to discount the value of the behavioural approach because learners may learn indirectly to be other-directed rather than self-directed.
However, the behavioural model does provide important insights into the intrinsic and reinforcing value of feedback, particularly when it relates to learners' anticipated outcomes of learning.

If any reader believes that behaviourist models have nothing to say to them, I would point out that behaviourist concepts underlie:

❖ the field of **instructional technology** concerning the development of sound educational resources such as instructional manuals, self-instructional learning modules, videotapes, etc. (Pratt, 1987);

❖ the development of **programmed learning modules and computer-based training programs** to assist learners to acquire and master skilled behaviour, such as word processing tutorials, computer-based simulations which teach pilots how to fly new types of airplanes, computer programs helping the learner change nutritional knowledge and eating behaviours, etc. (Heermann, 1984; Block & Anderson, 1975);

❖ **programs designed to modify behaviour** such as assertiveness training (Joyce & Weil, 1986); and

❖ **biofeedback programs** designed to help the learner change behaviour such as high blood pressure otherwise inaccessible to normal learning activities (Brown, 1980).

Information-Processing Models

Information-processing models (also called *cognitivist* or *mentalist models*) are related to:

❖ cognitive or intellectual development;

❖ cognitive activities for processing and using information;

❖ the knowledge framework associated with a specific discipline or area of study (Flannery, 1993a; Brandt, Farmer & Buckmaster, 1993; Huber, 1993; Yanoff, 1976; DiVesta, 1974; Norman, 1973).

Models based on a learner's cognitive or intellectual development, such as increasing cognitive complexity, tend to assume that adults are capable of using certain information-processing and thinking strategies solely because of their age or experience. This assumption ignores the fact that some adults have never acquired these strategies, and others have acquired them but do not use them. Cognitive development is discussed in detail in Chapter Four.

Models based on cognitive activities for processing and using information employ a series of facilitating activities based on *logical* and/or *analogical thought processes*. Cognitive processes include:

❖ perceiving (sensing, attending, recognizing patterns);
❖ remembering (representing, storing, retrieving); and
❖ thinking (classifying, understanding, meaning-making, analyzing, synthesizing, assessing).

Information processing models assume that if we understand how learners process information, we will also know how to present information as a stimulus for learning, the best sequence for specific cognitive activities, and how to facilitate using these sequences. Information processing models are often highly structured in process terms, but can vary widely in content.

Facilitators need:

1. command of both process and content,
2. knowledge about individual differences in cognitive styles, and
3. skills for facilitating the relevant processes.

The content can be provided either by expert resources (books, the facilitator, films, etc.) or can be provided by the learner as a result of analyzing personal problems and experiences.

Models based on the knowledge framework of a specific discipline or area of study, use as guiding structures, both the concepts and skills to be learned.

For example, in studying History, learners are encouraged to use the historical method of inquiry. In adult education, **guiding structures** might include learning, program planning, problem-solving, small group development and communication processes, since these concepts are basic conceptual structures in the field.

If **problem-solving skills** are to be learned, the model calls for learners to first solve a problem while "walking through" a typical series of problem-solving strategies. Then, through reflection, learners think about what happened and develop an understanding of what problem-solving involves. This understanding might include a conceptual framework, skills and strategies for further problem-solving, a set of values about the process, and some methods for helping other learners solve problems (Stouch, 1993; Joyce & Weil, 1986).

Discipline-specific models are typical in professional development programs such as teacher education or medical training. Adults learning how to help other adults learn, need to experience the relevant activities in the same way as adult learners with whom they will work.

Much professional development of adult educators consists of doing the appropriate methods and then reflecting on that doing.
In the vernacular of the field, this reflecting is referred to as "processing the experience."

I have found that information processing models help me appreciate the complexity of cognitive processes and to avoid taking for granted that all adult learners can use all cognitive processes. Facilitators who rely on these models, however, may look at adult learners from only a cognitive point of view, ignore emotionality and stress, disavow the importance of the social and spiritual aspects of learning, and not understand the holistic and integrated nature of learning.

Information processing models include, among others, such techniques as:

❖ **inquiry training** involving the process of investigating and explaining unusual phenomena through asking questions, gathering relevant information, and analyzing the information logically (Joyce & Weil, 1986).

❖ **mind mapping,** a visual depiction of a network of ideas. Using radiant (divergent) thinking, a mind map usually has a central image, idea or concept from which main themes radiate outward as major branches. Each major branch comprises a key image or word from which smaller branches radiate representing associated ideas or images (Buzan & Buzan, 1995).

❖ **concept attainment** (or deductive thinking) involving the search for and listing of attributes that can distinguish examples of various categories from non-examples. **Concept formation** (or inductive thinking) involves creating new categories on the basis of uncategorized information (Joyce & Weil, 1986).

❖ **advance organizers** providing "intellectual scaffolding" that structures ideas and facts related to a central concept and guides the manner in which the learner will think about this concept.

❖ **mnemonic devices** used to help in memorization through the use of association techniques. Many association techniques link ideas to be remembered to visual images ("one is a bun, two is a shoe") or rhymes ("i before e except after c") (Norman, 1969).

❖ **lateral thinking** "the process of using information to bring about creativity and insight restructuring" (deBono, 1977). Lateral thinkers are concerned with restructuring or changing patterns of concepts, ideas, thoughts or images so as to develop more effective patterns.

❖ **problem-solving,** according to), a design process improving existing conditions and finding a clear path out of dilemmas (Koberg and Bagnall 1981). To improve existing conditions, learners must:

❖ become aware of the problematic state;
❖ identify the essential component of the problem; and
❖ be able to use the skills and methods required to manipulate the problem condition into a better state.

The same process works for finding a way out of a dilemma but one must also know how to keep a cool head (Koberg & Bagnall 1981, p.8).

Humanistic Models

Humanistic or person-centred models focus on the whole person, on learning which involves body, mind and spirit, and cognitive, affective and motor components.

These models have two general overall objectives:

1. to help learners discover, explore, and create personal meanings and values, skills and strategies used to facilitate personal learning; and
2. to help learners develop a positive self-concept and high self-esteem, contributing in positive ways to further learning.

Humanists tend to view learning as an inside-out process controlled and directed by the learner rather than an outside-in process controlled and directed by the facilitator.

Humanistic models assume that humans have a natural potential for learning. They also assume that learning is facilitated when learners participate responsibly in the learning process through

* choosing their own directions,
* discovering their own learning resources,
* formulating their own problems,
* deciding their own course of action, and
* living with the consequences of their choices.

Further, they assume that learning involving the whole person is the most pervasive and lasting; and that the most useful learning is learning how to learn (Knowles, 1990; Brookfield, 1990; Joyce & Weil, 1986; Coleman, 1976; Kidd, 1973a).

Humanistic approaches shift facilitators' attention away from correct answers, achievement levels, extrinsic reward systems (grades and certification), reinforcement schedules, cognitive processes, and education technologies. These models do not work well in contexts constrained by the prescriptive demands of occupations or where the facilitator must work with very large groups of learners.

Humanistic approaches work best when working with individuals or small groups and when the learning outcomes can be flexible.

Facilitating strategies focus on what learners need and want from their learning activities. The learner can be assisted indirectly through interpersonal relationships based on trust, rather than directly through a set of structured activities or laid-on content.

As a facilitator, the humanistic model reminds me that I have important responsibilities to:

❖ create a climate valuing learning and reducing disincentives or obstacles to a minimum;

❖ help the learner to clarify learning needs, purposes, and objectives;

❖ organize and make available the widest possible range of resources;

❖ present myself as a flexible resource to be used by the learner;

❖ behave in simultaneous roles — as a co-learner who can and will learn from and with the learner; an objective observer who can respond to the individual needs and feelings of the learner; and a subjective participant who will act on and share feelings, needs, and personal values.

Humanistic models, therefore, demand that the facilitator be highly skilled in process facilitation and highly committed to personal involvement in the learning-facilitating interaction. Since much of the content is based on individual need, the facilitator does not need to be a content specialist, although it helps.

Humanistic models do not propose a sequence of activities; rather the design is emergent.

❖ The facilitator must wait to discover what the learner needs before learning activities and content can be planned.

❖ Learning processes and activities are shaped collaboratively as learners select and implement their own goals.

❖ Most humanistic models also include provision for some structured activities at the beginning of the learning program which assist both learner and facilitator to clarify learning objectives and directions. These objectives or directions may relate to any aspect of the learning process — content, strategies, processes, activities, experiences, and so on.

Humanistic models are based on the value orientation that each learner not only is unique but also is worthy of respect and acceptance, and of being treated with dignity. This orientation suggests that facilitators must be willing to acknowledge learners are as much a potential resource for learning as facilitators and that all share rights and responsibilities which are equal and reciprocal in nature.

Since facilitators are expected to be able to respond to individual needs and learning styles, the most essential element of facilitating is learning about learners. Humanistic models require that teachers be able to respond to individuals, develop supportive climates and facilitate learning processes for both individuals and groups

---

Suggestions on how to use humanistic models with children generally begin with the assumption that children do not have all the necessary knowledge and skills and will learn them through activities characterizing the model. When the same models are applied to adults, however, implementation suggestions tend to assume that an adult, to be respected and treated with dignity, should not be thought of in child-like terms. The tendency is to assume that adults already possess all the necessary knowledge and skills.

Sometimes little consideration is given to how a facilitator would implement a humanistic model in a group setting when the individuals in the group range from those with none of these characteristics to those with all of them.

Humanistic models are most relevant to the affective and social dimensions of learning and can lead to attitude changes, understanding and awareness of personal meanings and values, and changes in both self-concept and self-esteem.

Dialectical Models

In Chapter One, as part of the definition of learning, I briefly discussed the dialectical nature of learning, and that learning is interactive, constitutive, and transformative.

1. Learning is **interactive** because we make meaning through exchanging information with our environment, most particularly with other persons.

2. Learning is **constitutive** because we endow both ourselves and the world around us with social meaning.

3. Learning is **transformative** because both our meanings and personal model of reality are changed during interactive and constitutive processes (Mezirow, 1991; Basseches, 1984; Riegel, 1976).

The interactive aspects of learning

Interactions can occur between the learner and his or her own model of reality, and/or between the learner and the facilitator, other learners, and learning resources.

The effectiveness of interactive processes rests on communication skills including active and empathic listening,
responding first to the other's ideas or feelings before disclosing one's own, and providing feedback.
In effective dialogue, each person responds to
the previous person's statement before adding something new.

Without this process, a conversation between two persons has a tendency to be reduced to two monologues in which neither listens to the other. When interaction is effective, participation is based on

❖ equality,
❖ cooperation,
❖ collaboration,
❖ shared power and control.

Both facilitator and learner must understand that such characteristics are not based on some altruistic process in which one "gives" equality, control and power to the other. Rather, both must assume that the other is capable of exercising equality, control and power while, at the same time, ensuring that both time and space are shared equitably.

Further, both participants learn and both facilitate and both must be able to use effective communication and cognitive skills. Inter-activity assumes that learning and facilitating processes modify each other through a continuing dialogue over time. Since nothing stays the same for long, theorizing about the nature of interactivity is difficult. Two relevant concepts are exchange and empowerment.

---

*Learning involves an **exchange of information**, meanings, energy, feedback, and reinforcements*
Concepts about exchange hold that individuals will continue to interact
as long as each person feels rewarded and as long as these rewards are
more valued than the personal costs incurred (Dowd, 1980).

The rewards one person desires or needs may not be apparent to a casual observer and are rarely the same for both persons. For example, we often speculate on why an abused person remains in an abusive relationship. Exchange concepts suggest that the abused person is gaining some "reward" or avoiding some alternative "cost" which is perceived as being greater than the pain of the abuse.

On the reward side, abusers often provide support or care for the abused person, and the recognition inherent in the abusive act may be perceived by the abused person as important. On the cost side, protesting the abuse may escalate it and leaving the relationship may be perceived as leading to loneliness and difficulties in supporting oneself. Only when the costs of staying in the relationship increase over the level of rewards or when the costs of leaving the relationship are perceived as being offset by potential rewards, will the individual leave the abusive relationship.

***Empowerment** involves a two-phase process.*
This two-phase process includes: (1) growing in personal confidence and
(2) acting congruently with one's own knowledge and values.

Empowerment in the learning process is associated with a number of different processes:

❖ **learning knowledge and skills** can enable individuals to be informed and skilled in new ways which can increase self-confidence. The conferring of credentials attests to this form of empowerment.

❖ **reflective learning and critical thinking** can help learners to become self-reliant through learning how to learn, thus making them better able to direct, manage and control their own learning processes (Candy, 1990).

❖ **self-reflective learning** can enable individuals to become more self-confident and assertive, to believe in and value themselves more, and to perceive themselves as agents of their own actions, better able to shape their own destiny in small and large ways.

❖ **emancipatory learning** can enable marginalized groups and their individual members to understand how their own culture or experience has become submerged within the dominant culture and experience, to work toward recovering those submerged realities, and as a result, to develop social actions designed to counter injustices and inequalities (Mezirow, 1991; Freire, 1973).

As a facilitator, I cannot give power to a learner but I can set up an environment and use facilitating activities which can help shift power from the facilitator to the learner.

The constitutive or interpretive aspects of learning

Interpretation provides an opportunity for individuals to share in the meaning-making process, to share personal meanings, and to use these activities to come to a better understanding of one's self and others.

Two relevant concepts are the negotiation of meaning and symbolic interactionism.

1. **Meanings are negotiated** between the interacting persons through the communication process. In theory, at the start of each dialogue, all meanings are open to modification and negotiation. In practice, dialogues never start with new meanings each time.

We tend to operate with our existing meanings until they don't work — then we negotiate.

The meaning making process proceeds most effectively if both persons

- ❖ clarify their own ideas,
- ❖ paraphrase what they have understood of the ideas of the other,
- ❖ share their own feelings,
- ❖ reflect the feelings of the other.

2. **Symbolic interaction** is a sociological concept explaining why persons in interactions remain relatively stable in spite of pressure to change (Marshall, 1980). When an individual engages in an interaction with another person, each brings their personal model of reality to bear, especially that component related to one's self-system.

This component is always composed of both self-reflective subcomponents (things I see in myself) and subcomponents which mirror what I think others think of me, as well as past (experienced) and future (aspired) subcomponents.

The interaction among all these subcomponents provides a dynamic entity which both acts on the world and is acted on by the world. The dynamic entity, "me-myself-and-I", must maintain some sort of cohesion over time, if only to maintain sanity in a constantly changing world. The self-system, therefore, is ultra-stable and keeps one feeling intact even while it is changing.

Whenever we interact in a learning-facilitating dialogue, we invest our self-system in the exchange of information and meanings. Between two persons, the possibility exists that their self-system will be challenged in some way as shared meanings are negotiated. To safeguard the integrity of each individual, another form of ultra-stability exists allowing for an exchange to occur without enormous cost to either person. We tend to travel through life looking for exchanges which simultaneously enhance and reaffirm our self-systems. We also tend to act in ways drawing certain behaviours from the other person, thus fulfilling our expectations. Within this ultrastability, the fact that many of us learn exciting and new things is often a miracle.

---

*To be open to the possibility of learning in interactions with others requires
that one be willing to take risks that
what will be learned is of greater value than what is being protected from change.*

The transformative aspects of learning

Transformations involve both changes in meaning schemes and changes in perspectives or frames of reference (Cranton, 1994; Mezirow, 1991).

---

*Our meaning schemes or implicit theories may be transformed because
we take time to critically reflect on the underlying assumptions which determine the meaning.
We usually come to this activity when we experience a growing sense of the inadequacy
of our old ways of seeing and understanding something.*

For example, I am learning to exercise control over my life at the university, give more time to students, and more time to myself for research and writing. I have recently begun to do something I once told myself I would never do — I have posted, on my office door, the days and times I will be available. Now, when I am in my office, I am available to students without trying to do two tasks at once; when I am at home, I get my research and writing done without feeling guilty and without interruption. In the process I have had to transform my meaning of "helpful", find ways to get my work done without feeling overwhelmed, and redefine my role as a professor.

Learning through perspective transformation involves transforming our personal model of reality and our frame of reference for viewing reality. Such learning begins when we encounter experiences, often in emotionally charged situations, that fail to fit our expectations and consequently lack meaning for us; or when we encounter an anomaly that we cannot understand by either learning within existing meanings schemes or learning new meaning schemes.

*Perspective transformations occur through
critically reassessing the assumptions that support the meaning schemes that
are not working and redefining the situation or problem.*

For example, when I was still a graduate student in adult education, I was often told that I "looked confident." Since I never felt confident inside, I questioned the ability of anyone to actually judge someone else's confidence. Then I became involved in a peer counselling session which was videotaped. When the tape was replayed, my first impression on seeing myself was "What a confident looking person!" Then I was trapped in an inner conflict. How could I present myself as a confident person on the outside when I felt very unconfident on the inside?

I reconsidered. Maybe, just maybe, I was able to do more than I had thought I was able to do. All my life I had seen myself as inadequate in interpersonal relationships, but maybe I had more skills than I was giving myself credit for. After that incident, each time I found myself feeling inadequate or lacking in confidence, I reassessed what I was doing and feeling. Eventually my perspective on myself changed and with that change I had to change almost all aspects of my self-system.

The idea of a perspective transformation is hard to understand until you have gone through one. In my example, one small change — related to feelings of self-confidence — promoted a massive revision of my self-concept and self-esteem.

Ethical dilemmas in facilitating dialectical learning

Transformations must evolve from within the learner.

Facilitating dialectical learning is more difficult to determine than facilitating the other three models I have discussed. As facilitators, we can

- ❖ set up opportunities for interactions among learners or between a learner and a facilitator,
- ❖ promote the sharing of meanings and the development of shared models of interpreting reality,

❖ encourage learners to assume control over their own learning and to see themselves as empowered to relate on an equal basis with others.

The facilitator's tasks are to provide activities, information and ideas, encourage critical reflection and self-reflection, participate in dialogues on issues of importance to the learner, and provide non-judgmental feedback. But whether or not a transformation will occur is very much dependent on the learner's willingness to

❖ be open to new ideas,
❖ cope with ambiguity,
❖ accept potential feelings of disconfirmation and personal disorganization, and
❖ redefine the situation or problem in new ways.

Of greater importance are three ethical dilemmas which confront facilitators in encouraging learners to engage in transformational learning (Taylor, 1990).

The first dilemma is whether I, as a facilitator, have the right to encourage you to think about introducing changes into your facilitating strategies and practices by thinking critically about them and about everything you read in adult education, including the ideas described here, without also doing something to change the fundamentally authoritative nature of educational institutions which tend to trap both facilitator and learner. The strategies I have proposed are cosmetic at best until we can work together to change the ways our institutions operate.

The second ethical dilemma is that the dialectical model carries with it the idea that the facilitator and the learner are equal in the learning-facilitating interaction; that the facilitator is also a learner engaged in learning about learners and about the nature of learning. The very best dialectical facilitators are concerned primarily about learners' needs, goals and styles, and adjust their facilitating strategies accordingly.

This implies an altruism that may negate the very nature of the dialectical process and may fly in the face of its underlying assumptions. The balance of power in the resulting interactions is never equal if facilitators are unprepared to critically, collaboratively and publicly examine their own personal model of reality and its underlying assumptions. I puzzle over how I can do that while, at the same time continue to be a productive, effective and supportive facilitator?

The third ethical dilemma is the frequently unquestioned assumption that all learners can benefit from transformational learning. Perhaps some learners do not benefit from such learning. Perhaps I, as a facilitator, have no right to deliberately encourage such learning through my facilitating strategies. This dilemma raises the question "Empowerment for what?" and "Emancipation from what?" I have no clear answers to these ethical dilemmas and would urge you to discuss them with your colleagues.

LEARNING AND FACILITATING PRINCIPLES

❖ Adults learn most productively when the facilitating mode matches their needs and/or preferred learning behaviours and styles.

❖ Adults' learning behaviours tend to change as a result of increasing familiarity with a learning program or content. Facilitating modes need to change in responsive ways at the same time.

❖ There is no "one best facilitating style" for use with adult learners. Each style is appropriate for some learners, in some settings and for some content.

PUTTING THE IDEAS TOGETHER

10

In Chapter One I began by explaining that my view of adult learning is very complex; that I viewed the complexities of adult learning in terms of the metaphor of a kaleidoscope. I talked about the colours I see in the learning process: red for emotional or affective learning, orange for physical or skill-based learning, yellow for cognitive or mental learning, greens and blues for social or relational learning, and indigo and deep purple for spiritual or transcendent learning.

In Chapters Two through Nine, I outlined some aspects of learning I believe are important, described my ideas and opinions, and reviewed ideas, theories and models found in the adult education literature. Now I would like to return to the metaphor of the kaleidoscope.

A kaleidoscope consists of many small coloured pieces of translucent material reflected back on themselves by a special arrangement of mirrors contained within a tube enclosed at one end with a translucent cover and at the other with an eyepiece. Looking through the eyepiece, I see intricate, coloured patterns made by the coloured pieces as they are reflected in the mirrors. If I shake the tube, the pieces rearrange themselves and a new pattern emerges. If I roll the tube around while looking through the eyepiece, I can see minute changes in the pattern as the coloured pieces shift position. The colours and patterns delight my eye; the shifts in patterns delight my mind.

For me, learning is like a kaleidoscope. If I take the idea of learning apart and set out its differentiated components, I find that the parts are of all sizes, shapes and colours. I can describe each separately without much trouble and can easily see how the various parts can be combined. Some ideas (patterns and colours) are repeated and reflected back on themselves in a variety of forms throughout the chapters of this book, just like the kaleidoscope.

For example, you may have noticed that the idea of "stress" occurs in several chapters. In Chapter Three, I talked about stress in relation to the body's arousal system; and in Chapter Four, I talked about how the brain down-shifts when the learner becomes distressed. The idea of stress is implied in other chapters as well. In Chapter Five, I implied that men and women are unlikely to learn effectively when asked to learn under conditions preventing or precluding them from making full use of their self-system, whether autonomous or relational.

Similarly, in Chapter Six, I suggested that the characteristics of physical learning preclude the productive learning of a new physical skill under time pressures. Skill learning requires practice; stress would interfere with the effective use of practice sessions. In Chapter Seven, the characteristics of spiritual learning suggest that when our ideas or experiences are adversely judged, we are unlikely to move beyond the limits of our self-system. Feeling judged usually leaves individuals feeling distressed. In Chapter Eight, we also found that Taylor (1987) included disorientation and confusion, two aspects of stress, as an integral part of the learning cycle.

We could trace other themes through the chapters. Some of these include:

- ❖ the differences between "self-directed"/autonomous and "other-connected"/relational learners or learning;
- ❖ the idea that learning is a constructive process in which the individual negotiates with others to make sense of experience and create meaning and knowledge;
- ❖ the idea that learning is as much a function of the learning environment as it is of the learner's characteristics;
- ❖ the idea that good facilitating involves matching facilitating strategies to learning strategies and so on.

For me however, the more interesting aspect of a kaleidoscope is that the characteristic shape and colour of the separate pieces matters much less than the combinations created as colours and shapes mingle.

The colours combine to form new colours and the various coloured pieces overlap each other to form new shapes —- colours and shapes could not have been predicted by an examination of the separate pieces of the kaleidoscope. In this chapter, I would like to address some themes emerging, not from an examination of the separate aspects of learning, but from seeing the combined colours and shapes in new ways. These themes are intended as practical advice for learners and facilitators.

THEMES FOR THE LEARNER

My themes for learners are ten:

1. Trust the process.
2. Stay open to new ideas and experiences.
3. Be prepared to take risks.
4. Enjoy the detours even if they are the result of non-successful endeavours.
5. Ask for help when you feel stuck, confused, anxious or upset.
6. Ask questions and think critically.
7. Reflect, reflect, reflect.
8. Share your ideas.
9. Have fun.
10. Take the time to facilitate the learning of others.

1. Trust the Process

It is not always essential to know where you are going in your learning or even what you are going to learn (although it helps), but it is essential to trust yourself as a learner and to put your faith in the learning process.

Learning will happen if

❖ you give the process enough time,

❖ you allow it to happen without placing unnecessary pressures on yourself or the process,

❖ you stay with the learner-centred approach and

❖ you trust your own brain, mind, body, emotions, self-system and spirit.

You may end up reaching a goal you had not originally intended, learning something you had not planned, but this goal may be even better than the original one.

Put another way, your brain and mind probably know more about how to learn
than you can ever know at a conscious level.
Whenever I attempt to control and direct my learning activities by replacing them with activities attempting
to consciously direct the process,
my learning becomes very limited and sometimes stops altogether.

Many learners, believing that analogical thinking is irrational, attempt to control their learning by using only logical, rational thinking. Competent, effective learning requires the involvement of both analytic and holistic cognitive styles. Your brain and mind know how to do this; so trust the process and let them get on with the learning in an integrated and synthesized manner.

However, you can exert some controls over the learning process. These controls include:

❖ refusing to accept the first answer which comes to mind, thereby thinking twice about ideas;

❖ refusing to judge yourself as incompetent if the learning takes longer than you planned or is not going as smoothly as you hoped;

❖ giving yourself permission to enjoy the process, even to have fun along the way.

2. Stay open to new ideas and experiences

The definition of learning being used in this book states:
Learning is a process of making sense of and giving meaning to life's experiences;
using these meanings in thinking, solving problems, making choices and decisions; and
acting in ways based on these choices and decisions as a means
for obtaining feedback to confirm or disconfirm meanings and choices.

An important assumption in this definition is that learning requires the learner to be continuously open to new experiences. These experiences are the sources of new information or ideas that could modify knowledge or meanings already developed. If ideas and experiences provide enough information, then variations on themes and patterns can emerge to assist in developing new meanings.

Lacking new ideas and experiences, the mind will behave as if it were *under-stimulated*, a condition possibly resulting in mental activities resembling those associated with distress or over-stimulation (see Chapter Three). In *over-stimulation*, the mind buckles under the onslaught of excessive information that cannot fit easily into the existing model of reality. Confused thinking is the result (Taylor, 1987). When under-stimulated, the mind invents ideas and images to fill the void.

Those who believe that they should never daydream, or
that invented ideas and images are the mark of mental ill-health and a form of disorientation,
will likely chastise themselves; and
in judging themselves in negative terms, they will stop learning.

At the same time do not expect to use all the information you gather from new ideas and experiences. When ideas and experiences are wholly new, you may be able to use only a small part. Rest assured that your mind will store the remaining information in memory for use at a later time, when you will be better able to make sense of it.

3. Be prepared to take risks

All learning activities carry some potential for confused thinking, anxiety about making changes, and apprehension about dealing with the unknown consequences of the learning. For this reason, competency in learning is always accompanied by a willingness to take risks such as looking and feeling foolish because you cannot perform a skill perfectly the first time, or feeling incompetent or "dumb" because you cannot express your thoughts in words.

As a graduate student, I recall one day walking through the halls muttering to myself because I felt upset. A professor asked me what was wrong. I told him that I was upset because I was on my way to a class and didn't understand the topic for discussion despite having studied all the readings. He laughed and reminded me that I was going to class for the express purpose of learning what it was I didn't already know, so I shouldn't get down on myself for not already knowing it!

As a student I realized that if I had already learned everything about adult education, there would be no point in continuing! Further, if I had known everything ahead of time, I would have allowed no room for a course leader to facilitate and extend my learning. Since I like to facilitate the learning of others, I decided I would give the course leader an opportunity to facilitate mine. Everyone needs a chance to shine, even the facilitator —- maybe even especially the facilitator.

Avoid seeing yourself as a failure just because you have not succeeded at a learning task.
In order to trust the process of learning,
you must also trust that you are capable of handling failure.

---

4. Enjoy the detours, even if they are the result of non-successful endeavours

If you do find yourself on a detour in the learning process, enjoy it. Remember that any plan for learning has options. It is not carved in stone and can be abandoned if you choose.

Remember also that as you embark on the learning journey, you are bringing your own unique perspective. If you get onto a detour in the planned learning process, you may be bringing personal meanings that have never been this way before. It is an opportunity to learn something totally new about yourself or to learn something no one else knows because no one with your experience has ever been on this particular detour. The sense you make of the events may lead to an important new perspective on existing knowledge.

I once wrote a lengthy paper on the development of my small learning group. The facilitator wrote back that he thought my ideas were excellent and had I read a particular author? When I read that author and found that my brilliant idea had been postulated by someone else about twenty years ago, I was mortified. However, the facilitator said I should congratulate myself for being as intelligent as a published author of note; and who knows, I might have come up with a new way to understand the development of small groups.

5. Ask for help when you feel stuck, confused, anxious or upset

Once you are feeling disoriented or confused, the way out of the confusion is to talk things over with someone else (Taylor, 1987). A good strategy is to allow yourself to ask for assistance. Many learners do not want to ask for help because they think they are supposed to be self-reliant and independent and this perception leaves them feeling like a fraud. Others do not ask for help because they don't want the person assisting them to solve the problem or even to offer good advice. McIntosh (1985) describes *feeling like a fraud as...*

> ...the feeling that in taking part in public life one has pulled the wool over others' eyes; that one is in the wrong place, and about to be found out; that there has been a colossal mistake in the selection and accreditation process which the rest of the world is about to discover...One feels apologetic, undeserving, anxious, tenuous, out-of-place, misread, phoney, uncomfortable, incompetent, dishonest, guilty (McIntosh 1985, p.1).

She suggests that feeling like a fraud is a two-edged sword: fraudulent feelings may be regrettable but they may also indicate an unwillingness to accept that having power or authority also means one has merit.

In learning situations, feeling like a fraud leads
to a situation in which the learner, feeling unable to ask for help,
may not obtain the necessary information to move forward in the learning process.

In asking for help, you do not want the assisting person to take over your learning. So protect yourself when asking for help. Explain to the assisting person that you want them to listen to you while you talk through a problem, or talk around a confusing issue. Ask them to reflect back to you what they have heard you say, without trying to solve the issue or name what it is that confuses you — a process which usually just increases the confusion.

If you say "I need help," the assisting person is likely to hear your request as a plea for a solution or for straightening out your thinking. Their solution may not work for your problem, and a better way to straighten your thinking is to talk through the issues out loud — even if the only person listening is yourself.

6. Ask questions about what you read and hear, and think critically

I have encountered students who believe that they are supposed to accept all statements and facts in print or that come from an expert without question; that they are supposed to answer questions, not ask them; and that they are certainly not supposed to question what an "expert" might have to say. This is the underside of the "feeling like a fraud" phenomenon. The underlying logic is: "If I, a learner, feel like a fraud, then experts must be authentic; and if experts are authentic, then I have no right to question what they know".

Learning to ask questions is difficult; but it is much more fun than answering them.
I like to ask what I refer to as "dumb questions" which are designed to help me obtain
the information I need to clarify some aspect of the topic under consideration.
I have found that by asking such questions,
I often open the way for others to ask similar types of questions.

Everyone can learn to ask questions and everyone is entitled to ask questions if their intent is to clarify the issue. Learning is never facilitated when questions are asked as a means of attacking the person to whom the question is addressed. I find that questions beginning with "Why?" are often used by the asker as a form of attack. Useful questions more often begin with what, how, where, when, how many, how often, how much, and the like. Questions also can be phrased as statements which begin "I don't understand..." or "Do you mean...?" or "The way I am understanding what you are saying is..."

Asking questions is the beginning of critical thinking, a process which attempts to identify underlying assumptions supporting the generalizations ideas, opinions, explanations, predictions, models, theories, and so on. Critical thinking is necessary if you, as the learner, wish to

❖ explore ideas further,
❖ challenge the experiential basis of ideas,
❖ expand your own knowledge, or
❖ change various aspects of your model of reality.

Without critical thinking you are doomed to be only a received knower for life.

7. Reflect, reflect, reflect

I believe strongly in reflection.
Looking back at what I have already done is
a means for understanding where I am now and where I might go next.

In Plato's *Apology* , Socrates tells us that the unexamined life is not worth living. Not looking back at your past experiences and what you have learned may work for a while. But if you don't look back, you are doomed to repeat the same mistakes over and over again.

The phrase "to learn from my mistakes" can mean never repeating a failure by never again trying the activity or event which led to it. The phrase could also mean examining how the mistake or failure occurred, and by modifying the related knowledge, skill or value, succeeding the next time. I like the second version of learning from my mistakes much better.

Some learners refuse to reflect because they claim they don't have time; others because they are afraid to confront their failures. Still others seem to believe that taking time to reflect on past experiences, may be perceived by others as unproductive. Such beliefs tend to be prevalent in workplaces where productivity is measured in terms of workers being seen as " doing something". Reflective activities require a certain amount of apparent inactivity which can be construed by some employers as non-productive or potentially threatening. I find that I can reflect and still appear productive by doing work which doesn't require mental effort — such as stuffing envelopes.

Reflection is a crucial key to learning. Without reflection, you will never know what you already know or can do. If you avoid reflecting on past behaviour, you may avoid confronting your failures, but you will also never know when you should be celebrating a success. So do yourself a favour. Reflect on your learning experiences as a means for sorting out successes from failures. Then learn from your failures and give yourself a pat on the back for your successes.

Steps for reflective learning

The process of reflective learning has a number of steps (Boyd & Fales, 1983) beginning with an inner discomfort, then moving on to

- ❖ identifying or clarifying the issue causing the discomfort;
- ❖ being open to new information from internal and external sources, while observing and taking in information from a variety of perspectives;
- ❖ allowing ideas to come together through integration and creative synthesis, without controlling the process or its outcomes;
- ❖ establishing connections between integrated ideas and the self-system and personal model of reality from the past; and
- ❖ deciding whether and how to act on the outcome of the reflective process in the future.

Ways to facilitate this process (Fales, MacKeracher & Vigoda, 1981) include:

- ❖ consciously paying attention to, and becoming aware of, day-to-day experiences through describing and recording these descriptions in suitable ways (keeping a journal, making notes, drawing, etc.);
- ❖ consciously paying attention to, and becoming aware of activities normally used to engage in reflection (driving a car, exercising, doing physically routine work, dreaming, etc.);
- ❖ increasing awareness of how experiences are turned into images, sounds and sensations through discussing how specific experiences are represented and stored in memory;
- ❖ becoming aware of significant current experiences and how these are or may be connected to past images, sounds and sensations;
- ❖ discovering the unspoken meanings we give to these connections through expressing these meanings out loud and sharing them with others; and
- ❖ considering how these meanings can be used in our future activities.

*The facilitator also needs to encourage learners to
take the time necessary to reflect and to
avoid judging reflective time as inactive or unproductive.*

8. Share your ideas

Learning is enhanced when you share your ideas.

Many learners are reluctant to share their ideas because they don't want others to be critical. That is, to think critically about such ideas. At its worst, "being critical" can involve attacking the ideas of others, a process not conducive to further learning. And when individuals whose ideas are being attacked perceive that their personhood is also being attacked, disconfirmed or devalued, they will almost certainly stop learning and may withdraw from others.

❖ If you don't understand someone else's ideas, ask them to talk more about it;

❖ if you think you understand their idea but want to be sure, paraphrase it back to them in your own words and with your own assumptions; and

❖ if you disagree, tell them "I don't agree because..." and then explain why.

Under no circumstances should you say something like, "You're really stupid if you believe that" or "You're confused." Such statements sound like an attack on the person rather than a disagreement with an idea.

As a listener, you are responsible for listening carefully to ideas proposed by others, whether learners or facilitators, and for responding to the idea rather than the person. On the other hand, if you are the one proposing the idea, you are responsible for trying to hear any critical comment, not as an attack on you personally, but either as a misunderstanding or a disagreement.

As a child, in response to my observations about the world around me, I was often asked, "Where'd you get a foolish idea like that?" For many years, this question echoed in my mind and heart as a statement that I was a fool as a person and that my ideas were unacceptable. I almost stopped relying on my own ideas, becoming instead very competent at receiving knowledge. Certainly I stopped sharing my "foolish ideas". It was later in an adult education program that I discovered my ideas were not just acceptable, they were even valued.

Sharing your ideas is risky. But if you don't, you may never find out which are unique, which may break new ground, or which may help others move forward in their learning. I tend to protect myself from very adverse criticism by prefacing my sharing with the admission that my ideas are half-baked at best. I find they are easiest to share in a learning environment based on mutual trust, an environment which Clinchy and Zimmerman (1985) describe as being like an informal conversation around the kitchen table over a cup of tea or coffee. A metaphorical "kitchen table" is the best place to share half-baked ideas.

Another way to share your ideas is to apply them in new settings. As learners, we have some responsibility for sharing the results of our learning with others. If you figure out how to build a better mouse trap, you need to share the mouse trap with those who need to rid their homes of mice.

9. Have fun

While you are learning, give yourself permission to have fun, to play, to use humour. In Chapter Four I pointed out that a good laugh is accompanied by synchronous activity in the two cerebral hemispheres, a process which makes learning more vivid, adds affect to whatever is learned, and makes the resulting knowledge easier to recall. Laughter, play and fun are aides to learning (Melamed, 1987; Wischnewski, 1883). Melamed (1987) describes play as a component of learning which:

❖ keeps learners open to new ideas and experiences,
❖ allows learners to be actively involved in their own learning process,
❖ stretches the limits of knowing,
❖ encourages and values learning from experience,
❖ supports holistic learning,
❖ involves intuitive or right hemisphere activity, and
❖ is empowering by encouraging transformative learning.

So enjoy your learning, and share the laughter with others.

10. Take time to facilitate the learning of others

*I discovered early in my career as an adult educator that
I learned the most when I facilitated the learning of others.
Nothing challenges my model of reality so much as having to describe it to someone else.*

As a brand-new secondary school teacher, I was assigned the responsibility of teaching botany to grade 13 students. While I had a sound background in zoology, I had never taken a course in botany. Throughout my first year, I kept one step ahead of my students through intensive reading and much angst. I learned a lot of botany, the knowledge is still with me today; but because of my anxiety, I was less sure about what my students learned. Students in adult education programs tell me that the topic they learn best is the one they have to research for a class presentation.

THEMES FOR THE FACILITATOR

My themes for facilitators are ten:

1. Carry a pair of binoculars.
2. Develop your own map.
3. Remember the three R's.
4. Be a responsive learner.
5. Facilitate both relational and autonomous learning.
6. Be passionate, enjoy yourself, cherish humour.
7. Think critically.
8. Self-reflect, self-reflect, self-reflect.
9. Engage in transformative learning.
10. Keep in mind that you are a model for learners whether you want to be or not.

1. Carry a pair of binoculars

No one can be conscious of all details of facilitating adult learning, or even of understanding all of one's own learning. When I engage in learning, whether for myself or in facilitating the learning of others, I try to keep a vision of what I am aiming for in the greater scheme of things. Schön (1971) calls such a vision a "projective image" or future focused image describing some future possibility. I continuously monitor my current activity by keeping that future focused image in view through the metaphorical binoculars I carry with me.

When I began as a facilitator of adult learning, my monitoring was conscious and tended to slow down my activities. But with practice, I learned to monitor my progress at some level below full consciousness. Now, as long as things progress as planned, my monitoring activities stay below consciousness. But when things go awry, a warning signal reminds me to deliberately start monitoring my current activities. When I have enough information to diagnose what has gone wrong, I can make a correction by changing my current activities. Sometimes I discover that my future focused image was wrong in the first place, but mostly I find that I have just gone off-track.

I have found that I need to think carefully about what my future focused image of learning or learners is by engaging in *preliminary planning*. This type of planning is important. Most planning involves establishing learning objectives, designing facilitating activities, and setting up assessment procedures.

Determining a future focused image is no different, but since many such images are unknown or hidden, the planning process needs something extra. You need to ask yourself a series of questions to determine the unarticulated goals you may be working toward unconsciously.

The questions also may bring answers which can become program goals or learning objectives. The type of questions I ask myself are:

1. What general long term goals of learning (in terms of knowledge, skills, strategies or values) do I assume are important for the learners to accomplish by the end of their program or in two or three years? What general long term goals do the learners desire for themselves? How am I accounting for any differences between my assumptions and their desires in my future focused imagery and planning?

2. What specific short term goals (in terms of knowledge, skills, strategies or values) do I have in mind for these learning activities (by the end of this course or program?) What specific short term goals do the learners have in mind for themselves? How am I accounting for any differences

between these two sets of goals in my future focused imagery and planning?

3. In what way are any short-term goals incompatible with any long term goals? What modifications need to be made in my future focused imagery or planned activities to ensure they are compatible?

For example, if I assume that the ultimate goal for learners is to become self-directed, then I must know how to encourage self-directedness in specific learning activities. I must know what 'self-directedness' means to them and whether they value its development as a long term goal as much as I do. I must know how skilled they are in being self-directed now, and whether these skills can be applied successfully in this specific learning context.

❖   If some learners do not value self-directness, how do I work with them? Do I require that they become self-directed?

❖   If self-directedness is an important goal for all of us, should I assume that learners are equally skilled in self-directed learning? If some learners do not have all the necessary skills, then how do I modify planned activities to assist them to acquire these?

Future focused images could relate to content to be learned, learning activities to be used, or desired outcomes. I recall one class session in which I suddenly became aware that I was leading students down a garden path of my own choosing. In fact, I discovered I had a hidden agenda to "teach a lesson" and they were not responding the way I expected. Once I realized what I was doing, I gave it up both as an activity which made no sense in terms of the course objectives and as a poor, even punitive facilitating strategy.

If this goal is really important, then I must design activities to lead to it over the duration of the program. If, however, I decide this goal is important for me but not for the learners, then I must ask myself why I am imposing self-directedness as a future focused image on each learner who comes into my programs and courses. It may be an important goal for some, but not for others.

I have found since, that
whenever I want to teach someone a lesson,
I may need to learn a lesson myself.

So carry a pair of binoculars and keep your eye on your own future focused image of what the learning-facilitating interaction is intended to accomplish.

2. Develop your own map

*Planning is absolutely crucial to good facilitating,
even if you hope to make your facilitating strategies look spontaneous.*

I have found that I can be more spontaneous and creative when I have a plan than when I have none. When I have a plan, I can abandon it at my choosing. When I have no plan, I lose my flexibility since I don't really know what I am trying to accomplish. I do not feel as free about abandoning activities planned by someone else since I don't know what each was intended to accomplish.

A good plan is like a map and a good map is an important tool to carry on any journey. The map tells you the shortest, easiest route to your destination and which parts of the territory to stay away from — like swamps and briar patches. A good map will also tell you if certain detours are likely to be interesting or whether they are dead-ends. So make a plan for facilitating, and have a back-up activity for each option just in case. As the facilitator, you will enjoy the journey much more with a map than without one.

3. Remember the three R's

*Roby Kidd, the noted Canadian adult educator,
admonishes facilitators to remember the three R's of good facilitating (Kidd, 1960).
These three R's are not reading, 'riting and 'rithmetic but
Relevancy, Relationship and Responsibility.*

Relevancy can be understood in terms of how the content relates to the learners' current and future life. If the content is directly relevant to some aspects of what they currently do, then learners are more likely to be motivated to look for connections and develop new meanings. Kidd comments that "without relevance, there will not be the kind of engagement that constitutes education" (Kidd 1960, p.2). If the content is not directly relevant to the learners in some way, then the facilitator must find a way to make it so through the use of metaphors and examples.

The learning process must also bear some relevancy to processes familiar to learners. If the learning process is new to learners, then facilitators must take time to explain why certain learning activities are being used.

Relationship can have two meanings. Where relevancy refers to *connections* between learning activities and the learner's present and future needs, *relationship* refers to how knowledge from past experiences connects to present learning. Relationship also refers to the learner's need to establish a *sense of belonging* within the social aspects of the learning environment by developing connections to other learners and to the facilitator, and using these as a basis for further learning.

A good facilitator, aware of both meanings of relationship, draws on past experiences, knowledge and skills of learners whenever possible and actively promotes the development of inter-learner and learner-facilitator connections.

Responsibility refers to our *obligations* to learn, to understand, to question, to undertake new inquiries, and to use what we have learned in our homes, our workplaces and our communities.

Good facilitators encourage a questioning attitude and critical thinking, especially when the critique is directed to them; and provide opportunities for learners to think about applying new ideas beyond the learning context. Facilitators have a responsibility to provide emotionally and physically safe environments for learners to learn and test new ideas and plans.

4. Be a responsive learner

Responsibility has a second meaning if we understand it to mean the ability to be responsive. Facilitators have an obligation to themselves and to the learners to be responsive to the needs of individual learners and learning communities. Being responsive requires that the facilitator be a learner too.

*Perhaps the most important thing that
facilitators can do, is to
consistently see themselves as learners.*

As facilitators, our tasks are to learn:

❖ about the learners we work with,

❖ more about the content area in which we have some expertise, and

❖ about the processes of facilitating and learning.

One aspect of our learning is the need to "flex" to the learners. In Chapter Eight we discussed Hunt's model for matching the facilitating process to the learning process and in Chapter Two we discussed Lewin's B-P-E model for matching facilitator behaviours to learner characteristics as one aspect of the learning environment. Responsiveness requires the facilitator to develop future focused imagery and flexible plans and to operate from a set of known and examined assumptions.

Roby Kidd created ten commandments which he suggested adult educators keep in mind in everything they do. The eighth of these commandments (Kidd 1973a, p. 306) states:

*"Thou shalt have no universal remedies nor expect miracles."
We could expand this commandment to state:
...nor use just one facilitating or learning style.*

To adopt this commandment and become more responsive, we must all learn to be multi-skilled and flexible by developing a range of facilitating strategies suitable for a variety of different learning styles and needs.

5. Facilitate both relational and autonomous learning
Kidd's fifth commandment (1973a, pp 306-307) states:

"Thou shalt help everyone become on the one hand, sensitive and compassionate, and also tough-minded."
A restatement of this commandment might be:
Thou shalt try to help learners become on the one hand, interdependent and empathetic learners, and
on the other hand, independent, critical and tough-minded thinkers.

In Chapter Five we considered differences among learners, particularly differences based on the gender-related development of self-concept. We found that both men and women develop some aspects of an autonomous as well as a relational self, with men tending to emphasize the autonomous self and women tending to emphasize the relational self.

These different self-concepts have important effects on learning. Many women prefer relationally-based learning involving discussions with others, while many men prefer autonomously-based learning involving self-direction. Kidd's admonition suggests that we need to develop a sense and sensibility about facilitating both types of learners.

6. Be passionate, enjoy yourself, cherish humour
Kidd's ninth commandment (1973a, p. 307) states:

"Cherish a sense of humour which may save you from becoming shocked, depressed or complacent."
I would like to add:...let your excitement and passion show.

Learners like to know that their facilitators (or teachers, instructors, trainers, counsellors, advisors and the like) feel enthusiasm and passion for them, for the content to be learned, and for the learning processes and activities to be used. When the learning-facilitating interaction involves a sense of well-being, the entire enterprise is enhanced. So do not be afraid to let your passion show.

In the process, you need to learn useful ways to direct your frustration into constructive activities. Never get angry with an individual learner in front of others. If you must let a learner know you are angry, do so privately; and always provide descriptive, non-judgmental and positively constructive feedback.

Learn to make positive uses of your own humour when you are facilitating. If you think that you have lost your sense of humour (everyone has one) then begin rediscovering it right now by promising yourself that you will find something humorous to laugh about at least once a day. Laugh at yourself, laugh with others, enjoy the moment and smile.

7. Think critically

Thinking critically is essential for understanding how a society and its learning communities organize themselves to enable or constrain learning and how an individual's learning is inexorably coupled to the interactive social contexts and relationships in which it takes place.

Rather than emphasizing the nature of individual learning processes, social learning theory emphasizes the nature of all the social processes involved in learning and facilitating. Two of these processes are socialization and enculturation. In socialization, individuals learn acceptable knowledge, skills and values for their anticipated and actual roles and relationships (Brim & Ryff, 1980). In enculturation, individuals learn the language, symbols and behavioural nuances of their culture (Barer-Stein, 1993).

In Chapter One I wrote that learning is non-normative and that within the same activity, what is learned by one differs from what is learned by another.

The consequences of socialization and enculturation are very strong and all members of a social group learn to perceive reality in similar ways because of the homogenizing effect of their shared social institutions, language and culture.

Hall (1976) tells us that we are our culture — who we think we are is constrained by what our culture encourages us to think we are. Any possibilities beyond these constraints normally lie beyond our conscious awareness and perception. Within these constraints we develop a view of reality which is distorted in favour of that espoused by the dominant group. As we have already seen in Chapter Five, the dominant view in Euro-American societies is based on the experience and knowledge of white, middle to upper class males. The experience and knowledge of non-whites, members of the working class, the poor and females tend to be subordinated to the dominant view and even perceived as irrelevant and sometimes deviant.

Default assumptions

Distortions in our shared model of reality often are built into the language itself. For example, traditional use of masculine nouns and pronouns to refer to a generalized person results in some very strange sentences such as, "Man is the only mammal who does not always suckle his young" (Hofstadter 1985, p.145). Hofstadter describes the use of masculine terms as a "default assumption", as something we assume unless the opposite is clearly specified. For example, if we talk about a surgeon, the default assumption is that the surgeon is male unless we specify a "female surgeon". The same holds true for terms which are assumed to refer to a female; a nurse is female unless we specify that he is a "male nurse".

Relying on default assumptions enables us to manage in a very complex world. In our daily lives, we do not take the time required to think critically about exceptions to our default assumptions or about the distortions in our personal model of reality.

You probably didn't take the time to consider, for example, whether or not the salt shaker you used at lunch might have been filled with something other than salt. As a facilitator, you may not have given much consideration to any of your assumptions about the way adults ought to learn — default assumptions that get many facilitators into trouble. To question our default assumptions or model of reality too frequently may result in unsettling disconfirming experiences, possibly threatening our sense of personal identity. Yet, our default assumptions are only one type of distortion which profoundly affects how we learn and facilitate.

Social learning theory

Social learning theory assumes that all societal institutions and social groups create interactive learning environments which enable or constrain the learning of individuals and which vary from miseducative to educative, autocratic to democratic, enabling to constraining. The essential processes operating within these shared learning environments are those which support interpersonal communication and distribute power among the learners involved. This leads to equitable opportunities for participating and for having individual rights to have ideas heard, accepted, validated and valued by others.

To examine how our taken-for granted default assumptions, language and culture, values, beliefs and knowledge limit our learning and facilitating, we must

❖ think critically about them,

❖ identify their limitations and distortions, and

❖ hopefully transform them.

The cognitive or reflective component of critical thinking is ineffective without a subsequent practical or action component.

Critical theory

Critical theory examines how our shared belief systems (democracy, productivity), societal structures (e.g., patriarchal families, hierarchical organizations), and cultural legacies (e.g., language, symbols) have limited and continue to limit not only the development of our individual and collective human potential, but also our understanding of groups with alternate belief systems, societal structures and cultural legacies.

Critical theory emerged from German intellectual thought typified by such writers as Immanuel Kant, Wilhelm Hegel, Karl Marx, and Jürgen Habermas. Kant and Hegel were philosophers who wrote about education as a secondary interest. Marx wrote about the dynamics of social order and encouraged his followers to take collective action to correct existing social conditions. Habermas placed learning at the centre of his understanding of critical theory and described knowledge as the outcome of human activity motivated by three natural needs and interests, or knowledge-constitutive interests, which guide the way knowledge is created (Carr & Kemmis, 1986):

1. Technical knowledge enables control over the conditions of one's existence; takes the form of descriptions, explanations and predictions leading to control over one's own actions and over the environment; and lies in the *instrumental domain* of learning.

2. Practical knowledge enables individuals to understand and interact with others; to make sense of the symbolic forms through which we communicate and of the meanings constituting our shared social reality. Such knowledge is not reducible to instrumental knowledge and lies in the *communicative domain* of learning.

3. Emancipatory knowledge is grounded in the human capacity to think reflectively and critically about the nature and consequences of both *technical-instrumental* and *practical-communicative* knowledge and to transform them by becoming aware of their distortions and limitations.

---

*The **instrumental** and **communicative domains of learning** are necessary to our daily functioning whether as self-directed and autonomous individuals or in cooperative and collaborative groups. The **transformative domain** is necessary if we are to free ourselves from the constraining influences limiting our development as individuals and as learning communities.*

Jack Mezirow (1995, 1991) has extended our understanding of emancipatory knowledge by describing the nature of transformative learning. Mezirow's theory, outlined briefly in Chapter One, keeps the focus on the learner and implies that the consequences of adult learning are, for the most part, politically neutral. Mezirow (1995) describes two types of transformative learning:

1. We reflect critically on our knowledge and ways of learning thereby transforming knowledge and ways of learning as *meaning schemes.*

2. We reflect critically on the premises or taken-for-granted assumptions underlying what we know (knowledge, beliefs) and how we know it (strategies, styles, processes); by transforming these premises, we also transform our *perspectives or model of reality.*

Michael Welton (1995, 1991) directs our attention to the importance of the communicative domain of learning. Individual development proceeds satisfactorily only in learning communities which enable

❖ non-distorted communication practices,

❖ equitable opportunities to engage in uncoerced interaction with others, and

❖ relationships based on equal empowerment among the actors.

Welton reminds us that the fate of education is tied to the quality of interchanges between the individual and the social and cultural contexts within which each lives and works.

Michael Collins (1990) points out that as facilitators, we cannot pretend that we have ferreted out all distortions and taken-for-granted assumptions in our knowledge and model of reality. Further, we need to "attend to our own education, especially as it pertains to pedagogical practices" (1995, p.75). Collins advocates becoming aware of how our facilitating practices can be examples of an "increasingly over-managed society and of the fractured communities depicted in [our] critical theorizing" which we are ostensibly working to heal and unify (p.75).

As facilitators, therefore, we need to engage continuously in critical thinking about what we are doing, how and why we are doing it in terms of both our work with individual learners and our concerns about the learning communities in which we and the learners must participate.

8. Self reflect, self-reflect, self-reflect

An essential component of critical thinking is reflection and self-reflection. While reflection allows us to reconsider what we know and how we know it, self-reflection asks that we critically examine our own behaviour.

Argyris and Schön (1974; Schön, 1987) encourage us to become reflective practitioners. They recommend that we critically examine specific cases of our own professional practice. The method they recommend for examining a critical incident or case is:

1. Divide a journal page in half vertically.
2. On the right side, describe specifically what happened, who was involved, what was said, and what the outcomes were.

3. On the left side, write out what you felt about that occurrence, thought about but did not say, wanted to but didn't do, and what outcomes were desired but did not occur.
4. Then compare what you have written on the two sides of the page and think critically and honestly about what limited your behaviour.

This process can help transform knowledge and strategies, and may also help transform the premises which guide how we facilitate and the perspectives (model of reality) which inform our ways of being and doing.

9. Engage in transformational learning

Deliberately engaging in critical thinking and self-reflection is potentially disconfirming, resulting in some anxiety and confusion.
However, such possibilities should not deter you from engaging in transformational learning. You can learn to manage the anxiety and confusion.

I try to set aside some time each week to reconsider all the disconfirming events and dysfunctional strategies that have recently accumulated. I have found that in any given time, most of the facilitating glitches and problems seem to relate to the same underlying issue. When I can identify that underlying issue, I can often resolve several problems simultaneously. So each week I reconsider everything. I try to avoid panic if I cannot identify the underlying issue and find that writing out my concerns in a journal is helpful to put anxiety behind me. I continue with my usual strategies and behaviours but put myself on mental alert for future related evidence. Sometimes two or three months go by before I recognize the issue which has eluded me; usually I need to talk over what has been happening with one of my colleagues. Once the underlying issue is identified, I always wonder why I didn't see it earlier. Then I get on with making changes in my facilitating strategies.

The process of transformative learning is slow.
Unlike learning a new skill or committing new information to memory, it does not occur at will and there is frequently no immediate evidence of its occurrence.

My practical experience tells me that transformative learning occurs in two ways:

1. The relatively small transformations in the details of my facilitating knowledge and strategies seem to occur every two or three months, often after a seemingly endless struggle with the details.
2. The larger transformations seem to occur spontaneously after several years of collecting miscellaneous ideas, experiences and small transformations which, when they occur may appear to have no relevance to each other. Then one day I will become aware that I have changed the way I look at the world and the way I see myself in that world.

The small, effortful transformations seem to be what Mezirow (1991) refers to as *transformations of knowledge* (content) *and strategies* (processes) which daily guide my facilitating behaviours. The large, apparently effortless transformations seem to be what Mezirow refers to as *perspective transformation.*

If you are attempting to engage in transformational learning,
don't chastise yourself if the small changes do not occur as quickly as you want them to occur.
Trust the process. The transformations will happen if
you keep reflecting on what you are doing, keep an open mind and be on the lookout for
new ways to make sense of your experience.

I recommend that you try not to force the large transformations to occur. All you can do is put the information into your learning system and then let all those multiple processing channels — including all the emotional, cognitive, social, physical and spiritual components of learning discussed throughout this book — go to work on your behalf while you get on with your daily life.

10. Keep in mind that you are a model for learners whether you want to be or not

For many facilitators, discovering that they are serving as a model for learners with whom they work is a potentially disconfirming experience. I initially rebelled at the idea; I didn't want to be a model for anyone. Then I realized that being a model was not a bad thing as long as I kept thinking critically, reflecting regularly on my own behaviour and knowledge, and continued to learn for my own benefit rather than because I thought it would benefit someone else. As long as I stay consistent and true to my own nature, I can be a congruent model for others without becoming self-conscious about my effect on them.

The first and last of Kidd's ten commandments inform us how we can be models for learners (1973a, pp. 306-307):

Thou shalt never try to make another human being exactly like thyself; one is enough. Thou shalt remember the sacredness and dignity of thy calling, and at the same time, "thou shalt not take thyself too damned seriously."

NOTES

CHAPTER 1

Note 1 Many adult educators like to avoid using terms such as "teacher" or "instructor" since these connote either highly directive behaviours or are viewed as being appropriate for pedagogical roles but not androgogical roles. To reduce complexities of using multiple terms such as "teacher/facilitator" and to avoid aggravating those who perceive words such as "teacher" as connoting ideas with which they do not agree, I have chosen to use the term "facilitator" to refer to those who roles include assisting adults with learning activities and "facilitating behaviours" or "facilitating activities" to describe their behaviours or activities while functioning in these roles. The reader should understand that the term "facilitator" also includes teachers, instructors, trainers, counsellors, planners, designers and the like.

Note 2 The idea of a "personal model or reality" is also described in the literature as a set of personal constructs (Candy, 1987; Kelly, 1955), a representational map (O'Connor & Seymour, 1990) and an evolving self-organizing system (Jantsch, 1980).

CHAPTER 3

Note 3 As an example of multiple processing: in learning about group development, the information the learner is processing might be obtained through reading theory, through observing and reflecting on the developmental sequence observed in group sessions, through listening to others talk about their experiences, through self-reflection on past experience, through encounters with personal descriptions in novels or films, and through many other directly or indirectly relevant experiences.

CHAPTER 4

Note 4 Over the years I have accumulated many interesting "facts" about how things work, but I rarely remember to keep a bibliographical reference for each. The key references for this and other facts presented here are unavailable.

CHAPTER 8

Note 5 A new instrument has been developed, called P.E.T. or Professional Effectiveness Technologies, which assesses both psychological type and provides information which integrates these types with responses to the learning environment (Dunn & Dunn, 1977), the activities of Kolb's learning cycle, Kolb's learning styles, and social interaction styles (Fuhrmann & Jacobs, 1980). The instrument has not yet been evaluated in the adult education literature.

PERMISSIONS

**Grateful acknowledgement
is made for permission to reprint quotes and/or information from the following:**

EXPERIENTIAL LEARNING: EXPERIENCE AS THE SOURCE by Kolb, David A., ©1984,
Adapted by permission of Prentice-Hall, Inc., Upper Saddle River , NJ
Excerpt from BETWEEN PSYCHOLOGY AND EDUCATION by David E. Hunt
and Edmund V. Sullivan,
©1974 by Holt, Rinehart and Winston, Inc., reprinted by permission of the publisher.
LEARNING TO TEACH, TEACHING TO LEARN by D.J. Clandinin, A. Davies, P. Hogan
and B. Kennard, ©1993
with permission of the publisher, Teacher's College Press, New York.
PERSONALITY TYPES: A MODERN SYNTHESIS by Alan Miller ©1991
with permission of the publisher, The University of Calgary Press, Calgary AB.
APPRECIATING ADULTS LEARNING edited by David Boud and Virginia Griffin ©1987
with permission of the publisher, Kogan Page Ltd., London UK.
With special thanks to Marilyn Taylor for permission to use drawings from her THESIS and the labels from her chapter in
Boud & Griffin's APPRECIATING ADULTS LEARNING ©1987.
WORKS IN PROGRESS NO. 12: THE DEVELOPMENT OF WOMEN'S SENSE OF SELF
by Jean Baker Miller
©1984 with kind permission of the publisher, The Stone Centre, Wellesley College, Wellesley, MA.
WORKS IN PROGRESS NO.18: FEELING LIKE A FRAUD by Peggy McIntosh ©1985
with kind permission of the publisher, The Stone Center, Wellesley College, Wellesley, MA.
HOW THE BRAIN WORKS by Leslie A. Hart ©1975, with kind permission of the publishers, Harpercollins, NY.
PHILOSOPHICAL FOUNDATIONS OF ADULT EDUCATION Second Edition by John L. Elias
and Sharan B. Merriam, ©1995
with permission of the publishers, Krieger Publishing Co., Malabar, FL.
LEARNING STYLES by James Keefe,©1987, with permission of the publisher, National Association of Secondary School
Principals, Reston VA. For more information about NASSP programs and services, call 703-860-0200 or 800-253-7746.
From the TRANSFORMATIONS OF CONSCIOUSNESS, ©1986 reprinted by arrangement with
Shambhala Publications, Inc. 300 Massachusetts Avenue, Boston MA 02115.
From the THE TRIARCHIC MIND by Robert J. Sternberg ©1988 by Robert J. Sternberg.
Used by permission of Viking Penguin, a division of Penguin Books USA Inc.
Excerpt from TEXTBOOK OF PSYCHOLOGY Third Edition by Donald O. Hebb ©1972
by Holt, Rinehart and Winston, Inc.,reprinted by permission of the publisher.
Messick, Samuel, "Personality Consistencies in Cognition and Creativity." p. 14. In S. Messick & Associates.
INDIVIDUALITY IN LEARNING: IMPLICATIONS FOR HUMAN DEVELOPMENT.
©by Jossey-Bass Inc., Publishers. Code 7609.
Ferro, Trenton R. "The Influence of Affective Processing in Education and Training," excerpt as submitted
from p. 26. In D.D. Flannery (ed.), APPLYING COGNITIVE LEARNING THEORY TO ADULT LEARNING.
New Directions for Adult Continuing Education, No. 59 ©1993 by Jossey-Bass Inc., Publishers.
Josselson, Ruthellen. THE SPACE BETWEEN US: EXPLORING THE DIMENSIONS OF HUMAN RELATIONSHIPS,
excerpt as submitted from p. 1 ©1992 by Jossey-Bass Inc., Publishers.
Candy, Philip C. SELF-DIRECTION FOR LIFELONG LEARNING: A COMPREHENSIVE GUIDE TO THEORY
AND PRACTICE, excerpts as submitted from pp. 125 and 130.
©1991 by Jossey-Bass Inc., Publishers. Code 9104.
Baxter Magolda, Marcia B. KNOWING AND REASONING IN COLLEGE: GENDER-RELATED PATTERNS
IN STUDENTS' INTELLECTUAL DEVELOPMENT. Table 2.1, p. 30.
©1992 by Jossey-Bass Inc., Publishers. Code 9264.
Hunt, David E. BEGINNING WITH OURSELVES, pp. 148–50, p. 156 and 157. Cambridge MA: Brookline Books.

BIBLIOGRAPHY

Abbey, D. S., Hunt, D. E. & Weiser, J. C. (1985) Variations on a theme by Kolb: A new perspective for understanding counselling and supervision.**The Counselling Psychologist, 13,** 477-501.

Adams, J. D. (1980) **Understanding and managing stress: A book of readings.** San Diego CA: University Associates.

Apps, J. (1973) **Toward a working philosophy of adult education.** Syracuse NY: Syracuse University, Publications in Continuing Education.

Arenberg, D. (1994) Aging and adult learning in the laboratory. In J. D. Sinnott (Ed.), **Interdisciplinary handbook of adult lifespan learning** (pp. 351-370). Westport CN: Greenwood Press.

Arends, R., Hersh, R. & Turner, J. (1978) Inservice education and the 6 o'clock news. **Oregon School Study Council, 21**(4).

Argyris, C. & Schön, D. A. (1974) **Theory in practice: Increasing professional effectiveness.** San Francisco: Jossey-Bass.

Arlin, P. K. (1986) Problem finding and young adult cognition. In R. Mines & K. S. Kitchener (Eds.), **Adult cognitive development: Methods and models** (pp. 22-32). New York: Praeger.

Baltes, P. B., Reese, H. W. & Lipsitt, L. P. (1980) Life-span developmental psychology. **Annual Review of Psychology, 31,** 65-110.

Barer-Stein, T.(1993) Culture in the classroom. In T. Barer-Stein & J.A. Draper (Eds.) **The craft of teaching adults** (2nd edition, pp. 145-164). Toronto ON : Culture Concepts Inc.

Barker, J. A. (1993) **Paradigms: The business of discovering the future.** New York: HarperCollins.

Basseches, M. (1984) **Dialectical thinking and adult development.** Norwood NJ: Ablex Publishing.

Bateson, G. (1972) **Steps to an ecology of mind.** New York: Ballantine Books.

Baum, G. (1978) "Adult education as a political enterprise". Address to the Alumni of the Department of Adult Education, Ontario Institute for Studies in Education, Toronto ON.

Baxter Magolda, M. (1992) "Knowing and reasoning in college". Address to the Alumni of the Department of Adult Education, Ontario Institute for Studies in Education. Toronto ON.

Belenky, M. F., Clinchy, B. M., Goldberger, N. R. & Tarule, J. M. (1986) **Women's ways of knowing: The development of self, voice and mind.** New York: Basic Books Inc.

Benne, K. D. (1964) History of the T-group in the laboratory setting. In L. P. Bradford, J. R. Gibb & K. D. Benne (Eds.), **T-group and laboratory method: Innovation in re-education** (pp. 80-135). New York: John Wiley & Sons.

Berg, C. A., Klaczynski, P. A., Calderone, K. S. & Strough, J. (1994) Adult age differences in cognitive strategies: Adaptive or deficient? In J. D. Sinnott (Ed.) **Interdisciplinary handbook of adult lifespan learning** (pp. 371-388). Westport CN: Greenwood Press.

Bergman, S. (1991) **Work in progress, no. 48. Men's psychological development: A relational perspective.** Wellesley MA: Wellesley College, The Stone Center.

Birren, J. E. & Bengtson, V. L. (Eds.) (1988) **Emergent theories of aging.** New York: Springer Publishing.

Birren, J. E. & Deutchman, D. E. (1991) **Guided autobiography groups for older adults.** Baltimore MD: John Hopkins University Press.

Birren, J. E. & Schaie, K. W. (Eds.) (1977) **Handbook of aging** (2nd edition). New York: Van Nostrand Reinhold.

Block, J. W. & Anderson, L. W. (1975) **Mastery learning in classrooms.** New York: Macmillan.

Bogen, J. E. (1977) Some educational aspects of hemispheric specialization. In M. C. Wittrock (Ed.) **The human brain** (pp. 133-152). Englewood Cliffs NJ: Prentice-Hall.

Bonham, L. A. (1991) Guglielmino's Self-Directed Learning Readiness Scale: What does it measure? **Adult Education Quarterly, 41** (2), 92-99.

Bortner, R. W. (Ed.) (1974) **Adults as learners.** University Park, PA: Pennsylvania State University, Institute for the Study of Human Development (ERIC Document ED 106 462).

Boshier, R. (1975) Behavior modification and contingency management in a graduate adult education program. **Adult Education, 26** (1), 16-31.

Boud, D. & Griffin, V. (Eds.) (1987) **Appreciating adults learning: From the learners' perspective.** London UK: Kogan Page.

Boud, D., Keough, R. & Walker, D. (Eds.) (1985) **Reflection: Turning experience into learning.** London UK: Kogan Page.

Boyd, E. M. & Fales, A. W. (1983) Reflective learning: Key to learning from experience. **Journal of Humanistic Psychology, 23** (2), 99-117.

Brammer L. M. & Abrego, P. J. (1981) Intervention strategies for coping with transitions. **The Counseling Psychologist, 9** (2), 19-35.

Brandt, B. L., Farmer, J. A. & Buckmaster, A. (1993) Cognitive apprenticeship approach to helping adults learn. In D. D. Flannery (Ed.) **Applying cognitive learning theory to adult learning.** New Directions for Adult and Continuing Education, vol.59 (pp.69-78). San Francisco: Jossey-Bass.

Brim, O. G. (1968) Adult socialization. In J. Clausen (Ed.), **Socialization and Society.** (pp.182-226). Boston MA: Little, Brown & Co.

Brim, O. G. & Wheeler, S. (1966) **Socialization after childhood: Two essays.** New York: John Wiley & Sons.

Brim, O. G. & Ryff, C. D. (1980) On the properties of life events. In P. B. Baltes & O. G. Brim (Eds.) **Life-span development and behavior** (volume 3, pp. 367-388). New York: Academic Press.

Brookfield, S. D. (1987) **Developing critical thinkers: Challenging adults to explore alternative ways of thinking and acting.** San Francisco: Jossey-Bass.

Brown, B. (1980) **Supermind.** New York: Harper & Row.

Brundage, D. & MacKeracher, D. (1980) **Adult learning principles and their application to program planning.** Toronto ON: Ontario Ministry of Education.

Bruner, J. (1986) **Actual minds, possible worlds.** Cambridge, MA: Harvard University Press.

Burge, E. J. (1993) Connectiveness and responsiveness. In **Feminist pedagogy and women-friendly perspectives in distance education** (pp. 86-102). Paper presented at the International WIN Working Conference, 10-13 June 1993. Umeå, Sweden: Umeå University, Women's Studies Center.

Buzan, T. & Buzan, B. (1995) **The mind map book: Radiant thinking** (Revised edition). London UK: BBC Books.

Caffarella, R. S. & O'Donnell, J. M. (1988) Research in self-directed learning: Past, present, and future trends. In H. B. Long and Associates, **Self directed learning: Application and theory** (pp. 39-61). Athens GA: University of Georgia, Adult Education Department.

Candy, P. C. (1987) Evolution, revolution or devolution: Increasing learner-control in the instructional setting. In D. Boud & V. Griffin (Eds.) **Appreciating adults learning: From the learners' perspective** (pp. 159-178). London UK: Kogan Page.

Candy, P. C. (1990) How people learn to learn. In R. H. Smith and Associates, **Learning to learn across the life span.** San Francisco: Jossey-Bass.

Candy, P. C. (1991) **Self-direction for lifelong learning.** San Francisco: Jossey-Bass.

Carr, W. & Kemmis, S. (1986) **Becoming critical: Education, knowledge and action research.** London UK: The Falmer Press.

Cawley, R., Miller & Milligan. (1976) Cognitive styles and the adult learner. **Adult Education, 26** (2), 101-116.

Chickering, A. W. & Reisser, L. (1993) **Education and identity** (2nd edition). San Francisco: Jossey-Bass.

Clinchy, B. & Zimmerman, C. (1985) **Work in progress, no.19. Growing up intellectually: Issues for college women.** Wellesley MA: Wellesley College, The Stone Center.

Coleman, J. S. (1976) Differences between experiential and classroom learning. In M. Keeton and Associates, **Experiential learning: Implications of cognitive style and creativity for human development** (pp. 49-61). San Francisco: Jossey-Bass.

Collett, D. J. (1990) Learning-to-learn needs for adult basic education. In R. M. Smith and Associates, **Learning to learn across the life span** (pp. 247-266). San Francisco: Jossey-Bass.

Collins, A., Brown, J. S. & Newman, S. E. (1989) Cognitive apprenticeship: Teaching the crafts of reading, writing, and mathematics. In L. B. Resnick (Ed.) **Knowing, learning and instruction: Essays in honor of Robert Glaser** (pp. 453-494). Hillsdale NJ: Lawrence Erlbaum Associates.

Collins, M. (1995) Critical commentaries on the role of the adult educator: From self-directed learning to postmodernist sensibilities. In M. R. Welton (Ed.) **In defense of the lifeworld: Critical perspectives on adult learning** (pp. 71-97). Albany NY: State University of New York Press.

Collins, M. (1990) **Adult education as vocation: A critical role for the adult educator.** New York: Routledge.

Combs, A. W. (1974) Humanistic approach to learning in adults. In R. W. Bortner (Ed.) **Adults as learners** (pp. 51-62). University Park PA: Pennsylvania State University, Institute for the Study of Human Development. (ERIC Document ED 106 462).

Connelly, F. M. & Clandinin, D. J. (1990) Stories of experience and narrative inquiry. **Educational Researcher, 19**(5), 2-14.

Cranton, P. (1989) **Planning instruction for adult learners.** Toronto ON: Wall & Thompson.

Cranton, P. (1994) **Understanding and promoting transformative learning: A guide for educators of adults.** San Francisco: Jossey-Bass.

Cropley, A. J. (1977) **Lifelong education: A psychological analysis.** Toronto ON: Pergamon Press.

Cross, K. P. (1976) **Accent on learning: Improving instruction and reshaping the curriculum.** San Francisco: Jossey-Bass.

Curry, L. (1983) An organization of learning style theory and constructs. In L. Curry (Ed.) **Learning style in continuing medical education.** (pp. 115-123). Ottawa ON: Canadian Medical Association.

Delahaye, B. L., Limerick, D. C. & Hearn, G. (1994) The relationship between andragogical and pedagogical orientations and the implication for adult learning. **Adult Education Quarterly,** 44 (4), 187-200.

Denis, M. & Richter, I. (1987) Learning about intuitive learning: Moose-hunting techniques. In D. Boud & V. Griffin (Eds.) **Appreciating adults learning: From the learners' perspective.** London UK: Kogan Page.

DiVesta, F. J. (1974) Information processing in adult learners. In R. W. Bortner (Ed.), **Adults as learners** (pp. 81-104). University Park: PA: Pennsylvania State University, Institute for the Study of Human Development. (ERIC Document ED 106 462)

Dowd, J. J. (1980) **Stratification among the aged.** Monterey CA: Brooks/Cole Publishing.

Draper, J. A. (1993) Valuing what we do as practitioners. In T. Barer-Stein & J. A. Draper (Eds.) **The craft of teaching adults** (2nd edition, pp. 55-67). Toronto ON: Culture Concepts Inc.

Dunn, R. & Dunn, K. (1977) How to diagnose learning styles. **Instructor, 87,** 123-144.

Edwards, B. (1979) **Drawing on the right side of the brain.** Los Angeles: J. P. Tarcher.

Eichler, M. (1988) **Non-sexist research methods: A practical guide.** Boston: Allen & Unwin.

Elias, J. L. & Merriam, S. B. (1995) **Philosophical foundations of adult education** (2nd edition). Malabar, FL: Krieger Publishing.

Engler, J. (1986) Therapeutic aims of psychotherapy and meditation: Developmental stages in the representation of self. In K. Wilber, J. Engler & D. P. Brown, **Transformations of consciousness: Conventional and contemplative perspectives of development** (pp. 17-51). Boston MA: Shambhala.

Entwistle, N. (1981) **Styles of learning and teaching: An integrated outline of educational psychology.** Chichester UK: Wiley.

Erikson, E. H. (1968) **Identity, youth and crisis.** New York: W. W. Norton.

Erikson, E. H. (1978) The life cycle of Dr. Borg. In E. H. Erikson (Ed.), **Adulthood** (pp. 1-31). New York: W. W. Norton.

Even, M. J. (1978) Overview of cognitive styles and hemispheres of the brain research. Paper presented at the Adult Education Research Conference, held at San Antonio, TX. (ERIC Document ED 152 992).

Fales, A. W., MacKeracher, D. & Vigoda, D. S. (1981) **Interpersonal skills for involvement with seniors — The ISIS Kit: Leader's manual.** Toronto ON: OISE Press.

Feringer, R. (1978) The relation between learning problems of adults and general learning theory. Paper presented at the Adult Education Research Conference, held at San Antonio, TX. (ERIC Document ED 152 992).

Ferro, T. R. (1993) The influence of affective processing in education and training. In D. D. Flannery (Ed.) **Applying cognitive learning theory to adult learning.** New Directions for Adult and Continuing Education, vol.59, pp. 25-34. San Francisco: Jossey-Bass.

Feuer, D. & Geber, B. (1988) Uh-oh...Second thoughts about adult learning theory. **Training, December,** 31-39.

Final Report (1975) The Declaration of Persepolis. International Symposium for Literacy. Persepolis, Iran.

Fiske, M. & Chiriboga, D. A. (1990) **Change and continuity in adult life.** San Francisco: Jossey-Bass.

Flannery, D. D. (1993a) Global and analytical ways of processing information. In D. D. Flannery (Ed.), Applying cognitive learning theory to adult learning. **New Directions in Adult and Continuing Education, vol.59** pp. 79-82. San Francisco: Jossey-Bass.

Fry, R. (1978) "Diagnosing professional learning environments: An observational scheme for matching learner style with situational complexity." Unpublished doctoral dissertation, Massachusetts Institute of Technology, Sloan School of Management, Cambridge MA

Fry, R. & Kolb, D. (1979) Experiential learning theory and learning experiences in liberal arts education. In S. E. Brooks & J. Althof (Eds.) **Enriching the liberal arts through experiential learning.** New Directions for Experiential Learning, vol.6, pp. 79-92. San Francisco: Jossey-Bass.

Fuhrmann, B. S. & Jacobs, R. (1980) **The learning interactions inventory.** Richmond, VA: Ronne Jacobs Associates.

Gavin, J. (1992) **The exercise habit.** Champaign IL: Leisure Press.

Gavin, J. & Taylor, M. (1990) "Understanding athletic injuries: A process model with implications for rehabilitation." Paper presented at the American Psychological Association Convention, Boston MA.

Gilligan, C. (1982) **In a different voice: Psychological theory and women's development.** Cambridge, MA: Harvard University Press.

Gorman, C. (1995) How gender may bend your thinking. **Time,** July 31, p.41.

Goslin, D. A. (Ed.) (1969) **Handbook of socialization theory and research.** Chicago: Rand McNally.

Gould, R. (1978) **Growth and change in adult life.** New York: Simon and Schuster.

Gregorc, A. G. (1982) **An adult's guide to style.** Maynard MA: Gabriel Systems.

Grow, G. O. (1991) Teaching learners to be self-directed. **Adult Education Quarterly,** 41(3), 125-149.

Guglielmino, L. M. (1977) Development of the Self-Directed Learning Readiness Scale. Unpublished doctoral dissertation, University of Georgia. **Dissertation Abstracts International, 38**(11A), 6467.

Hall, C. S. & Nordby, V. J. (1973) **A primer of Jungian psychology.** New York: New American Library.

Hall, E.T. (1976) **Beyond culture.** New York: Anchor Press.

Hanna, R. W. (1987) Personal meaning: Its loss and rediscovery. In R. Tannebaum, N. Margulies, & F. Massarik (Eds.) **Human systems development** (pp. 42-66). San Francisco: Jossey-Bass.

Hart, L. A. (1975) **How the brain works: A new understanding of human learning, emotion, and thinking.** New York: Basic Books.

Hart, L. A. (1983) **Human brain, human learning.** New York: Longman.

Harvey, O. J., Hunt, D. E., & Schroder, H. M. (1961) **Conceptual systems and personality organization.** New York: John Wiley & Sons.

Hebb, D. O. (1972) **Textbook of psychology** (3rd edition). Toronto ON: W. B. Saunders Co.

Heermann, B. (1984) Computer-assisted adult learning and the community college response. In D. A. Dellow & L. H. Poole (Eds.), **Microcomputer applications in administration and instruction.** New Directions for Community College, vol. 47. San Francisco: Jossey-Bass.

Hersey, P. & Blanchard, K. H. (1982) **Management of organizational behavior: Utilizing human resources** (4th edition). Englewood Cliffs NJ: Prentice-Hall.

Hiemstra, R. (1988) Translating personal values and philosophy into practical action. In R. G. Brockett (Ed.), **Ethical issues in adult education** (pp. 178-194). New York: Columbia University, Teachers College.

Hofstadter, D.R. (1985) **Metamagical themes: Questing for the essence of mind and pattern.** New York: Bantam Books.

Hopson, B. & Adams, J. (1976) Toward an understanding of transition: Defining some boundaries of transition dynamics. In J. Adams, J. Hayes & B. Hopson (Eds.) **Transition: Understanding and managing change** (pp. 3-25). London UK: Martin Robertson.

Houle, C. O. (1961) **The inquiring mind: A study of the adult who continues to learn.** Madison, WI: University of Wisconsin Press.

Houle, C. O. (1972) **The design of education.** San Francisco: Jossey-Bass.

Houston, J. (1982) **The possible human: A course in enhancing your physical, mental and creative abilities.** Los Angeles: J. P. Tarcher.

Hoyer, W. J. (1974) The adult learner: An operant perspective. In R. W. Bortner (Ed.), **Adults as learners.** University Park: PA: Pennsylvania State University, Institute for the Study of Human Development. (ERIC Document ED 106 462).

Huber, K. L. (1993) Memory is not only about storage. In D. D. Flannery (Ed.) **Applying cognitive learning theory to adult learning.** New Directions for Adult and Continuing Education, vol. 59, pp. 35-46. San Francisco: Jossey-Bass.

Huff, P., Snider, R. & Stephenson, S. (1986) **Teaching & learning styles: Celebrating differences.** Toronto ON: Ontario Secondary School Teachers' Federation.

Hunt, D. E. (1971) **Matching models in education. Monograph Series 10.** Toronto ON: Ontario Institute for Studies in Education.

Hunt, D. (1987) **Beginning with ourselves: In practice, theory and human affairs.** Toronto ON: OISE Press.

Hunt, D. E. & Sullivan, E. V. (1974) **Between psychology and education.** Hinsdale IL: Dryden Press.

Imara, M. (1975) Dying as a last stage of growth. In E. Kübler-Ross (Ed.) **Death: The final stage of growth** (pp. 147-163). Englewood Cliffs NJ: Prentice-Hall.

Inglis, A. (1994) A new paradigm for the future. In M. S. Parer (Ed.), **Unlocking open learning.** Churchill Australia: Monash University, Gippsland Campus, Distance Education Centre.

James, W. B. & Blank, W. E. (1993) Review and critique of available learning-style instruments for adults. **New Directions in Adult and Continuing Education, 59,** 47-57.

Jantsch, E. (1980) **The self-organizing universe: Scientific and human implications of the emerging paradigm of evolution.** Oxford, UK:Pergamon.

Jarvis, P. (1985) **The sociology of adult and continuing education.** London UK: Croom Helm.

Jarvis, P. (1987) **Adult learning in the social context.** London UK: Croom Helm.

Jones, R. M. (1968) **Fantasy and feeling in education.** New York: Harper Colophon Books.

Josselson, R. (1992) **The space between us: Exploring the dimensions of human relationships.** San Francisco: Jossey-Bass.

Joyce, B. & Weil, M. (1986) **Models of teaching** (3rd edition). Englewood Cliffs NJ: Prentice-Hall.

Jung, C. G. (1964) **Man and his symbols** (Edited by M-L von Franz). Garden City, NY: Doubleday & Company

Kasworm, C. E. (1983) Self-directed learning and lifespan development. **International Journal of Lifelong Education, 2** (1), 29-46.

Katz, D. & Kahn, R. L. (1970) Communication: The flow of information. In J. H. Campbell & H. W. Hepler (Eds.) **Dimensions in communication: Readings** (2nd edition). Belmont, CA: Wadsworth.

Keefe, J. W. (1987) **Learning style theory and practice.** Reston VA: National Association of Secondary School Principals.

Kegan, R. (1982) **The evolving self: Problem and process in human development.** Cambridge MA: Harvard University Press.

Keirsey, D. & Bates, M. (1984) **Please understand me: Character and temperament types.** Delma CA: Prometheus Nemesis Books.

Kelly, G. A. (1955) **The psychology of personal constructs** (2 volumes). New York: W. W. Norton.

Kennard, B. (1993) Restorying the expert-novice relationship. In D. J. Clandinin, A. Davies, P. Hogan & B. Kennard (Eds.), **Learning to teach, teaching to learn: Stories of collaboration in teacher education.** New York: Teachers College Press.

Kidd, J. R. (1960) "The three R's — Relevance, relationships, responsibility." Speech to the Annual Spring Encaenia, of the Thomas More Institute, 16 May 1960, Montreal, QU.

Kidd, J. R. (1973a) **How adults learn** (revised edition). New York: Association Press.

Kidd, J. R. (1973b) **Relentless verity: Education for being-becoming-belonging.** Syracuse NY: Syracuse University, Continuing Education.

Kidd, J. R. (1995) **Roby Kidd: Adult education 1915-1982. Autobiography of a Canadian Pioneer.** Toronto ON: Oise Press.

Klopf, G. J., Bowman, G. W. & Joy, A. (1969) **A learning team: Teacher and auxiliary.** Washington DC: Office of Education (DHEW). (ERIC Document ED 031 438).

Knowles, M. S. (1990) **The adult learner: A neglected species** (4th edition). Houston TX: Gulf Publishing Co.

Koberg, D. & Bagnall, J. (1981) **The revised all new universal traveller** (revised edition). Los Altos CA: William Kaufmann, Inc.

Koestler, A. (1964) **The act of creation.** New York: Macmillan.

Kohlberg, L. (1973) Continuities of childhood and adult moral development. In P. B. Baltes & K. W. Schaie (Eds.) **Life-span developmental psychology: Personality and socialization** (pp. 179-204). New York: Academic Press.

Kolb, D. A. (1984) **Experiential learning: Experience as the source of learning and development.** Englewood Cliffs NJ: Prentice-Hall.

Kolb, D. A. (1985) **Learning style inventory.** Boston: McBer & Company.

Koplowitz, H. (1987) Post-logical thinking. In D. N. Perkins, J. Lockhead & J. C. Bishop (Eds.) **Thinking: The second international conference.** Hillsdale, NJ: Lawrence Erlbaum Associates.

Kübler-Ross, E. (1970) **On death and dying.** New York: Macmillan.

Lam, Y. L. J. (1976) Transitional analysis of adult learners' needs. **Alberta Journal of Educational Research, 22** (1), 59-70.

Levinson, D. J. (1978) Growing up with the dream. **Psychology Today,** January, 20-31.

Levinson, D. J. (1986) A conception of adult development. **American Psychologist, 41** (1), 3-13.

Levinson, D. J. and Associates (1978) **The seasons of a man's life.** New York: Alfred A. Knopf.

Lewin, K. (1951) **Field theory in social science.** New York: Harper & Row.

Loevinger, J. (1976) **Ego development.** San Francisco: Jossey-Bass.

Lyons, N. P. (1988) Two perspectives: On self, relationships and morality. In C. Gilligan, J. V. Ward, & J. M. Taylor (Eds.), **Mapping the moral domain.** Cambridge MA: Harvard University Press.

MacKeracher, D. (1993) Women as learners. In T. Barer-Stein and J. A. Draper (Eds.) **The craft of teaching adults** (2nd edition, pp. 69-86). Toronto ON: Culture Concepts Inc.

Marshall, V. W. (1980) **Last chapters: A sociology of aging and dying.** Monterey CA: Brooks/Cole Publishing.

Maudsley, D. B. (1979) "A theory of metalearning and principles of facilitation." Unpublished doctoral dissertation, Ontario Institute for Studies in Education, University of Toronto, Toronto ON.

McCarthy, B. (1985) **The 4MAT system: Teaching to learning styles with right/left mode techniques.** Barrington IL: Excel, Inc.

McCarthy, B. (1986) **Hemispheric mode indicator: Right and left brain approaches to learning.** Barrington IL: Excel, Inc.

McClusky, H. Y. (1970) An approach to a differential psychology of the adult potential. In S. M. Grabowski (Ed.) **Adult learning and instruction** (pp. 80-95). Syracuse, NY: ERIC Clearinghouse on Adult Education.

McIntosh, P. (1985) **Work in progress, no.18. Feeling like a fraud.** Wellesley MA: Wellesley College, The Stone Center.

McKenney, J. L. & Keen, P. G. W. (1974) How managers' minds work. **Harvard Business Review, 52** (3), 79-90.

McKenzie, L. (1977) The issue of andragogy. **Adult Education, 27** (4), 225-229.

Melamed, L. (1987) The role of play in adult learning. In D. Boud & V. Griffin (Eds.) **Appreciating adults learning: From the learners' perspective.** London, UK: Kogan Page.

Messick, S. (1976) Personality consistencies in cognition and creativity. In S. Messick and Associates, **Individuality in learning: Implications of cognitive styles and creativity for human development** (pp. 310-326). San Francisco: Jossey-Bass.

Mezirow, J. (1991) **Transformative dimensions of adult learning.** San Francisco: Jossey-Bass.

Mezirow, J. (1995) **Transformation theory of adult learning.** In M.R. Welton (Ed.) In defense of the lifeworld: Critical perspectives on adult learning (pp. 39-70). Albany NY: State University of New York Press.

Miller, A. (1991) **Personality types: A modern synthesis.** Calgary AB: University of Calgary Press.

Miller, J. B. (1984) **Work in progress, no.12. The development of women's sense of self.** Wellesley MA: Wellesley College, The Stone Center.

Miller, J. B. (1986) **Toward a new psychology of women** (2nd edition). Boston MA: Beacon Press.

More, W. S. (1974) **Emotions and adult learning.** Lexington MA: Lexington Books.

Morstain, B. R. & Smart, J. C. (1977) A motivational typology of adult learners. **Journal of Higher Education, 48** (6), 665-679.

Neugarten, B. L. (1976) Adaptation and the life cycle. In N. K. Schlossberg & A. D. Entine (Eds.) **Counselling adults** (pp. 34-46). Monterey, CA: Brooks/Cole Publishing.

Neugarten, B. L. & Datan, N. (1973) Sociological perspectives on the life cycle. In P. B. Baltes & K. W. Schaie (Eds.) **Life-span developmental psychology: Personality and socialization** (pp. 53-69). New York: Academic Press.

Novak, J. & Gowin, D. (1984) **Learning how to learn.** New York: Cambridge University Press.

Novak, M. (1993) **Aging and society: A Canadian perspective** (2nd edition). Scarborough: Nelson Canada.

O'Connor, J. & Seymour, J. (1990) **Introducing neuro-linguistic programming: The new psychology of personal excellence.** London UK: Mandala.

Oddi, L. F. (1986) Development and validation of an instrument to identify self-directed continuing learners. **Adult Education Quarterly, 36** (2), 97-107.

Oltman, P. K., Raskin, E. & Witkin, H. A. (1970) **Group embedded figures test.** Palo Alto, CA: Consulting Psychologists Press.

Ornstein, R. (1972) **The psychology of consciousness.** San Francisco: W. H. Freeman.

Perry, W. G. (1970) **Forms of intellectual and ethical development in the college years: A scheme.** New York: Holt, Rinehart & Winston.

Peterson, D. A. (1983) **Facilitating education for older learners.** San Francisco: Jossey-Bass.

Pine, G. J. & Boy, A. V. (1977) **Learner centered teaching: A humanistic view.** Denver CO: Love Publishing Co.

Pratt, D. D. (1979) "Instructor behavior and psychological climate in adult learning." Paper presented to the Adult Education Research Conference, held at Ann Arbor, MI.

Pratt, D. D. (1988) Andragogy as a relational construct. **Adult Education Quarterly, 38** (3), 160-181.

Randall, W. (1995) **The stories we are: An essay on self-creation.** Toronto ON: University of Toronto Press.

Restack, R. (1979) The other differences between boys and girls. **Student Learning Styles.** Reston, VA: National Association of Secondary School Principals.

Riegel, K. W. (1973) Dialectical operations: The final period of cognitive development. **Human Development,** 16, 346-370.

Roberts, T. B. (1975) **Four psychologies applied to education.** Cambridge MA: Schenkman Pub.

Roberts, T. B. & Clark, F. V. (1975) **Transpersonal psychology in education.** Bloomington IL: Phi Delta Kappa Educational Foundation.

Rogers, C. (1969) **Freedom to learn.** Columbus OH: Merrill.

Rowe, C. J. (1975) **An outline of psychiatry** (6th edition). Dubuque IO: Wm. C. Brown Co.

Sagan, C. (1977) **The dragons of Eden.** New York: Random House.

Schaie, K. W. (1977-78) Toward a stage theory of adult cognitive development. **Journal of Aging and Human Development, 8** (2), 129-138.

Schlossberg, N. K. (1984) **Counseling adults in transition: Linking practice with theory.** New York: Springer.

Schlossberg, N. K. (1987) Taking the mystery out of change. **Psychology Today,** May, 74-75.

Schön, D. A. (1971) **Beyond the stable state.** New York: Random House.

Schön, D. A. (1987) **Educating the reflective practitioner.** San Francisco: Jossey-Bass.

Schutz, W. C. (1967) **Joy: Expanding human awareness.** New York: Grove Press.

Seagal, S. & Horne, D. (1991) **An introduction to human dynamics.** Topanga CA: Human Dynamics International.

Selye, H. (1956) **The stress of life.** New York: McGraw-Hill.

Sheehy, G. (1976) **Passages: Predictable crises of adult life.** New York: E. P. Dutton.

Simpson, E. (1979) **Reversals: A personal account of victory over dyslexia.** New York: Washington Square Press.

Skinner, B. F. (1971) **Beyond freedom and dignity.** New York: Alfred Knopf.

Sloboda, J. (1993) What is skill and how is it acquired? In M. Thorpe, R. Edwards & A, Hanson (Eds.) **Culture and processes of adult learning** (pp. 253-273). London, UK: Routledge.

Smith, D. H. (1989) Situational instruction: A strategy for facilitating the learning process. **Lifelong Learning: An Omnibus of Practice and Research,** 12 (6), 5-9.

Smith, R. M. (1982) **Learning how to learn: Applied theory for adults.** New York: Cambridge Book Company.

Smith, R. M. (1990) The promise of learning to learn. In R. M. Smith and Associates, **Learning to learn across the life span.** San Francisco: Jossey-Bass.

Springer, S. P. & Deutsch, G. (1985) **Left brain, right brain.** New York: W. H. Freeman & Co.

Squires, G. (1993) Education for adults. In M. Thorpe, R. Edwards & A. Hanson (Eds.), **Culture and processes of adult learning** (pp. 87-108). London UK: Routledge.

Steinem, G. (1992) **Revolution from within: A book of self-esteem.** Boston MA: Little, Brown & Company.

Sternberg, R. J. (1988) **The triarchic mind: A new theory of human intelligence.** New York: Penguin Books.

Stouch, C. A. (1993) What instructors need to know about learning how to learn. In D. D. Flannery (Ed.), **Applying cognitive learning theory to adult learning.** New Directions for Adult and Continuing Education, vol. 59, pp. 59-68. San Francisco: Jossey-Bass.

Suessmuth, P. (1985) A learning styles inventory. **Training Ideas, 44,** 2-20.

Surrey, J. L. (1985) **Work in progress, no.13. The "self-in-relation:" A theory of women's development.** Wellesley MA: Wellesley College, The Stone Center.

Sutcliffe, J. (1990) **Adults with learning difficulties.** Leicester UK: National Institute of Adult Continuing Education.

Tannen, D. (1990) **You just don't understand: Women and men in conversation.** New York: William Morrow and Company.

Taylor, M. (1979) "Adult learning in an emergent learning group: Toward a theory of learning from the learner's perspective." Unpublished doctoral dissertation, University of Toronto, Ontario Institute for Studies in Education, Toronto ON.

Taylor, M. (1987) Self-directed learning: More than meets the observer's eye. In D. Boud & V. Griffin (Eds.) **Appreciating adults learning: From the learners' perspective** (pp. 179-196). London UK: Kogan Page.

Taylor (1990) Notes on empowerment for formal education. **Proceedings of the Canadian Association for the Study of Adult Education.** Victoria BC: University of Victoria.

Thibodeau, J. (1979) "Adult performance on Piagetian tasks: Implications for education." Paper presented at the Adult Education Research Conference, held at Ann Arbor, MI.

Thomas, A. M. (1991) **Beyond education: A new perspective on society's management of learning.** San Francisco: Jossey-Bass.

Toffler, A. (1970) **Future shock.** New York: Random House.

Tough, A. M. (1978) Major learning efforts: Recent research and future directions. **Adult Education,** 18 (4), 250-263.

Tough, A. M. (1979) **The adults' learning projects** (2nd edition). Toronto ON: OISE Press.

Tulving, E. (1985) How many memory systems are there? **American Psychologist,** 40, 385-398.

Vaillant, G. E. (1977) **Adaptation to life.** Boston MA: Little, Brown and Co.

Vanier, J. (1970) **Tears of silence.** Toronto ON: Griffin House.

Walker, G. A. (1984) "Written with invisible ink: Women in the adult education knowledge base." Unpublished manuscript, School of Social Work, Carleton University, Ottawa.

Watzlawick, P., Weakland, J. & Fisch, R. (1974) **Change: Principles of problem formation and problem resolution.** New York: W. W. Norton.

Weiler, K. (1988) **Women teaching for change: Gender, class and power.** South Hadley MA: Bergin & Garvey

Welton, M.R. (1991) Shaking the foundations: The critical turn in adult education theory. **Canadian Journal for the Study of Adult Education,** V (Winter, Special Issue), 21-42.

Welton, M.R. (1995) In defense of the lifeworld: A Habermasian approach to adult learning. In M.R. Welton (Ed.) **In defense of the lifeworld: Critical perspectives on adult learning.** Albany NY: State University of New York Press.

West, C. K., Farmer, J. A. & Wolff, P. M. (1991) **Instructional design: Implications from cognitive science.** Englewood Cliffs NJ: Prentice-Hall.

Wilber, K. (1986) The spectrum of development. In K. Wilber, J. Engler & D. P. Brown, **Transformations of consciousness: Conventional and contemplative perspectives on development.** Boston MA: Shambhala Pubs.

Wingfield, L. & Haste, H. (1987) Connectedness and separateness: Cognitive style or moral orientation. **Journal of Moral Education,** 16 (3).

Wischnewski, M. M. (1983) **Humour: Why educators should take it seriously.** Toronto ON: Ontario Ministry of Education.

Witkin, H. & Goodenough, D. (1977) Field dependence and interpersonal behavior. **Psychological Bulletin, 84,** 661-689.

Wlodkowski, R. (1985) **Enhancing adult motivation to learn.** San Francisco: Jossey-Bass.

Wonder, J. & Donovan, P. (1984) **Whole-brain thinking: Working from both sides of the brain to achieve peak job performance.** New York: Ballantine Books.

Yanoff, J. M. (1976) The functions of the mind in the learning process. In M. L. Silberman and Associates (Eds.) **Real learning: A sourcebook for teachers.** Boston: Little, Brown & Co.

Zimbardo, P. G. & Ruch, F. L. (1978) **Psychology and life** (9th edition). Glenview IL: Scott, Foresman & Co.

Zinn, L. (1990) Identifying your philosophical orientation. In M. W. Galbraith (Ed.) **Adult learning methods: A guide to effective instruction.** Malabar FL: Krieger.

INDEX